IT WAS NEVER ABOUT THE BABE

The Red Sox, Racism, Mismanagement,
and the Curse of the Bambino

Jerry M. Gutlon

Skyhorse Publishing

Skyhorse Publishing books may be purchased in bulk at special discounts for sales promotion, corporate gifts, fund-raising, or educational purposes. Special editions can also be created to specifications. For details, contact the Special Sales Department, Skyhorse Publishing, 555 Eighth Avenue, Suite 903, New York, NY 10018 or info@skyhorsepublishing.com

www.skyhorsepublishing.com

10 9 8 7 6 5 4 3 2 1

Library of Congress Cataloging-in-Publication Data

Gutlon, Jerry M.
  It was never about the Babe : the Red Sox, mismanagement, and the curse of the Bambino / Jerry M. Gutlon.
     p. cm.
  ISBN 978-1-60239-349-3 (alk. paper)
  1. Boston Red Sox (Baseball team)--History. 2. Boston Red Sox (Baseball team)--Management. 3. Superstition--Massachusetts--Boston. I. Title.
  GV875.B62G88 2009
  796.357'640974461--dc22
                              2008053343

Printed in the United States of America

This book is dedicated to my loving, long-suffering wife, Kristie Gayle Gutlon, who always believed . . . sort of.

I also dedicate this work to the memory of my pop, Irving Isaac Gutlon, who introduced me to the game of baseball, and persisted in bringing me to Fenway Park, the home of the Boston Red Sox even though we never saw them win in person—ever!

Lastly, I want to dedicate this book to my precious friend, Lloyd "Bud" Gayton, who passed during the editing process of this book, and whom I'll see again in glory.

CONTENTS

INTRODUCTION

Introduction

THE WORLD TURNED
UPSIDE DOWN

I'm sure my wife Kristie meant no harm when she darted out onto the porch of our home in west central Georgia to attempt to comfort me that chilly October night in 2003. It was either that, or that she wanted to salvage the other lawn chairs, since I'd just smashed one of the inanimate beasts into little pieces.

But her words did nothing but fan my frenzy, because my beloved Boston Red Sox had just thrown away another American League Championship—and to the hated New York Yankees, to boot.

Unbelieving Phillies fan that she is, she whispered words that were intended as a salve, but instead cut like razor wire: "It's only a game."

"'Only a game'!" I shrieked. "'Only a game'? Do you know how long I've waited for this team to win a World Series? How can you say 'only a game'?"

But, all things considered, unless you were brought up a Red Sox fan, it's very difficult, if not impossible, to comprehend what their fans endured from 1919 through 2003.

Neither a lengthy hitch on active military duty nor having spent most of my adult life in print and broadcast news diminished my love

I T   W A S   N E V E R   A B O U T   T H E   B A B E

for the team that annually broke my heart. And although we haven't made New England our home since October 1997, I continued to regularly put down my thoughts concerning the Olde Towne Team.

Such as: Who could have known that Sox manager Grady Little's firing in the wake of the club's 2003 American League Championship Series collapse would prove to be the beginning of the final, sorry chapter in eighty-six years of perpetual heartache for Sox fans. Perhaps Little's leave-taking provided the ultimate exclamation point of how futile it's been for Red Sox fans over those years.

Leaving Pedro Martinez in Game Seven after he was obviously out of gas meant that instead of a solid 5–2 victory propelling the Sox into the World Series, the team suffered an eleven-inning, 6–5 defeat at the hands of the despised Yankees.

I can't honestly say that as I watched the game on TV, I was screaming at Little to pull Pedro before any more damage was done. When my buddy, Steve (a Chicago Cubs fan), started bellowing that Little should have given Martinez the hook, I countered, "Look, Little just asked him if he wanted to continue, and Pedro nodded."

Of course, at the time, nobody but the Sox brain trust knew that Little had been ordered to remove Martinez after seven innings or 100 pitches, whichever came first. His refusal to do so cost Little his job, a gaffe one sportswriter characterized as "catastrophically moronic."

Martinez had been *the* premiere starter since a very unhappy Roger Clemens coasted during his last several seasons in Boston. Even though Pedro had recently suffered physical problems, he remained the staff ace . . . so Little left him in the game. At the time I really couldn't blame him. A multiple Cy Young Award winner on the mound—even if he's short on gas in a must-win game—deserves to be given enough rope to hang himself. Sad to say, that's exactly what happened. Although it quickly became apparent that Pedro was finished, Little stubbornly remained in the Sox dugout until the game was tied at 5–5. By then, those of us old enough to remember Bucky ("Bleeping") Dent's dying-quail home run off Mike Torrez in the infamous 1978 one-game playoff against the Yanks were frantically searching for the nearest exhaust pipe to suck on. I was having flashbacks of '78—even after Mike Timlin dodged a slew of bullets to retire the Yankees, and Tim Wakefield followed to throw his dancing knuckle ball. Two innings later, Wakefield threw a knuckle ball that didn't knuck, and Aaron Boone hit it into the left-field stands.

Better luck next time. Wait till next year.

I could've screamed. Because that's what I'd lived with for more than forty-five years, ever since I fell in love with the sport of baseball, specifically with Boston's Back Bay team, the very same club that held a massive fire sale following its last World Series championship in 1918. A fire sale that saw many of the best in baseball sold off, predominantly to the Yankees. Several future Hall of Famers went from Boston to New York over the next fifteen years, but of course the one everyone remembers—the one that no one can forget—is Babe Ruth.

Instead of remaining a perennial pennant contender, the Red Sox became the doormats of the American League. While they had their near-great seasons, Boston always came up short in their quest for another World Series title. True Red Sox fans seemingly never lost heart, telling themselves that another championship would eventually ensue, but not in 2003.

However, a year later it *did* happen when a self-proclaimed ragtag "bunch of idiots" led by a quartet of big-name stars did something no team in Major League Baseball had *ever* done. They came back from an unprecedented three-game deficit in the best-of-seven American League Championship Series to win four in a row and capture the pennant.

To this day, Red Sox fans the world over savor that historic milestone, especially because the team that had the Sox in its stranglehold were the Bronx Bombers, otherwise known as the New York Yankees (not to mention countless unprintable names coined in New England).

Sox hurler Curt Schilling put it so perfectly when he prepared to pitch in the ALCS at Yankee Stadium, declaring, "I just want to make fifty-five thousand Yankee fans shut up." He did that, and then some.

Boston then went on to sweep the 2004 World Series from the St. Louis Cardinals in four games. Finally, after nearly nine fruitless decades, the Sox brought a world championship back to Boston.

||||||

Now, maybe my pop can finally rest in peace.

He was almost five years old when Red Sox owner Harry Frazee shipped an overgrown problem child named George Herman Ruth to the New Yorkers, but my dad didn't live long enough to see another world championship banner fly over Fenway Park. Yet Dad would reminisce of the beauty of watching Ted Williams hit. "That swing," he'd say in a faraway voice. "That swing." And he spoke of a chance meeting he had while on a cross-country World War II troop train preparing to ship out for Europe. On the same train was a hulking ex-Red Sox power hitter named Jimmie Foxx. "Old Double X," Dad would tell us. "He really was a nice guy."

Pop also stewed over how the Red Sox bungled the handling of a promising young rookie named Jimmy Piersall, who ended up in a mental institution because of the cavalier way he was treated. "What a mess they made of that boy," he said. "It was criminal."

There was one other Red Sox ballplayer my dad used to rave about all the time—George Herman Ruth.

Pop used to crack up my friends by grandly announcing, "Sure, I saw Babe Ruth play . . . (pause . . . beat . . . beat) . . . for the Yankees." But after a while it didn't seem so funny. Or sit so well.

||||||

Between 1919 and 1952, the year of my birth, the Sox would play in one, and only one, World Series. That was in 1946, against the very same Cardinals they beat in the 2004 Fall Classic. Naturally, the Sox lost it in seven.

Yet New England baseball fans cherish the team like no other. In the words of *Boston Herald* columnist Mike Barnicle, "Baseball isn't a life-and-death-matter, but the Red Sox are." And baseball chronicler Roger Angell termed the passion of Red Sox Nation as, "the profound New England seriousness of Following the Sox."

Growing up in suburban Boston, I was always cognizant that a New England–based sports fan could count on the Celtics to win. Period. As for the Sox, the Bruins, and the Patriots, one-for-four meant you were hitting .250, which was a good enough average to keep you in Major League Baseball at the time.

So I became inured to the trials and tribulations of the Sox, always looking for a silver lining, but never expecting too much. I remember the games I went to with my dad as a kid and—without fail—I never witnessed a Red Sox victory. It was to be expected. But the thing I remember the most was the stoicism we showed in the wake of loss after loss.

Then came 1967, the "Impossible Dream" year, when the Sox won the AL pennant on the last day of the season after battling down to the wire in a four-club slugfest: the Sox, Tigers, Twins, and White Sox. The exhilaration was entirely foreign.

Naturally, the Cards beat Boston in a seven-game series for the world championship again. Oh, sure it hurt, but in our hearts the club had finally come into its own, and there was always next year.

The only problem was "next year" didn't come again for eight years. After 1975, we waited yet another eleven years for the next "next year." And, after 1986, "next year" proved to be 2004. When the Boys in the Red Hose finally brought home the championship.

Now life will never be the same.

|||||

I just wish my dear old dad had lived to see it, although he probably would have turned off the television in October 2004 because yet another season seemingly was on the ropes. Like an outclassed, battered prizefighter, the Red Sox were three outs away from closing out another postseason as an American League also-ran.

And once again the Boston nine had been thoroughly humbled by the Yankees, the best team money could buy.

Both of the Sox marquee starters, Curt Schilling and Pedro Martinez, failed to win the first two games of the ALCS. Despite a valiant attempt at a come-from-behind victory in Game One, a late inning Red Sox rally fell short, and Boston lost, 10–7. Then, in spite of a solid outing by Pedro Martinez, the Yankees took Game Two, 3–1.

But the roof *really* caved in during Game Three. The Bronx Bombers lived up to that name, overwhelming the Sox with nineteen runs in the supposedly home-team friendly confines of Fenway Park. Down three games to none with the prospect of being swept at home by your arch nemesis was the ultimate train wreck dreaded—indeed, *expected*—by every Sox fan.

No team in the history of Major League Baseball had *ever* rallied from a three-game deficit to win a best-of-seven series. In fact, no team had ever come from being behind by three games to even force a seventh game.

Certainly the star-crossed Sox couldn't be expected to make history, especially against the New York Yankees, a team that under owner George Steinbrenner proved to be a relentless force constantly re-arming to maintain a perennial stranglehold on the American League.

The morning after the Game Two loss I appeared on a radio talk show with several of the area's high school football coaches, in my capacity as sports editor for the *Griffin Daily News* in Griffin, Georgia. Knowing I was from Boston, Kirk Hoffman, the one coach I most respected, turned to me after the broadcast and declared the ALCS all but over.

"Gee, I don't know, Kirk," I retorted. "I'm just not ready to throw in the towel yet."

He reacted as if I required bundling off to the nearest psych unit. "There is no way the Red Sox can beat the Yankees," he twitted. "Bet me money."

I declined, but added, "I'm not convinced it's over yet."

He burst out in laughter. "Stick a fork in them, they're done," Kirk declared.

"Not quite," I snapped. "We'll see how they do tonight."

That was the night the Yankees took the Sox to the woodshed with the 19–8 drubbing. If ever a team was on the ropes, it was my beloved Red Sox. Not only had Boston's starting pitchers failed, but the team's hitting had become spotty at best.

New York had manhandled Martinez throughout the latter part of the season, to the point that he made the statement he may forever be linked with: "I've got to tip my cap to them. The Yankees have been my Daddy."

If that wasn't enough to make Red Sox fans cringe, the injury Curt Schilling suffered while pitching against the Angels in the divisional series had Sox lovers setting aside one last bullet for the *coup de grâce.* Moving off the mound after a grounder, Schilling tore the sheath around the tendon on the back of his right ankle. Although no one outside the ballclub was aware of the seriousness of the injury at the time, Schilling's horrible performance in Game One of the ALCS was the direct result of his inability to push off on that foot. For a power pitcher, the injury was the kiss of death.

And even though Martinez pitched well in Game Two, the Yankees' Jon Lieber threw the game of his life, shutting down the Sox, 3–1. Yankee fans mercilessly hounded Pedro all evening, chanting, "Who's your Daddy? Who's your Daddy?"

But with the debacle in Game Three, even the most stouthearted Red Sox fan had to take pause.

Yet hope rekindled when in Game Four, Boston engineered a miraculous comeback, beating the detested Yankees, 6–4. Three outs shy of elimination, trailing New York 4–3 in the bottom of the ninth inning, the somnolent Red Sox bats finally stirred, at least enough to score one run on two walks, a stolen base, a sacrifice bunt, an error, and one measly run-scoring single by third baseman Bill Mueller. Even at that, being the fatalist I was, I feared the Sox would *still* figure out a way to lose.

But I was wrong. David Ortiz, a.k.a. "Big Papi," rocketed a moonshot into the seats at Fenway to win the game in the bottom of the twelfth inning.

In a flash, baseball pundits repeatedly reminded Red Sox Nation that never in the history of Major League Baseball had a team come back from a three-game hole to even play a seventh game. With virtually nothing to lose, a seemingly relaxed Red Sox squad took the field the following night. And, once again, "Big Papi" came through when the team needed it most, slicing a single to drive in the winning run in the fourteenth inning.

Game Six at Yankee Stadium provided arguably the gutsiest pitching performance in playoff history. Red Sox stalwart Curt Schilling took the mound with the postseason at stake. The sheath in his right ankle had been *sutured* to hold the tendon in place. Schilling proceeded to shut down New York for seven innings, bad ankle and all. With blood visibly seeping through his sanitary hose, Schilling didn't make a mistake until he gave up a solo home run to Bernie Williams in the bottom of the seventh inning.

Meanwhile, several Red Sox regulars who hadn't produced all series came through when it counted the most. With the game scoreless in the fourth inning, first baseman Kevin Millar hammered a double, scoring on a single by catcher Jason Varitek. Then, with two runners aboard, second baseman Mark Bellhorn hit a three-run homer into the left-center field bleachers. At first, the umpires called Bellhorn's hit a ground-rule double, but then they huddled together and determined that the drive didn't deflect from the field into the crowd, but vice-versa.

Perhaps more critically, the collaboration among the members of the umpiring squad proved to be a portent of things to come, for in the eighth inning, Alex Rodriguez blatantly knocked his batted ball out of the glove of Boston pitcher Bronson Arroyo, then threw a tantrum when the umpires correctly called him out. Yankees captain Derek Jeter was obliged to return to first resulting in an argument from both Jeter and manager Joe Torre. Again, Bronx cheers accompanied another Bronx tradition—that of burying the playing field in refuse.

Arroyo had replaced Schilling in the eighth inning. With Sox fans praying he would redeem himself after his abominable showing during the 19–8 massacre the previous Saturday, Arroyo gave up one run to make the score 4–2. But the karate chop Rodriguez delivered to Arroyo's left wrist ultimately knocked the wind out of the Yankees' sails. The Yankees did not score again after that play, with Sox closer Keith Foulke striking out Tony Clark on a 3–2 pitch after walking two men in the ninth.

"I don't think any of us have any idea what [Schilling] went through to pitch tonight," Red Sox manager Terry Francona declared following the game. "For him to go out there and do what he did, his heart is so big."

The series was now in the questionable right hand of Derek Lowe, a twenty-one game winner two years earlier, but a disappointment in 2004.

The odds were against him and the Red Sox. Of the previous twenty-five teams that fell behind 3–0 in a best-of-seven series, twenty lost the fourth game, three lost in five, and the other two in six.

But that's why they play the game. And this Game Seven would make baseball history.

Johnny Damon, who to that point in the ALCS had hit about as well as slight gymnast Keri Struggs, smashed a grand slam and a two-run homer. Mark Bellhorn homered for the second straight night, and Jason Varitek got a couple more hits. Lowe, who had amassed an earned run average of more than five runs allowed per nine innings pitched during the regular season, mesmerized the Yanks.

Finally, Pedro Martinez pitched the seventh inning and, although New York touched him for three hits and two runs, the Yankees learned they're not *really* his Daddy. Indeed, Boston fans remained in the stands chanting, "Who's *your* Daddy?" again and again, after the Yankees quietly retired to their clubhouse.

Just how unlikely the comeback was is hard to fathom. Only two teams in the history of three major team sports had ever come back from a three-game deficit to win a seven-game series; both were in the National Hockey League. Elsewhere, seventy-three National Basketball Association teams failed to win a seven-game series after being down by three. And the overall record for comeback seven-game victories in the National Hockey League is 2–138. Before the Sox engineered their historic comeback, the overall total in MLB, the NHL, and the NBA was two wins in 236 tries.

Furthermore, in the history of the franchise the Red Sox had never won a decisive Game Seven on the road. And since the inception of the seven-game league championship format the Yankees had never lost a seventh game—until 2004.The unprecedented comeback was well-recognized.

Red Sox first baseman Doug Mientkiewicz asserted, "We've been playing Game Seven since Game Four."

General manager Theo Epstein echoed the sentiments of players and fans alike when he remarked, "I hope Ted Williams is having a cocktail upstairs." Williams, who died in July 2002, starred with the Sox from 1939 through 1960, missing five years due to military service in two wars. He never won a World Series ring, playing only in the 1946 Fall Classic against the Cards, and batting just .200.

Finally, Sox president Larry Lucchino, who the previous fall had famously referred to the Yankees as the "Evil Empire," got in the last word on the matter in the fall of 2004. "All empires fall sooner or later," he declared.

Indeed, one could almost hear the strains of a British band playing "The World Turned Upside Down."[1]

Four games later, the 2004 Red Sox swept the Cardinals and
were champions of the world for the first time since 1918.

---

1 After the American Army defeated Lord Cornwallis at Yorktown to secure the country's
freedom from Great Britain in 1781, the British band played a song titled "The World
Turned Upside" as the English Army retired from the battlefield following its surrender. The
ultimate rout of the British began in Boston in 1775, where the colonists had stood up to
British tyranny by taking up arms against the crown at Lexington and Concord.

THE CURSE OF THE BAMBINO

Erroneously believing that slandering American icons would somehow infuriate our troops in the Pacific during World War II, Japanese attackers sometimes assaulted U.S. positions while screaming, "To hell with Babe Ruth!"

Well, "To hell with the *curse* of Babe Ruth!"

In the wake of Boston's first world championship in eighty-six years, one thing had to be made perfectly clear: There never was a curse. Or, in the words of former Red Sox right fielder, Trot Nixon, "To us, it was just a five-letter word."

Over the previous twenty years various pundits had termed the annual Red Sox swan dive "The Curse of the Bambino," creating the illusion that Ruth's leave-taking saddled the Sox with a cloud darker and more persistent than the one that hung over that Lil' Abner cartoon character, Joe Btfsplk.

In 1986, *Boston Globe* writer Marty Nolan was the first to theorize that a psychic connection might exist between the sale of Ruth and Boston's yearly nosedive. *Globe* writer Peter Canellos also alluded to such a curse, then it was mentioned by *New York Times* sportswriter George Vecsey after the Sox lost the 1986 World Series to the Mets, a Series Boston had all but won.

In Seth Mnookin's book, *Feeding the Monster*, he theorized that Vecsey's suggestion might very well have engraved the "curse" theory in stone. "Vecsey helped introduce the idea of Ruth's curse, and the power and prestige of the *Times* helped cement the notion that [Red Sox owner Harry] Frazee's sale of the team's star was tied to his theatrical aspirations."

Then *Boston Globe* sportswriter Dan Shaughnessy penned his 1990 fairy tale, *The Curse of the Bambino*. Since that time Shaughnessy has been routinely criticized as being among the first who publicly posed the myth. Even today, many diehard Red Sox fans remain furious with him, claiming Shaughnessy "financed his kids' college educations" from the sale of that book.

Notwithstanding, after *The Curse of the Bambino* was published, the fable took on a life of its own, although fifteen years after its publication, Shaughnessy qualified his theory, stating, "Probably the reason that Boston has not won is that they have not been good enough." But in his 2005 book, *Reversing the Curse*, Shaughnessy continued to try to validate the myth, which he claimed he originated. Virtually the entire introduction to the book centers on the so-called curse, implying that Red Sox Nation was absolutely bedeviled by the thought.

However, a number of astute authors have put the lie to Shaughnessy's rush to judgment.

Wrote Mnookin, "Shaughnessy's book focused almost exclusively—some might say masochistically—on the Red Sox's misery, as he repeated many of the inaccuracies that had hardened into perceived fact. Failing to acknowledge that some contemporary articles and editorial cartoons had argued it was better for the team that Ruth had been sold, Shaughnessy wrote how the sale of the slugger was almost universally seen as a horrible move at the time it occurred. He quoted the *Times* obituary that said that Frazee's estate "did not exceed $50,000" when he died, but left out what followed in the *Times'* account—that "it may be much larger after Mr. Frazee's interests in Boston and Chicago are appraised."

In fact, the *Times* was forced to run a correction in the wake of the original Frazee obituary.

Mnookin continued, "In order to support his strained hypothesis that all of the team's misfortunes could be traced to an event that had occurred six decades earlier, Shaughnessy ignored the many problems of Tom Yawkey's ownership of the team, even going so far as to whitewash Yawkey's troubled history with black ballplayers."

Even in *The Rivals: the Boston Red Sox vs. the New York Yankees*, a collaborative effort between writers from the *Boston Globe* and the *New York Times*, Shaughnessy persisted in attempting to bolster the conclusions he made way back when.

"In recent years, much has been made of the 'fallacy' that Frazee sold Ruth to the Yankees in order to finance a play titled *No, No, Nanette*," he wrote. "The debunkers point out that the Ruth deal was struck in 1919 and that the hit play didn't debut until 1923. The Frazee family has embraced these facts as proof that Big Harry did not sell out Boston in order to produce a hit play. It's also been pointed out that American League president Ban Johnson didn't like Frazee and the Sox owner dealt almost exclusively with New York as part of an alliance against the league president. While the limitations of Frazee's options are certainly a factor, and the cause-and-effect of the Ruth sale and the timing of *Nanette* are open to argument, the fact remains that Frazee cared more about his

Broadway shows than about his baseball team and struck a deal that was good for him and bad for the Boston ball team."

But the facts don't support Shaughnessy's assertions. Bill Simmons, in *Now I Can Die in Peace,* put the uninitiated on warning. "We need to set the record straight about The Curse for three reasons:

1.) It's *The Blair Witch Project* of sports legends. In other words, the vast majority of people don't understand it, so it has assumed a life of its own.

2.) The only people who keep mentioning The Curse are members of the media and uneducated non-Boston fans.

3.) Sox fans don't discuss The Curse—not because we're afraid of it but because it's so absurd, we wouldn't bother discussing it in the first place."

Certainly.

The recent new, hands-on Red Sox ownership overhauled the manner in which the Sox operate at a breakneck speed. We've witnessed the dawning of a new age of Boston baseball.

And it's high time.

When named general manager in 2002, Theo Epstein declared, "The Curse of the Bambino doesn't exist. Just give us a couple of years and we're going to win a World Series and that'll satisfy those troubled people who continue to believe in curses."

"The Curse of the Bambino?" posed minority owner Tom Werner in 2001. "We prefer to think of it as a spell we intend to break."

Boston pitcher Tim Wakefield, a member of the club since 1995, said the "curse" was simply hogwash. "We never believed in a curse here anyway," he declared. "It was the figment of some writer's imagination. We'd simply run into some bad luck here and there. We knew we'd win eventually."

Sages often say history tends to repeat itself, so an examination of how the Red Sox got to this point is appropriate and necessary.

In reality, the "curse" involved more than small doses of bigotry, cronyism, and mismanagement. The abject failure of the media to hold the team responsible not only for its plethora of bad—indeed, outright stupid—trades, but more importantly, for the miserable way the team avoided social change bordered on the criminal.

Many journalists persist in claiming that Ruth was sold so Red Sox owner Harry Frazee could use the money to underwrite a Broadway musical entitled *No, No, Nanette*. In reality that fable is the result of prejudice, pure and simple.

Babe Ruth was sold to the Yankees because he was a problem child and, in spite of his prodigious abilities, a disruption on the club. Constantly jousting with management, he was in the process of being converted from a pitcher to an outfielder. After hammering twenty-nine home runs for Boston in 1919 as a part-time outfielder, the Babe didn't want to continue pitching, even though the Sox were in decline and desperately needed him to pitch on occasion. Plus, despite having just signed a lucrative, multi-year contract extension, Ruth decided he wanted to renegotiate *another* contract.

Boston manager Ed Barrow, a disciplinarian of the first order, tried his best to keep the exuberant lout on a short leash, another matter Ruth incessantly whined about. (Ruth had no serious rivals in the whoring and drinking departments then or later, at least until his second wife reined him in.)

A theatrical producer by trade, Frazee did *not* sell Ruth to underwrite a play, as legend has it. In actuality, the theater magnate had previously hit the jackpot several times with Broadway productions, and his biggest hit, *No, No, Nanette*, was an overwhelming success in 1925, two years *after* he sold the Red Sox franchise.

Yes, the so-called curse is nothing more than a myth. And the truth is much uglier, a dirty little secret.

American League president Ban Johnson was a major league *bigot*. Further, he had been instrumental in ignoring the actions of the infamous 1919 Black Sox—simply out of spite toward Charles Comiskey, the owner of the American League franchise in Chicago. Johnson, who regularly used his position to defame people, did his best to ruin those who crossed him. And ultimately it was Johnson who drove Frazee out of his ownership of the Red Sox—because he believed Frazee was a Jew.

The anti-Semitic falsehood (Frazee was Presbyterian) was also nationally disseminated by Johnson's pal, Henry Ford, through the *Dearborn Independent*, the automaker's controversial Michigan-based weekly newspaper.

The rumor was further perpetuated by Fred Lieb, a longtime baseball writer. In fact, Lieb actually reported that Frazee admitted to him that he was forced to sell Ruth. But after Lieb's death, he was universally discredited as a reliable reporter, and a vast number of credible journalists have proven that Lieb often made up quotes out of whole cloth.

Another interesting note is that, at the time of Ruth's sale, Yankees owner Jacob Ruppert was the only American League owner who'd deal with Frazee. Frazee and Ruppert, along with Comiskey, were constantly running afoul of the imperious Johnson. The three were the only team owners in the American League who had the temerity to challenge Johnson's right to govern as he saw fit.

The bad moves by Boston Red Sox management neither began nor ended with the sale of Ruth to the New York Yankees. The franchise literally disposed of several of the greatest stars in the history of Major League Baseball, sending marquee players from several generations packing and getting little or nothing in return: Cy Young, Tris Speaker, Red Ruffing, Waite Hoyt, Herb Pennock, and, of course, the Bambino.

IIIIII

The second part of the story involves overt racism. The Sox have the distinction of being the last major league team to integrate. Among the Negro League stars they passed over were Jackie Robinson and Willie Mays. Instead, their first black player was infielder Elijah "Pumpsie" Green, a marginal player destined to have little more than "a cup of coffee" in the majors.

Imagine instead an outfield of Mays, Dom DiMaggio, and Ted Williams, and an infield featuring Robinson, along with the likes of Bobby Doerr, Johnny Pesky, Gene Stephens, Walt Dropo, and Billy Goodman.

The second African-American ballplayer to make the Red Sox was a right-handed power pitcher named Earl Wilson. But the Sox dumped Wilson in 1966 after the Marine Corps veteran was ordered out of a Central Florida lounge because he was black. His military service apparently counted for nothing. He couldn't stop off at a bar for a cold one after training solely because of his color. And although Wilson strove mightily to play down the confrontation, he became bitter at the club's refusal to address the matter.

When Wilson shared his thoughts with the press, the story unleashed a firestorm that rivaled the ascension of Pumpsie Green. Naturally, the Sox blamed Wilson, subsequently trading him to Detroit (along with African-American outfielder Joe Christopher) for an aging power hitter named Don Demeter, who was clearly in the twilight of his career, and minor league pitcher Julio Navarro, who never pitched a single inning for the parent club. (Under Tom Yawkey's ownership, the Sox always had an even number of African-Americans so they wouldn't have to room a black ballplayer with a white man.)

Wilson, who was originally signed as a catcher, proceeded to hit more home runs than Demeter. The pitcher also went on to lead the American League in victories in 1967 for the Tigers, tying his former teammate, Jim Lonborg of the Red Sox.

Unfortunately, the franchise's approach to integration mirrored the general mood of the city of Boston. From the late sixties through the mid-nineties the city was constantly torn by racial strife.

In 1975 Red Sox pitching ace Luis Tiant declared, "When I'm in the ballpark, I'm a hero—I'm El Tiante. A block away from the ballpark, if I try to get a cab, I'm just another black man nobody will stop for."

Longtime Red Sox owner Tom Yawkey was a drunk and, most likely, a closet racist. The management personnel he hired largely became his drinking buddies, cronies he enjoyed hanging out with and tipping a few.

In his book *Why Not Us?* published following Boston's 2004 world championship, Leigh Montville surmised, "The Red Sox were never a star-crossed operation. They were bumblers and stumblers, everything run in secret as if this were some kind of fraternal lodge instead of a business model. Skeletons hung in half the closets. The other half were stocked with liquor."

"There was always a sense of decadence around this team, an awful lot of odd behavior that had nothing to do with any freakin' curse," television journalist Clark Booth told Montville.

Yawkey hid behind three general managers—Eddie Collins, Joe Cronin, and Mike "Pinky" Higgins—in order to plausibly deny he was bigoted. Publicly, the Red Sox mantra was that they'd put an African-American man on their roster if they found one who was worthy to play for the team.

Booth said that, if a curse existed, it had nothing to do with Babe Ruth. "I hate those simple, Mickey Mouse explanations," he declared.

"They cover up sixty to seventy years of incompetence with this franchise. If there was any curse, it was the 'Curse of Tom Yawkey.'"

Some argue that, because the New York Yankees didn't integrate until the mid-fifties, the Red Sox were justified in failing to acquire African-American ballplayers.

"Yawkey had the heft and the weight that could've allowed him to integrate before [Brooklyn general manager Branch] Rickey did it. The team certainly had the money as well," declared baseball historian Glenn Stout. "Once the Dodgers did it, certainly there was no reason not to integrate, particularly when [the Red Sox] were that close to overtaking the Yankees. That the Yankees dragged their feet to integrate has always been the excuse Red Sox apologists use."

Edward R. Murrow, the groundbreaking broadcast journalist for the CBS network, explained his philosophy of news coverage as providing the public with a flawless mirror so the audience accurately saw itself, including all its warts and blemishes.

Unfortunately, for decades the Boston media failed to call the Red Sox front office on the carpet for its attitude toward minority baseball players. For the most part, writers assigned to cover the Red Sox never reported the "tryouts" afforded several African-American ballplayers who were legitimate Negro League stars. In fact, those ballplayers would never have even received their so-called tryouts if it hadn't been for a city councilor (who happened to be Jewish) who badgered the team into giving Jackie Robinson and two other African-American ballplayers a tryout. He employed all the leverage he could to force the Sox to conduct those tryouts, even threatening to put a halt to Sunday baseball.

The tryout reportedly concluded with someone high up in the stands behind home plate—never definitively identified—ending the audition by shouting, "Get those niggers off the field!"

Clif Keane, a *Boston Globe* Red Sox beat writer, attended the tryouts. The story he wrote on the incident never saw the light of day. In fairness to the *Globe,* it has never been determined whether or not management killed the article.

Even such an esteemed sports journalist as the late Will McDonough of the *Globe*, insisted—to the very end of his life—that Tom Yawkey was no racist. McDonough claimed the team simply couldn't find any African-American ballplayers who could help the club. "The only problem the Red Sox have ever had with blacks," McDonough once told Stout, "was finding blacks who could play. All right?"

Yet as a teen and young adult one of Yawkey's earliest mentors was none other than Tyrus Raymond Cobb, a notorious racist who publicly beat, stabbed, and shot African-American men and women. His intense hatred of African-Americans is legendary, and unfortunately all too true.

In fact, it was Cobb who first encouraged Yawkey to buy a major league team. Yawkey took Cobb's advice and acquired a club that became derisively known as "The Plantation."

A long-time Red Sox ballplayer, Mike "Pinky" Higgins, initially an infielder but later manager and general manager (and one of Yawkey's drinking buddies) publicly declared that no black would ever take the field while he was manager. He was right. Pumpsie Green joined the team after Billy Jurges took over the managerial reins mid-season in 1959.

Higgins returned to manage the following year, as without fail Yawkey always took care of his sycophants. Ironically, the Sox ended up with more black ballplayers under Higgins then they did during the late eighties and early nineties. Jim Rice was the lone African-American for nearly four years during the late eighties, and

Ellis Burks was the only African-American throughout the 1990 season and into 1991.

Yet Sox apologists maintain the team never had a "racial problem." A number of baseball analysts say those within the organization were largely blind to the inbred prejudice.

Shortly after Higgins left organized baseball, he killed a African-American man while driving drunk. Pinky died of a heart attack two days after his parole from prison.

"The place was filled with some wonderful characters," opined long-time Boston broadcaster Clark Booth, "but underneath it all there was this strain of darkness with the Yawkeys. It was all very weird."

Until the demise of America's daily newspapers, nearly every major metropolitan city sported a half-dozen or more dailies. It wasn't until after World War II that the daily newspapers' humongous readership base began to erode, as broadcast news and sports began cutting deeply into circulation.

During my lifetime the Boston-based dailies shrunk from six daily newspapers to two—and at this writing, one of those papers continues to hang on to existence by a thread, in spite of the deep pockets of its owner, media mogul Ruppert Murdock. A third daily newspaper, a freebie, was started in 2007 but folded in April 2008 after less than a year, despite "increased circulation and revenue," according to *BostonNOW* executives. While Babe Ruth toiled for the BoSox, there were nine daily newspapers.

For decades the media was pretty much hamstrung in objectively covering Major League Baseball. The clubs picked up the tab for those traveling with the teams. Early in the twentieth century the family that owned the *Boston Globe* owned the Red Sox. Even today, the *New York Times* owns the *Globe*, which in turn is a minority owner of the Red Sox. Now each newspaper makes its own travel arrangements as opposed to doing so through the team. But before the demise of most of those dailies years ago, editorial management, vying for numbers, gave their columnists unbelievable leeway in what they wrote and how they presented the information they wanted to convey. Examples of journalistic mayhem from the founding of the Red Sox through the mid-fifties are rife.

One of the primary reasons Ted Williams—undoubtedly the greatest baseball player ever to don a Red Sox uniform—had such a bad attitude toward the press was because he was constantly vilified by, among others, a drunken scribe named Dave Egan, who wrote for the *Boston Record*. Egan, nicknamed "The Colonel," a Harvard Law School graduate, often slandered Williams outright, going far, far beyond name-calling. (Ironically, Egan *defended* Williams during Ted's two greatest crises.)

Meanwhile, the hapless ineptitude of the Sox was typified by the theory offered by field manager Billy Herman, who ran the club from 1964 through 1966. (In 1965 the team lost an even 100 games, the most since 1932.)

"For Red Sox fans," pontificated Herman, "there are only two seasons: August and winter."

So much for a winning attitude.

Noted Simmons, "Red Sox fans [didn't] define themselves by the eighty-six-year drought, we [were] *defined* by the 86-year drought." Tom Yawkey, his wife Jean, and his trust controlled the club for sixty-eight years, never winning a single World Series—and competing in but four.

It didn't take long for the consortium headed by the new principal owner, John Henry, to reverse that trend.

"How long have the new owners been here?" asked the sagacious Booth, in the wake of the franchise's 2004 world champion-ship. "Three years. That's how long it took once the Yawkey orga-nization was out of the picture. That's your curse."

Bigotry ran deeply throughout the major leagues from its incep-tion. During the early decades of the twentieth century, the Red Sox squad was polarized into two camps: Catholics and Protestants. And the Sox weren't the only team that this schism proved to be an un-derlying fact of life, as the Pittsburgh Pirates—a franchise owned by a Jew, Barney Dreyfuss—was similarly fractured.

With rare exception under the Yawkey ownership, the Red Sox never wavered in their quest for success. The franchise's corner-stones were predominantly made up of hefty right-handed hitting sluggers who could take potshots at the inviting left-field wall, in actuality only 305 feet down the left-field line.

Much of this story ain't pretty, but perhaps it will prompt a re-solve to never view such things through rose-colored glasses again. And those of us in the press need to take an objective, unvarnished and factual look at the club's history—and the poor job the media performed in covering the Sox—so we won't get fooled again.

2

THE BIG BAN

B yron Bancroft Johnson, the founder of the American League, was a gargantuan man with bold dreams and sweeping vision, without whose drive, determination and cunning the league might never have come into existence.

Wrote Bob Considine after Johnson's death, "Johnson [was] a ruthless dreamer who lived and died believing that baseball was perfected in order to serve him as a gigantic chess board on which to move his living pieces."

Born in Newark, Ohio on January 5, 1864, Johnson attended Marietta College, where he played baseball, serving as a catcher— without protective gear—during the era that pitching was still entirely underhand.

Transferring to the University of Cincinnati Law School after a year at Marietta, Johnson quit college to take a job as a sportswriter at the *Cincinnati Commercial Gazette* in 1887, where he later became "sporting editor." Johnson parlayed that position into a minor league baseball executive job. Ironically, one of his most fervid backers at the time was Charles O. Comiskey, who later became a Johnson antagonist.

At the behest of Comiskey and Cincinnati owner John T. Brush, Johnson was named president of the Western League in 1894. Brush, a bitter enemy of Johnson's, saw it as a means of getting the younger man out of Cincinnati and out of his hair. Johnson had routinely attacked Brush in print for failing to spend enough money on the Reds, claiming Brush colluded with the other National League owners to ensure maximum profits and damaging the best interests of baseball. He called Brush the "master of parsimony" and a "representative of interests best divorced from baseball."

The Western League was comprised of teams in Indianapolis, Kansas City, Milwaukee, Minneapolis, Toledo, Grand Rapids, Detroit, and Sioux City. After Comiskey's contract as Cincinnati's field manager expired, he bought the Sioux City franchise and moved it from Iowa to Minnesota, relocating the club to St. Paul.

Under Johnson, the Western League became known as the best-run minor league circuit in the country. Johnson exercised a free hand in all league matters, including the drafting of schedules and travel contracts, signing players, and shifting of franchises. His word was law, and the individual club owners went along with his rulings because they began making lots of money.

Once ensconced as the master of the Western League, Johnson moved to broaden his influence, and he and Comiskey began plotting further expansion.

Indeed he telegraphed his intentions to the National League owners on February 29, 1896, asserting, "The Western League has passed the stage where it should be considered a minor league . . . it is a first-class organization, and should have the consideration that such an organization warrants."

As a result of Johnson's strict enforcement of decorum, Western League games quickly were considered family entertainment because fans would not witness violent behavior or hear bad language. Those changes dramatically increased attendance. And as the Western League improved its image, the twelve-team National League increasingly saw a decline in attendance. Both the Cleveland Spiders and Baltimore Orioles had raised rowdyism to an art form, and warfare among the owners, a blatant disregard for the public, and the ill treatment of players outraged the National League's fan base.

In 1899, when the NL pared back to eight teams by dropping Cleveland, Washington, Louisville, and Baltimore, Johnson spied his opportunity. At a meeting of Western League officials in October, the league changed its name to the American League to give it more of a national character. Johnson then announced that the league would expand by establishing one franchise in Cleveland and moving Comiskey's St. Paul club to Chicago. The National League's Orphans—later renamed the Cubs—were already situated in Chicago, but its owner agreed to the invasion of Comiskey's club, ceding the city's south side.

Initially, Johnson attempted to broker a deal with National League owners in order to establish a sister league, but the owners rebuffed his overtures. It was no doubt the most egregious miscalculation of their collective lives, as Johnson proceeded to create a major league of his own. Nevertheless, as late as November 1899, Johnson still tried to settle things amicably, proposing player exchanges with a view to giving the public new attractions. Foolishly, the National League moguls instead set a $2,400 salary cap, prompting eighty-seven players to jump to the new circuit.

Johnson was awarded a ten-year contract as AL president in 1901, initially placing teams in Philadelphia, Buffalo, Baltimore, and Washington, while retaining the Cleveland, Chicago, Detroit, and Milwaukee franchises. He then moved the Buffalo franchise to

Boston, and a year later relocated the Milwaukee-based club to St. Louis. In 1903 the New York Invaders, later the Highlanders—who were then renamed the Yankees—replaced the Baltimore franchise. Dealing with the Players Protective Association, each AL team was limited to fourteen players per team, with a 140-game schedule. And the American League contracts limited player service to five years.[2]

Although a few National League owners realized that a second league could spur greater interest among the fans, increase attendance, and make postseason contests a possibility, most simply preferred to crush their new rivals. For two years a "war" raged between the leagues, but the NL never had a chance. Johnson shored up weak franchises by finding financial backers and moving star players to struggling teams.

By 1902 the American League had surpassed the National League in attendance, essentially forcing the latter's owners to make peace with Johnson.

Johnson ruled the American League with a mailed fist, the ultimate imperialist. For the most part, he badgered and bullied club owners until he got his way. In fact, mimicking the Western League's approach, individual AL owners made Johnson the *de facto* owner of every club. Johnson used that power regularly, vetoing trades and ordering player movements. No sports executive in the history of organized team sports ever exercised such sway.

David Lee Poremba, in his book, *The American League: The Early Years*, said of Johnson, "As boss, Johnson found no task too large or too small to merit his attention. He located millionaires to bankroll his teams, came down hard on rowdies and roughhousing on the field, appointed managers, arranged trades, and apportioned players. He arranged schedules to spread travel costs equitably, inter-

2 Johnson later amended the fourteen-player rule, expanding rosters to fifteen players at the behest of six of the AL clubs.

preted rules, levied fines and suspensions, issued statistics, and even recruited William Howard Taft as the first President to throw out an Opening Day ball. One of his most important contributions was to enforce respect for umpires as symbols of baseball's integrity."

Johnson quickly took action when he suspended Baltimore first baseman Burt Hart on August 7, 1901, for striking umpire John Haskell, stating, "This is the first time a player in the American League has struck an umpire, and it is an offense that cannot be overlooked." Hart never appeared in another major league game.

Unhappy with the location of some of the American League teams, Johnson constantly tinkered with the league's make up. His moving the franchise from Baltimore to New York City incensed the legendary John J. McGraw. In a preemptory strike, a furious McGraw had bolted to the National League's New York Giants (as player-manager) before the Baltimore club could be moved, earning Johnson McGraw's lifelong enmity. Despite his previous promises, McGraw then raided his old Maryland-based franchise to pirate away some of its best ballplayers.

A year after the landmark first AL-NL World Series between Boston and Pittsburgh, McGraw refused to face the Boston Americans in the 1904 World Series. "The Giants will not play a postseason series with the American League champions. Ban Johnson has not been on the level with me personally, and the American League management has been crooked more than once," McGraw declared. "When we clinch the National League pennant, we'll be champions of the only real major league."

Responded Johnson, "No thoughtful patron of baseball can weigh seriously the wild vaporings of this discredited player who was canned from the American League."

Once the bloodletting ceased and the two leagues agreed to work in tandem, a three-man National Commission, comprised of both league presidents and a third party, was established. Johnson's influence was such that he was dubbed the "Czar of Baseball," and the game's popularity soared during the first two decades of the twentieth century.

"He did it all with little grace and no humor. Johnson was hottempered, bullheaded, imperious and uncompromising, not unlike many other tycoons of his time," wrote Poremba. "His owners voted him $25,000 a year and presidency for life."

Ultimately things soured for Johnson, yet during his tenure as league president, only three owners dared to directly challenge him: Comiskey, Yankees owner Jacob Ruppert, and Red Sox owner Harry Frazee.

Frazee and Ruppert went into action after Johnson negated the trade of Red Sox pitcher Carl Mays to New York. The Yanks obtained a court order upholding the player move.

Both Comiskey and Frazee would pay dearly for defying Johnson: Comiskey would lose eight players due to the 1919 Black Sox scandal, while Frazee was eventually forced to sell his baseball club.

Johnson's lack of tolerance for Frazee, in large part due to his belief that the theatrical magnate was Jewish, was reflected in the pages of the *Sporting News*, which railed against "a lot of dirty, long-nosed, thick-lipped and strong-smelling [i.e., Hebrew] gamblers [who] butted into the World Series." Ironically, the weekly was attempting to refute charges that the 1919 World Series had been fixed,—ignoring the fact that the gambler initially involved was Irish-American!

Johnson truly was a force to be reckoned with.

Old friend Charles Comiskey once said, "Ban Johnson *is* the

American League!" But after a Johnson ruling caused Comiskey to lose pitcher Jack Quinn to the Yankees, Comiskey thundered: "I made you, and by God I'll break you!"

Years later, Comiskey told the *Cleveland Plain Dealer* that his falling out with Johnson wasn't due to the Quinn imbroglio. However, he refused to be specific about what actually caused their rift.

In *Eight Men Out*, author Eliot Asinof suggested that Johnson and Comiskey had their first significant disagreement in 1905, when Johnson suspended Chicago's James "Ducky" Holmes on short notice. Comiskey became angry because he wasn't notified of the suspension until just prior to a game. "If Comiskey doesn't like the punishment, he is at liberty to pull out of the American League!" retorted Johnson. "I regard the whole matter as closed!"

After the subsequent suspension of another White Sox ballplayer in 1907, Johnson blithely sent Comiskey a dozen bass. Snapped Comiskey, "Does Johnson expect me to play fish in my outfield?"

In spite of repeated peace entreaties, the Quinn affair signaled the end of détente between the two men. Yet in an unpublished autobiography, Johnson claimed that he could think of only one feud with Comiskey that permanently soured their relationship: the refusal of AL owners to immediately end the 1918 season after the U.S. entered World War I. After the War Department forced the major leagues to stop play in September 1918, Johnson termed it "very humiliating" to the game.

When Comiskey suspected that his Chicago White Sox were throwing the 1919 World Series, his appeals to Johnson fell on deaf ears. Johnson responded to Comiskey's pleas with "That's the yelp of a beaten cur!"

Nevertheless, despite evidence to the contrary, years later Johnson asserted Comiskey never approached him after Game Two of the 1919 World Series. "If there was any gossip of a questionable nature [after Game One] I do not recall it," wrote Johnson. "Nor was there any brought to our attention after the second game."

Johnson biographer Eugene Murdock challenged Johnson's version of the events surrounding the fix coming to light, citing journalists Hugh Fullerton and Taylor Spink, National League president John Heydler, White Sox team secretary Harry Grabiner, and Comiskey himself.

In Johnson's memoirs—published in part much later in the *St. Louis Post-Dispatch*—he admitted, "Looking back, one can see that repeated warnings had been given us." He was even more forthcoming in his unpublished autobiography. "The most sensational happening to occur during my tenure of office as president of the AL was the successful attempt of eight members of the Chicago White Sox team to 'throw' the World Series of 1919 in the interest of a group, or rather of two groups, of professional gamblers." [3]

Ironically, Johnson also alluded to a failed attempt on the part of a St. Louis–based gambler to fix the 1918 World Series—the last World Series won by the Red Sox until 2004.

Although Johnson later launched an investigation of the 1919 Black Sox scandal, team owners moved to replace the ruling triumvirate with a single commissioner, Judge Kenesaw Mountain Landis, appointed in 1920 after the 1919 Black Sox scandal came to light.

In Landis, Johnson finally met his match. Just as imperious as the American League founder, Landis handed down edicts like a Roman emperor. Bristling at the encroachment of what he perceived as his

---

3 1919 wasn't the first time conclusive evidence of players throwing World Series games came to light. In the very first World Series—between the Boston Americans and the Pittsburgh Pirates—it was very evident that players on both squads colluded to draw out the nine-game series for as long as possible. Ultimately, the Americans won the initial face-off, giving Boston its first world championship.

territory, Johnson's jousting with the former federal judge was legendary. "The hiring of Landis was the thing that turned Johnson into a screaming harridan, and had Ban been just a little less arrogant, he might have saved himself the crushing burden of dealing with the equally arrogant Landis," recalled long-time major league umpire Bill Klem.

Time magazine published a lengthy report on Johnson's ouster in December 1929.

"For many, many years he was a sort of Grand Khan of the sport. He . . . fought many battles during his career as president of the American League, serene in the confidence of his own ability to deal properly and effectively with whatever situation might arise," asserted the authors of the piece. "In 1920, the two major leagues (National and American) made Judge Landis 'Tsar of Baseball,'" setting the stage for Johnson's abrupt departure, triggered by another alleged gambling scandal involving the New York Giants. Once Johnson lost his bid to stop the 1920 World Series, the major league owners removed him from the National Commission after he called Landis a "wild-eyed crazy nut."

The last straw occurred when Johnson made additional accusations, charging that, in addition to the notorious eight "Black Sox," Ty Cobb and Tris Speaker, star players *and* managers, were likewise involved in gambling fixes. Landis unceremoniously shoved Johnson out the door.

After being temporarily replaced as American League president in early 1927, the founder of the American League officially retired because of ill health on October 17. He passed away due to complications from diabetes on February 28, 1931.

Johnson's influence was posthumously lauded in Spink's *Sporting News*.

"The voice of the lion is stilled. They say the lion was getting old, that his roar had become a mumble. It may be so. But never, maybe, will be heard again such a voice. The roar that struck terror to evil-doers, in high estate or low, and thrilled to new encouragement those who had ideals and the vision Ban Johnson had."

FOUNDATIONS

3

The American League franchise now known reverentially as the Red Sox was originally called the "Boston Americans," so-named to differentiate it from its cross-town rival, the Boston Braves of the National League. Boston's NL club had already been in place for a quarter century before the AL arrived.

The Braves were known as the "Red Caps" in 1876 when the initial "Boston Base Ball" franchise was established, but the nickname "Red Stockings" likewise dates back to the 1870s. They went by many names in the first two decades of their existence, but eventually they discarded the name "Red Stockings," ultimately settling on the Braves.

Various sources referred to the early Boston American League franchise as the "Pilgrims," "Puritans," "Plymouth Rocks," or the "Somersets," but baseball researcher Bill Nowlin determined that none was ever in popular use, and that "Pilgrims," regarded today as the most popular of the early names, was barely used at all. From 1901 through 1907 the team was universally known as the "Boston Americans."

Ban Johnson had several acquaintances with deep pockets, including a timber and shipping magnate named Charles Somers, whom he enticed into investing in both the Boston *and* Cleveland franchises. Somers became the majority owner of the Americans, and a minority owner of Cleveland (now known as the Indians, but who went by their own array of names in the early days of the AL). Johnson also convinced Somers to loan money to Connie Mack, who co-founded the Philadelphia Athletics, and to Charles Comiskey, sole owner of the Chicago White Sox. Ultimately, Somers put up about $5 million in the fledgling league.

By the turn of the century professional baseball was in utter disarray, and National League fans abandoned the game in droves. The greed of the existing NL clubs was boundless. In particular, Boston Braves owner Arthur Soden took his fan base for granted.

Although Boston wasn't initially on the short list of cities slated to receive an American League club, the Braves fan base had eroded so badly that Ban Johnson quickly shifted his proposed Buffalo franchise to Boston. Somers immediately proceeded to raid the Braves roster and even enticed the greatest pitcher of the era, Cy Young, to leave the St. Louis Cardinals for Boston.

Other marquee players Somers enticed included outfielder Chick Stahl, first baseman Buck Freeman, and third baseman Jimmy Collins, who would become the squad's first manager.

The first indicator that perhaps the Red Sox would prove snake-bitten occurred when Chick Stahl's former girlfriend, Lulu Ortman, was arrested in Indiana after attempting to shoot the Boston center fielder in the winter following the club's first season.

Ground was broken for a new field, located on what is now the campus of Northeastern University, a short distance from the Braves' stadium. The Americans began playing at the Huntington Avenue Grounds in 1901.

At first, Soden and his fellow National League owners remained oblivious to the onslaught. Instead, they established a rival league called the American Association, hoping that the upstart AL would quickly die on the vine. Indeed Johnson foresaw losses through the first five years. However, he underestimated the stupidity and greed of the National League moguls, who persisted in turning away Johnson's requests to allow the American League to go head-to-head with the NL. They also rebuffed the players, who had requested minor concessions.

In Boston, Soden completely misread the situation, counting on his loyal fan base of Irish-Americans. But his ballplayers drank regularly with these most rabid fans, known as the Royal Rooters—and those diehards were well aware of the liberties taken at the expense of the players. In addition, the blatant game fixing had taxed even their tolerance. The primary topic of discussion during the winter of 1900–1901 centered on the new baseball league.[4]

Somers decided to divest himself of the club after a single season so Johnson cast about for another owner for the new Boston club. He convinced Milwaukee attorney Henry Killilea to purchase a majority of Somers's stock. After the two leagues made peace in 1903, Killilea bought out Somers's entire interest.

The rival leagues also decided to stage a new kind of season finale. This was not entirely unprecedented because the original American Association and National League had played postseason series each year between 1884 and 1890. After the demise of the AA, the top two NL teams had played each other in postseason series.

The finale, the *Chronicle-Telegraph* Cup in 1900, had pitted Brooklyn against Pittsburgh. The Pirates, who'd lost that series,

---

4 The predominantly Irish-Catholic Royal Rooters congregated at a tavern called the Third Base owned by their unofficial leader, Ned "'Nuf Said" McGreevey. The Third Base earned its name because it was termed "the last stop before one headed home." McGreevey was known as "'Nuf Said" because he'd terminate arguments about baseball by crying, "'Nuf said!"

were the most formidable team in the NL when they faced the Boston Americans in the 1903 "World Series," a best-of-nine playoff.

Gambling and rowdyism dominated the first World Series. Even Pirates owner Barney Dreyfuss placed numerous wagers.

On October 3, Boston fans crashed Game Three by jumping the fence and taking over the outfield. Boston police and ticket-holders battled the gatecrashers; the police were eventually forced to use baseball bats to help control the crowd, but they still couldn't clear the field of spectators. Accordingly, the game continued under the stipulation that balls hit into the crowd would be ground-rule doubles. Johnson had officially barred gambling at American League parks effective August 17, 1903, but to little avail. Although he would later claim that league officials were successful in prosecuting "thirty-three of thirty-three [gambling] arrests . . . and convictions," the move largely proved to be a futile gesture.

In spite of Ban's ban, the Boston newspapers became preoccupied with the wagering that dominated the 1903 World Series. Much more print was expended concerning the gambling epidemic than upon the games themselves. Widespread reports indicated that Boston's ballplayers spent an inordinate amount of time consorting with gamblers at local watering holes. Following Game One, the *Boston Post* noted, "many around town last evening asked if Boston lost on purpose." Boston's play in the rest of the World Series was less than stellar, and the Boston media ultimately leveled outright charges that the games had been fixed.

"Boston sports [fans] today are wondering if they got their money's worth—if Boston really played their best to win," reported the *Post*. "Wholesale charges of throwing the games have been making the rounds of the city since Saturday evening."

Despite the team's questionable play, the Americans ultimately prevailed, winning the best-of-nine series five games to three. Even so, the American League players were disgruntled despite their victory. Although owner Henry Killilea honored his promise of paying each player a share of $1,182.34, Dreyfuss gave *his* Pirates $1,316.00, angering Boston's ballplayers because the losers earned more than the winners.

The dispute soured Killilea on ownership of the club, and he quickly sought a buyer. The front-runner was John "Honey Fitz" Fitzgerald, a local Irish powerbroker, later elected Boston's mayor and grandfather of President John F. Kennedy.

But Johnson feared that "Honey Fitz" might prove too difficult to control, so in spite of Johnson's assurances that Fitzgerald held the winning bid for the club, Fitzgerald—later the unofficial head of the Royal Rooters—lost out on the franchise to General Charles Taylor,[5] the owner of the *Boston Globe*, who immediately placed the team in the incapable hands of his son, John I. Taylor. The younger Taylor had the well-earned reputation of being a notorious playboy and drunkard, and his tenure as owner of the franchise did nothing to alter that perception.

Ban Johnson found he had his hands full. Instead of bowing to Johnson's wishes, Taylor failed to honor the league president's dictums and began dumping Boston's talented ballplayers for lesser ones.

Yet Taylor wasn't altogether to blame in making mindless player moves.

Worried that Boston would continue to dominate league play and hurt the fan base in other AL cities, Johnson himself decreed that the team send hard-hitting outfielder Patsy Dougherty to New York to make up for an earlier trade that the Highlanders had complained about. Boston had sent "Long" Tom Hughes, a right-handed

---

5 Taylor, a Civil War veteran, had been seriously wounded in the Battle of Port Hudson as a sixteen-year-old Union soldier. His rank of general was attained as a member of the Massachusetts State Militia.

pitcher who had a solid season in 1903, to New York for lefty Jesse Tannehill. Hughes's season promptly went belly-up, while Tannehill became one of Boston's top starters.

Embroiled in a struggle with the National League's New York Giants for the entertainment dollar, Johnson wanted to level the playing field for the team, still called the "Invaders" by some New York papers. Finally John Taylor caved, trading Dougherty to New York for utility man Bob Unglaub.

The move hurt Boston badly. Dougherty, an outfielder who was immensely popular with Boston's Irish-American community, had hit .342 and .331 in his two full seasons with the Americans. In return, Boston received Unglaub, a utility infielder who had played in all of six major league games. In three seasons with the Boston franchise, Unglaub hit .154, .223, and .254.

Yet despite the unpopular trade, Boston held off New York to claim the AL pennant for the second straight year. Boston was denied the chance to retain its world championship when the New York Giants refused to face them. There would be no 1904 Fall Classic.

The chaos continued. Boston shortstop Freddy Parent later called Taylor a constant disruption to the team, charging that the newspaper scion "was drunk half the time." Player-manager Jimmy Collins, also continually at odds with Taylor, went as far as barring the team president from the clubhouse.

But the players were growing old, and Taylor didn't help matters when he sent top prospect George Stone to the St. Louis Browns for the aging Jesse Burkett, who was definitely on the decline. Stone led the league in hits in 1905, was the AL batting champion in 1906, and remained one of the game's best hitters throughout the rest of the decade. Burkett retired after playing in Boston for one year, during which he batted .257.

By early 1905, rumors were rife that Johnson was campaigning for the sale of the club. The rumors were correct, but Taylor's father intervened to forestall the sale.

The two-time defending AL champs barely broke the .500 mark in 1905. Young Taylor showed his petulance by refusing to make any meaningful trades, defying manager Jimmy Collins's wishes to trade some of his thirty-something players while they still had some market value. Taylor shunned making any significant deals from January 1905 through June 1907. Even though the General stepped in to rectify some of his son's many miscues, he had neither the time nor the patience to deal with club policies; he was preoccupied with matters involving his newspaper.

Things grew worse in 1906. The Americans went 49–105 and plummeted to last place. The season also saw a twenty-game losing streak, from May 1 through May 24, the second-longest losing streak in league history.

Altogether, Boston was shut out twenty-eight times that year, eight times at the hands of White Sox pitchers. They went 1–10 against the fifth-place St. Louis Browns[6] at home. Pitcher Joe Harris lost fourteen consecutive games, finishing the season at 2–21. Third baseman Red Morgan and shortstop Freddy Parent combined for ninety-seven errors, leading the team, which committed 303 errors, all told.

After three consecutive shutouts Collins disappeared for a week, beginning on July 7. He was suspended, then returned but again left without notice in August, with Chick Stahl filling in as manager. Taylor fired Collins, naming Stahl manager.

When Stahl committed suicide on March 28, 1907, Taylor announced that he would run the team himself as field manager. A furious Ban Johnson forced Taylor to rethink the move. So Taylor

---

6 Later the Baltimore Orioles

appointed a reluctant Cy Young as interim manager during the 1907 season until a permanent replacement could be named. Taylor then hired George Huff, a virtual unknown, who'd never played *or* managed in the big leagues. Huff lasted just eight games, losing six, after which infielder Bob Unglaub was selected to helm the club.

Johnson stepped in again after the team went 9–20 under Unglaub's direction. In June, "Deacon" McGuire took the reins as Boston's fifth manager of the season.

Taylor's next bonehead move occurred on February 18, 1909. He traded twenty-one game winner Cy Young, who sported an ERA of 1.26 the previous year, to Cleveland for cash and pitchers Charlie Chech and Jack Ryan. Though Young would turn forty-two that season, he won nineteen games for Cleveland in 1909. The pitching pair the Red Sox received won a total of eleven.

John I. Taylor did make two substantive contributions to Boston's AL franchise. He renamed them the "Red Stockings," later shortened to "Red Sox," in late 1907, and he built Fenway Park in 1912. The new stadium, which replaced the old Huntington Avenue Grounds leased by the club, remains the oldest ballpark in the major leagues.

The stadium was financed by his father, General Taylor. Reflected John I. Taylor, " . . . it's in the Fenway [section of Boston], isn't it?" The park was constructed on an odd-shaped piece of property owned by the Taylors, accounting for its short left-field fence. By comparison, both right field and center field were monstrous. (Future owner Tom Yawkey would shorten right field, in part through the addition of two bullpens, during the Ted Williams era.)

Aside from the aberrant twenty-five-foot-high wooden wall, left field was best known for its upslope. The outfield plot became known as "Duffy's Cliff," rivaling the left-field wall for difficulty in gauging its play. But in the dead-ball era, neither the wall nor the cliff came into play very often.

Years later, Duffy Lewis described playing left field.

"At the crack of the bat you'd turn and run up it," remarked Lewis. "Then you had to pick up the ball [visually] and decide whether to jump, go right or left or rush down again. It took plenty of practice. They made a mountain goat out of me."

By 1912, catcher-manager Lou Criger had retired after the General had temporarily shipped his drunken son to Europe. But the elder Taylor then welcomed back the younger man.

The curtain fell on the Taylor regime when the General sold the club to former Washington Senators manager James McAleer and Ban Johnson's secretary, Robert McRoy, although in reality Johnson bankrolled the deal himself.

The change in ownership ushered in a new era of Red Sox baseball. McAleer, as front man, immediately began strengthening the team, adding first baseman–manager Jake Stahl (no relation to Chick) and luring catcher Bill Carrigan out of retirement. He also signed a Mexican-American pitcher, Carlos Clolo, known as Charlie "Sea Lion" Hall to disguise his background, another sign of the times.

As the team assembled for spring training, only Tris Speaker was absent because he was holding out for more money. (Taylor had nearly lost Speaker during his term as team president when he failed to send "Spoke" a contract.)

The rest of the team was ready to challenge Connie Mack's Athletics for the 1912 pennant. The ever-confident Mack predicted his squad would secure its third consecutive title and break its wins record. But it just wasn't in the cards.

The Sox jumped out to a fast start and didn't look back. Boston moved into first place on June 18 and never relinquished it.

Behind pitchers Smoky Joe Wood, rookie Hugh Bedient, and sophomore Buck O'Brien, the Sox were seemingly unstoppable. Both Bedient and O'Brien won exactly twenty games.

Wood and the legendary Walter Johnson, pitching for the Washington Senators, both began winning streaks on July 3 to go undefeated for seven straight weeks. The two squared off on September 6 at Fenway Park.

The crowd attending the Wood-Johnson duel, once said to have been the largest in Boston history, watched the two hurlers match each other pitch for pitch until the Sox managed a single run in the bottom of the sixth inning. Wood shut down Washington entirely to emerge as the 1–0 winner over the magnificent "Big Train," as Johnson was known. Anchored by the "Million Dollar Outfield" of Speaker, Harry Hooper, and Duffy Lewis, the Sox handily rolled to the AL championship.

Ultimately, Boston established a won-loss record of 105–47, and prepared to square off against the New York Giants. Boston had a score to settle, as its players and fans had never forgotten the Giants calling them "a bunch of bush-leaguers" in declining to play the 1904 World Series.

And indeed, the Sox—behind Wood (who threw more than 360 innings all told during 1912), defeated the New Yorkers in eight games (including a tie).

Nevertheless, the team alienated many fans because of its questionable play during the seventh game. "Not since the opening game of the first World Series nine years earlier had a Boston team turned in a performance with such an unpalatable stench," wrote Richard Johnson and Glenn Stout in *Red Sox Century*.

Many of the "Royal Rooters" didn't even bother to show up on Opening Day the following June to see the raising of the world championship pennant. In part, they were outraged because management had sold off their reserved seats during the Series, a gaffe that caused a riot.

And the Boston club was torn by dissention because of religious beliefs. The team was split into two factions—Catholic and Protestant.

Leading the Catholic faction were Lewis, Carrigan, Hooper and O'Brien, while Speaker and Wood led the Protestant clique. The ten local newspapers chronicled the feud by referring to the two sectarian groups as "the Knights" (short for Knights of Columbus) and "the Masons."

Even through the eighties and nineties, the Red Sox predominantly have mirrored the prejudice dividing the city itself. It was no different in 1912. The only variant was that religion was the dividing point instead of race.

Things went south quickly for the Boston nine in 1913, and they ended the season in fourth place, with Joe Wood suffering injuries that effectively ruined his pitching career.

After Boston again nose-dived in 1914, Johnson soured on McAleer's ownership of the club. While McAleer was overseas following the season, Johnson quietly engineered a transfer of ownership to Quebec native Joseph L. Lannin.

Again Johnson had flexed his muscles and proven he still pulled all the strings. The AL founder remained incensed that a ticket fiasco during the 1912 World Series had cost him money and hurt attendance, but of greater importance, a group announced it was forming a third major league: the Federal League. The newly-minted circuit began signing ballplayers from both the National League *and* the American League; even players who simply talked to the Feds wound up getting juicy raises. It cost Lannin and John I. Taylor, inexplicably still with the club as vice president, the princely sum of $36,000 to retain Tris Speaker for two years, a far cry from the pittance that players were making only a decade previous.

Joseph Lannin bought out all the common stock holdings of the Taylor family on May 14, 1914, and became the sole owner of the Red Sox. A new era in Boston baseball was dawning.

4

ENTER THE BABE

The Federal League was directly responsible for Boston's acquisition of one George Herman Ruth.

Ruth, pitching for the Baltimore Orioles of the International League, was a prized prospect, but owner-manager Jack Dunn found himself in dire financial straits after the Feds opened a new stadium directly across the street from his ballpark. Attendance was down markedly and Dunn was forced to sell off his best talent, most notably pitchers Ruth and Ernie Shore, along with catcher Ben Egan, in 1914.

Sox manager Bill Carrigan, who received glowing reports on the two minor league pitching phenoms, urged Lannin to purchase their contracts. Lannin traveled to Baltimore and spent approximately $25,000 to buy the three players.

Ruth's proclivity for hitting was widely noted from the outset of his professional baseball career, even though he was signed as a pitcher.

"The main topic of conversation is the work of Lefty Ruth and the prodigious hit he made in practice yesterday afternoon," wrote one scribe in the *Baltimore American* during Ruth's first-ever spring training.

Teammates and coaches alike didn't know what to make of the naive and uncouth nineteen-year-old southpaw. "He looked like a big, overgrown Indian," declared coach Freddy Parent, who had been shortstop on the 1903 world champion Red Sox.

Dunn, who signed Ruth while the youngster was still a ward of the Saint Mary's Industrial School for Boys in Baltimore, was absolutely smitten with the baseball prodigy. "He'll startle the baseball world if he isn't a rummy or a nut," Dunn told reporters. And to a priest at the school, he declared, "Brother, this fellow Ruth is the greatest young ballplayer who ever reported to a training camp."

Babe immediately displayed his reckless side. After Ruth crashed a bicycle into the back of a horse-drawn wagon Dunn lit into him. "You want to go back to that school? You behave yourself, you hear me? You're a ballplayer—not a circus act!" Dunn roared.

Ruth arrived in Boston on July 11, 1914, boasting of a 14–6 record with the Orioles. Manager Carrigan immediately threw Ruth into the fray, starting him against the Indians that very afternoon. Ruth blew through Cleveland's lineup for six innings but was clobbered in the seventh. After that outing he was used sparingly throughout the summer while the more seasoned Shore emerged as an ace. At one point Ruth was shipped to Boston's International League farm team in Providence, but he rejoined the parent club at the end of the season for another taste of the majors.

Carrigan recognized that Ruth, although completely out of his element, was a diamond in the rough. "Babe was crude in spots," Carrigan admitted. "Anybody could see he'd quickly develop into a standout with a little more experience. He had a barrel of stuff, his speed was blinding, and his ball was alive."

Ruth's naïveté quickly assumed legendary proportions. He lost a preseason game in 1915 because he thought a "waste pitch" was a "waist pitch."

Hall-of-Famer Harry Hooper discerned something special in the budding star, but he wasn't completely convinced of Ruth's phenomenal talent. "I saw a man transformed from a human being into something pretty close to a god," he said. "If somebody had predicted that back on the Boston Red Sox . . . in 1914, he would have been thrown into an insane asylum."

Meanwhile, bigotry continued to rear its ugly head on the club. Ruth, a Roman Catholic and unlettered at best, was a prime target of Wood and Speaker, leaders of the Protestant clique. In addition, Ruth was constantly harassed by many of the Sox veterans, including infielder Jack Barry, later the player-manager. Barry made surreptitious remarks about Ruth at team meetings, calling him a "big baboon." Once a tearful Ruth stood and challenged his unknown tormenter to a fight.

"I felt sorry for the kid," Hooper later said. "I went up to Barry afterward and told him that I knew it was him. I said if he didn't stop it, I would tell the kid who was doing it."

Babe definitely had his rough edges. "He had never been anywhere, didn't know anything about manners or how to behave among people . . . just a big, overgrown ape," said Hooper.

Pitcher Waite Hoyt agreed that Ruth was a mystery to his teammates. "There [were] a hundred facets to Ruth's complex character, yet he was so simple as to be difficult," said Hoyt, who was a Red Sox rookie during Ruth's final year in Boston and in later years rejoined him as a teammate in New York.

Even Ruth's new wife poked fun at him. Babe, who married a waitress named Helen Woodford, once visited a local zoo in

Boston. When a monkey mimicked Babe imitating the monkey, Helen declared, "Look Babe! He knows you."

As early as 1915, certain writers began publicly lobbying for the Babe to become a position player. "Ruth appears to be one of the best natural sluggers ever in the game, and might even be more valuable in some regular position than he is on the slab—a free suggestion to Manager Carrigan," suggested Paul Eaton in *The Sporting Life*.

The 1915 version of the Sox featured a pitching staff ranked among the best of all time. Joining Ruth and Shore on the mound were Dutch Leonard, Ray Collins, Rube Foster, Carl Mays and Vean Gregg. Then the club picked up future Hall-of-Famer Herb Pennock on waivers. His addition to the staff would prove useful as the team faced a spate of doubleheaders. Five Sox hurlers won fifteen or more games that year.

Although the club trailed early on during the season, it overtook Chicago and Detroit to garner another pennant. The team steamrolled over the hapless Phillies in five games in the 1915 World Series.

Ruth didn't appear in the World Series, although Carrigan later refuted the claim that he didn't use Ruth because Ruth was a problem child. "I don't know what effect keeping him out of that Series might have had," he declared in 1943, "but it wasn't because I was thinking of his [past behavior]." Carrigan explained that the team didn't use Ruth because Ruth was a lefty—and the Phillies feasted on left-handed pitching.

However, Ruth's non-conventional behavior did draw attention. "There is one player on the Red Sox team who doesn't need to acquire any 'pep,'" noted Arthur Duffy in the *Boston Post* on September 12, 1915. "This is Babe Ruth, whose eccentricities in the past have kept the manager and half the team stirred up."

|||||

The Federal League folded after the 1915 season, allowing team owners to again slash salaries. Lannin found himself trying to justify significantly cutting the pay of both Tris Speaker and Joe Wood. (Wood actually sat out the 1916 season, never again to appear in a Red Sox uniform. Despite his ruined arm, he would later return to the game as an outfielder in Cleveland.)

But Ban Johnson had other plans for Speaker. The AL president had loaned money to the new owner of the Indians, thus quietly obtaining a piece of the club for himself. Before anybody else was the wiser, Johnson engineered the purchase of Speaker for his own franchise. It was, at that point, the biggest purchase price ever paid for a ballplayer: $50,000 plus two players, pitcher "Sad" Sam Jones and infielder Fred Thomas. Jones went 64–59 for the Red Sox over six years. Thomas, a minor leaguer, played in forty-four games for Boston in 1918, hitting .257. Speaker played through 1928 when he retired with a career batting average of .345, one of the greatest hitters and defensive outfielders the game has ever known. He is still the all-time leader in doubles with 792.

The affair outraged Red Sox fans, and there was evidence that Johnson coerced Lannin into making the deal. It soured relations between the two men and engendered resentment against Johnson throughout the rest of the league.

In spite of Speaker's loss, the Sox remained strong. The division along religious lines had blurred, since Speaker and Wood had been the primary instigators of the rift. But Ruth drew some early season criticism.

After three successive poor starts, Paul Shannon of the *Boston Post* noted, "Ruth is overweight and when he gets rid of that surplus poundage, he will be the same tough proposition of last year to solve."

However, the Babe was getting more recognition for his hitting prowess. Noted the *Boston Globe,* "Some one of these days Babe Ruth may become an outfielder."

Pitching continued to carry the club, and the Red Sox faced Brooklyn in the 1916 World Series, after cruising to the pennant. And again they prevailed in five games with Ruth, making his post-season pitching debut, throwing a still-standing record fourteen innings to win Game Two.

More changes were in the wind; Lannin grew tired of Johnson's meddling, so he negotiated the sale of his club weeks after Boston's second consecutive World Series victory. The sale was announced December 4, 1916. To Ban Johnson's everlasting chagrin, Lannin sold the team to Broadway impresario Harry Frazee.

Harry Harrison Frazee, a native of Peoria, Illinois, was born in 1880. Reports indicate he was a pretty fair country third baseman in high school, but he left home at age sixteen for a job as assistant business manager at the Peoria Theater. His first involvement with professional baseball occurred when he booked a barnstorming tour on behalf of Peoria's minor league club in 1899.

Frazee's initial theatrical success occurred when he produced a show entitled *Mahoney's Wedding.* He cleared $14,000, the first step on his way to making a small fortune.

By 1907 Frazee owned his own Chicago-based theater, and then headed for New York City. His first coup in the Big Apple was a musical, *Madame Sherry,* which netted him around $250,000, followed by four additional Broadway hits.

He established the practice of organizing tour companies while his shows were still hot items on Broadway, specializing in farces and light comedies. In addition, he bought more theaters.

Frazee lusted after a Major League Baseball club, making unsuccessful bids for the Red Sox (during the Taylor regime), the Braves, the Cubs, and the Giants.

Over twenty years of producing plays, in addition to promoting prizefights, everything Frazee touched made money, so he finally made his winning bid for the big leagues. Late in 1916, Frazee and partner Hugh Ward offered the enormous sum of $675,000 for the BoSox, half in cash, the other half in promissory notes, finalizing the deal on November 1, 1916. The *Globe* predicted, "Messers Frazee and Ward will no doubt win their way to the hearts of Boston fans."

But Ban Johnson had another take on the matter. He was appalled, fearing Frazee would immeasurably drive up costs for every club. Johnson tried to stymie the deal, but failed.

Thus Johnson fired the first shot, charging that Frazee was "the champion wrecker of baseball." Alluding that Frazee was Jewish, he declared Frazee "too New York" for his liking (the rumor that Frazee was Jewish ultimately caught on).

Frazee didn't help his own cause when he rescinded the club's policy of free admission for local politicians. Even worse, he penalized sports reporters by making *them* pay their own way into the park if they wrote disparaging articles about the Sox. Frazee also cut off perks such as free liquor and food for the press.

Many local writers were Ban Johnson allies, and they didn't take kindly to Frazee's decidedly unfriendly changes. At first the newspapermen retaliated with a whisper campaign, referring to the "mystery" of his faith. In Brahmin and Catholic Boston, the rumor that Frazee was Jewish didn't go over well at all. Frazee completely ignored the jibes, refusing to publicly announce that he was a Presbyterian and a Mason. For its part, the media never bothered to ascertain the truth about him. It didn't make "good copy."

Ruth was proving to be quite newsworthy, but not for the right reasons. On June 23, 1917, before more than 16,000 fans could settle into their seats, Ruth walked Washington leadoff batter Ray Morgan on four consecutive balls. He challenged home plate umpire Brick Owens, charging the plate and bellowing, "If you'd go to bed at night . . . you could keep your eyes open long enough in the daytime to see when a ball goes over the plate!"

Owens threatened to throw Ruth out of the game, to which Ruth retorted, "Throw me out and I'll punch you right in the jaw." After Owens gave him the thumb, Ruth swung wildly, hitting the umpire behind the ear and knocking Owens to the ground. The Babe was ejected, fined, and became a footnote to history when his replacement didn't allow another batter to reach base.[7]

Ruth received a week's suspension and a $100 fine, yet Babe's problems weren't over for the year. While cruising around in his automobile early one November morning "accompanied by a young lady," he tried to beat two trolley cars across several tracks. His car was caught between the trains. A newspaper reported the vehicle was "smashed to a shapeless mass," and the woman was rushed to the hospital.

Ruth averaged at least one significant car wreck every season he spent in Boston. Cracked the *Boston Herald*, "Babe can hit telegraph poles as hard as he hits the horsehide. But we love him just the same."

Harry Hooper said it didn't take long for the innocent Ruth to become corrupted in the ways of the world. "He didn't drink when he came to Boston, and I don't think he'd ever been with a woman. Once he found out about [those vices], though, he became a bear."

Years later Babe's teammate Chick Shorten agreed. "You'd see

---

7 Morgan was thrown out trying to steal second base, and Ruth's replacement, Ernie Shore, proceeded to pitch a perfect game, retiring the next twenty-six batters.

Babe only at game time . . . as soon as it was over he'd take off for a party and have more fun. It never seemed to affect his ability and there was a saying among the Sox that 'He does everything right on the ball field and everything wrong off [of] it.'"

Player-manager Carrigan said the Babe was a money sieve. "He had no idea whatsoever of money," he later remarked. "You have to remember his background."

Frazee's club fell short in 1917, with Charles Comiskey's Chicago White Sox taking the AL crown. The 1918 season was an entirely different story, as the Red Sox handily won the pennant in a season shortened due to World War I. Yet the year was marred by constant intrigue and turmoil.

The Babe, feeling his oats and emerging as a dangerous home run threat, was unhappy with the money he was earning, so he jumped the team on July 3, declaring he was going to play for a semi-pro squad sponsored by a Pennsylvania shipyard. Frazee forced him to return to the club.

Meanwhile, Johnson sought to assist Philadelphia's Connie Mack—and attempted to put Harry Frazee in a cash flow bind—by orchestrating a multi-player sale to the Sox. The Athletics sent pitcher Joe Bush, catcher Wally Schang, and outfielder Amos Strunk to Boston for $60,000 and three minor players. When the owners of the Yankees found out, they were incensed. Johnson had again incurred the wrath of New York owners Tillinghurst l'Hommedieu Huston and Jacob Ruppert, a beer magnate. From then on, the Red Sox, White Sox, and Yankees were aligned against Johnson, while the other American League clubs, termed the "Loyal Five," referred to the three dissidents as the "Insurrectos."

Frazee openly fought Johnson when the American League presi-

dent tried to unilaterally shut down play in 1918. Frazee's antago-
nism toward Johnson prompted Johnson to try to terminate Boston's
league membership due to gambling in the stands at Fenway, even
though the problem wasn't any worse in Boston than anywhere else.

In another grievous miscalculation, Johnson proposed that eighteen players per club be exempted from the military draft, alienating
the public and threatening the entire season. Attendance during 1918
was halved due to the war, yet the jousting between the "Insurrecto"
club owners and Johnson seemed to double.

The buzzards were circling. It would take the disgraceful act
of throwing the 1919 World Series by eight of Comiskey's players
to set the stage for Johnson's ouster. Comiskey's comment about
breaking Johnson ultimately came true.

But that was two years in the future. Meanwhile the Red Sox again
prevailed in the 1918 World Series over the Chicago Cubs. Disciplinarian Ed Barrow had taken Boston's managerial reins, and George
Herman Ruth absolutely bristled. Teammate Harry Hooper said Barrow commanded respect. "We called him Simon Legree. He was a
strict disciplinarian and merciless with people who didn't produce."

Barrow, literally born in a covered wagon as his parents migrat-
ed westward, was a hefty former boxer who broached no nonsense.
"The former bare-knuckle fighter," wrote Ty Waterman and Mel
Springer, "was a pioneer of the game of baseball. He set up the first
minor league night game in 1896, promoted the only woman ever
to pitch in organized baseball (Lizzie Arlington, in 1897), was the
first man to paint distances on outfield fences, discovered Honus
Wagner, and switched Babe Ruth to the outfield. He also served as
general manager and president of the New York Yankees from 1921
to 1945, masterminding them to fourteen flags and ten world championships . . . [and] was elected to the Hall of Fame in 1953."

Barrow's spring training regimen was indicative of how forceful he was. "Three hours work on the diamond and we'll start them home about 1:30 [PM], and they will take the course over the mountains [on] the return trip," he directed while the team trained in Arkansas. "Then the famous Hot Springs baths will follow and, after the usual hour of rest, the boys will be ready to descend full strength upon the dining room."

Barrow hired former major league standout Heinie Wagner as a coach simply to baby-sit the impetuous Ruth. Early in the 1918 season the Babe jumped the team in Baltimore, and Wagner was dispatched to retrieve him. Both returned to the club in only their cups, disgusting the teetotaler Barrow.

In early July, Ruth and Barrow nearly came to blows in the dugout. According to the Babe, "The whole fuss was started over a play in the field. I hit at the first ball and [Barrow] said something about it being a bum play. Then we had words and I thought he called me a bum, and I threatened to punch him. He told me it would cost me $500 and then I made a few more remarks and left the club."

A day later Ruth compounded his problems with his manager by telling the *Herald*, "I got mad as a March hare and told Barrow then and there that I was through with him and his team. I knew I was too mad to control myself, but suiting the action to the word, I did leave the team and came home."

His teammates were now fed up. "Not a single player on the team is in sympathy with him and the Red Sox first and last are disgusted with the actions of a man whom they say has his head inflated with too much advertising and his effectiveness impaired by all together too much babying," reported the *Boston Post*. Yet, at that point in the season Frazee actually awarded the Babe a bonus, and promised the big man an extra $1,000 if the Sox won the pennant.

Ruth's home-run hitting had begun to stun the baseball world. By then Ruth was playing the outfield regularly while being used on the mound as well. He still hadn't attained much hitting prowess against left-handers, and many suspected his superior slugging was only because of the dearth of quality pitching during the war years. Of course, time would prove his doubters wrong—very, very wrong.

When Ruth quickly tired of serving double duty and complained that his left arm was tired. Barrow exploded. "Tired? Of course you're tired! You're running around all the time! If you'd stop carousing at night, you could play every day and never feel it!"

Barrow had legitimate concerns about the Babe, both on and off the diamond. Ruth had jumped the club twice during the 1918 season, and his hitting was streaky. He had trouble hitting at Fenway Park, and was decidedly becoming a detriment to team chemistry. Infielder Larry Gardner's wife, Margaret, said Ruth was no lovable lout. "He was a mess," she said flatly. "He was foul-mouthed, a show-off, very distasteful to have around." And pitcher Herb Pennock's wife pointedly asked Helen Ruth, "What do you feed that man?"

The next brouhaha occurred when baseball officials succeeded in shortchanging the ballplayers playing in the 1918 World Series, and the two teams declined to take the field in the midst of the Fall Classic. The individual shares of the revenue were slashed 10 percent to donate to war charities, but the owners didn't kick in anything. They also held the line on ticket prices, as well as reducing the percentages of gate receipts for the players—and this was after the games in Chicago had been moved to Comiskey Park to accommodate more people (the Red Sox had done the same thing in 1915-16 by playing those World Series at Braves Field). Part of what was left went to the second, third and fourth place teams in each league.

When the players refused to take the field before Game Five, Ban Johnson himself showed up in the Sox clubhouse, drunk as can be, according to numerous sources. Physically supported by two cronies, Johnson approached player representatives Harry Hooper, who represented the Red Sox, and Leslie Mann of the Cubs.

"Harry, old boy, old boy," he slurred, throwing his arms around the outfielder. "Whyn't you stop all this and play ball?"

Hooper proposed that *everybody* donate *all* proceeds to the American Red Cross. Needless to say, Johnson ignored Hooper's counter proposal.

"We will play not because we think we are getting a fair deal . . . but for the sake of the game, for the sake of the public . . . and for the sake of the wounded soldiers and sailors who are in the grandstand waiting for us," Hooper declared.

League officials later denied the Red Sox their World Series emblems (the equivalent of today's World Series rings), although the powers-that-be had promised that no repercussions would be exacted after the abortive players' strike.[8]

In spite of the behind-the-scenes machinations, the fans enjoyed the on-the-field spectacle, aptly described by Ruth biographer Robert Creamer: "The crowd was making more noise than any Boston crowd had since the Colonials took two from the British at Lexington and Concord."

The Babe responded, winning twice and setting a World Series-record twenty-nine and two-thirds scoreless inning mark that lasted more than three decades. The 1918 World Series would be the last one the Sox would win until they whitewashed the Cardinals in the wake of their miraculous comeback victory in the 2004 ALCS, eighty-six long years later. And exactly two months after the Sox

---

8 Descendants of the players eventually received them—in 1993.

won their fifth world championship, World War I was over. Yet one short year later the Sox faced an uncertain future.

Sox hurler Carl Mays was having an atrocious year in 1919, although he was the best pitcher on the team. Beset by a paucity of support at the plate, he lost five consecutive games via shutout, despite giving up only twelve runs during that five-game span. And the club proved extremely error-prone whenever Mays took the mound.

Angered by a heckler in Philadelphia, a frustrated Mays fired the ball into the stands, earning a $500 fine from Ban Johnson. Mays refused to pay. After the White Sox beat him on July 13 due to some particularly poor fielding and his subsequent loss of composure, he packed his bags and left the team. Once back in Boston, he popped off to the *Boston Herald*: "I'll never pitch another game for the Red Sox."

In stepped Johnson, who decreed that Mays was ineligible to be dealt away until Boston disciplined him. Frazee, who had other ideas, sent Mays to the Yankees for $40,000 and two players. Johnson ordered the deal nullified, and indefinitely suspended the hurler. So New York took the AL president to court, obtained an injunction, and Mays donned a Yankees uniform.

As for the Babe, he had obtained a significant raise in salary after clearly signaling his intentions during the off-season. "I'm going to ask for a figure in my contract that may knock Mr. Frazee silly," Ruth told reporters. "But, nevertheless, I think I am deserving of everything I ask."

At first Frazee termed Ruth's demands ludicrous, asserting, "I have done everything possible to talk [Ruth] into a reasonable frame of mind, yet he . . . demands a contract that is absolutely out of the question. I will have no man on the team . . . dictate terms to the management."

But ultimately, the Babe got a substantial pay hike.

He'd earned $7,000 in 1918; initially Frazee bumped up Ruth's pay $2,000 for the 1919 season. But the theater magnate, realizing that Ruth was essentially doing double duty (and drawing large numbers of fans with his home run hitting), tore up the contract mid-season and gave Ruth his much sought after three-year contract at $10,000 per year.

Yet Ruth continued to play the prima donna.

So Barrow hired Dan Howley to ride herd on the Babe. "Don't worry, Mr. Barrow," declared Howley. "I'll take care of that guy if I have to put a ring through his nose." However, he had no more success at taming Ruth than anyone else did.

Perhaps the best-known altercation between Barrow and Ruth occurred when the manager, having been tipped off by a hotel porter that the Babe had snuck into the hotel long after hours, caught Ruth in bed—drunk and smoking a pipe—at 6 AM. Barrow stomped out of Ruth's room, declaring that he'd see the wastrel at the ballpark.

Arriving at the clubhouse, Ruth threatened Barrow. "If you ever come to my room again . . . I'll punch you in the nose," he hollered. Others in the locker room separated the two, and Barrow suspended the Babe.

Another notable altercation also stemmed from Barrow's dim view of Ruth's off-the-field behavior during the season. The manager chewed out the team one day in the clubhouse, and the other players smirked at Ruth, giving him pointed looks.

That's when Ruth allegedly challenged Barrow in front of the entire squad. "I'll flatten your nose over your mouth to close it!" he cried. Barrow ordered the clubhouse cleared. A physical brute of a man himself, Barrow might well have given the Bambino-to-be a good beating. Instead Ruth sheepishly headed off to the playing field with the rest of the team.

Ruth began lobbying for Jack Barry, who guided the club until he was drafted into the U.S. Navy, to be reappointed as field manager, which made him even more enemies. His blatant machinations also soured Harry Hooper on Ruth, as Hooper had his own aspirations to manage the team.

Babe Ruth appeared in a Red Sox uniform for the last time on September 27, 1919. In one, last ironic touch, Frazee awarded Ruth a $5,000 bonus after the conclusion of the season.

Robert Smith, author of *Babe Ruth's America*, charged that several players from the Chicago White Sox had urged Ruth to demand $20,000 per year from Frazee. These were the same White Sox who threw the 1919 Series, and were later banned from baseball.

Inadvertently, those Black Sox who goaded Ruth to seek that additional money may have saved the very game whose existence they'd threatened. Barrow and Frazee had had more than enough from the temperamental pitcher-turned-slugger in spite of his record-setting twenty-nine home runs in 1919. Fearful that Ruth's attitude would ultimately contaminate the entire club, they saw good reason to ship him off to the Yankees in the most infamous player move in the history of professional sports.

Despite the three-year contract he inked in 1919, Ruth began posturing for more dough even before the season ended. "I will not play with the Red Sox unless I get $20,000 [a year]," announced Ruth. "I feel I made a bad move last year when I signed a three-year contract to play for [a cumulative] $30,000. The Boston club realized much on my value, and I think I am entitled to twice as much as my contract calls for."

Ruth told *The Sporting News* he was fully justified in ignoring his previously hard-won, three-year contract. "A player is worth just as much as he can get," declared the Babe, incensed that Ty Cobb had publicly termed him "a contract violator."

"[Ruth] has . . . arrived at the conclusion that a contract is not binding on a baseball star who chooses to disregard it," the *Sporting News* reported.

There was, however—or so some claimed—another reason to trade Ruth. Years later, author Leigh Montville claimed the oft-told stories of Harry Frazee's financial woes and single mindedness toward his theatrical ventures were gospel.

In his 2006 book, *The Big Bam*, Montville wrote, "Frazee was in a financial bind," alleging that Frazee was overextended fiscally and missed making a payment to former Sox owner Joe Lannin because of a cash crunch. "The money from the sale of Ruth, plus the money from the loan [i.e. the Fenway Park mortgage], was used to pay off Lannin and keep Frazee's theatrical interests viable."

Based in part on a statement Waite Hoyt made in an interview for the Hall of Fame, Montville wrote that Frazee used the $100,000 he got from the sale of Ruth to produce a play called *My Lady Friends*, which was later set to music, becoming Frazee's biggest hit, *No, No, Nanette*.

But Frazee had long asserted he'd refused to pay Lannin the scheduled November 1, 1919 installment on the team's sale because Lannin had failed to make good on a commitment to cover a cash settlement negotiated with the operators of the defunct Federal League. Frazee had already stopped paying Lannin interest on the notes held by the former Sox owner.

However, attendance in 1919 was 417,291, the highest mark during Frazee's seven years of ownership, and an increase of nearly 168,000 over 1918. And Frazee reportedly had been offered $1.2 million for the franchise he'd acquired two years earlier. A sale of the club at that point would have netted him a handsome profit of more than $500,000.

Barrow claimed in his own book, *My Fifty Years in Base-*

ball, that he told Frazee the Sox owner was making a mistake in selling Ruth.

"Maybe I am but I can't help it," Frazee allegedly conceded. "Lannin is after me to make good on my notes. And my shows aren't going so good. Ruppert and Huston will give me $100,000 for Ruth, and they've agreed to loan me $350,000. I can't turn that down. But don't worry, I'll get you some ballplayers, too."

After the Ruth sale was announced, Frazee issued a 1,500-word statement, declaring that the Babe "had become impossible and the Boston club could no longer put up with his eccentricities. While Ruth without question is the greatest hitter that the game has seen, he is likewise one of the most inconsiderate men that ever wore a baseball uniform."

He termed Ruth a malcontent who was a bad influence on both veteran players and rookies. "Had he possessed the right disposition, had he been willing to take orders and work for the good of the club like the other men on the team, I never would have dared let him go," Frazee said. "Twice during the past two seasons, Babe has jumped the club and revolted. He refused to obey orders of the manager."

Frazee further declared, "The Boston club can now go into the market and buy other players and have a stronger and better team than if Ruth had remained with us."

Predictably the Babe had some choice words for Frazee.

"Frazee sold me because he was unwilling to meet my demands, and to alibi himself with the fans he is trying to throw the blame on me."

An incensed Ruth sent telegrams to four of the largest dailies in the city, blasting Frazee, claiming Frazee's statements were "absolute falsehoods . . . meant to poison the minds of the Boston people against me."

He offered to pay Frazee $100 for every player who'd attest that Ruth was a disturbing element, and then threatened to sue for slander.

"This propaganda has been sent out to try and pacify the Boston people over the sale," the Babe charged. "It is a rank injustice to both them and me, for there is not any of it true."

The headline of the January 6, 1920, edition of the *Boston Post* blared, "Babe Ruth Sold to the Yankees," but a sub-headline read, "Ruth Termed a Handicap, Not an Asset." Writer Paul Shannon asserted the Babe had proven too difficult to rein in, even for Barrow. "Ruth . . . would never have been allowed to leave Fenway Park had it been possible for the Boston club to handle him. Ruth's failure to respect the club's training rules, his unwillingness to submit to any form of discipline, and the bad example he set for the other men formed a combination that President Frazee could no longer endure."

The *Post* took an altogether benign look upon the sale. "It is believed that practically every man on the Boston team will be pleased at Ruth's sale to New York," Shannon continued. "Popular as Ruth was, on account of his big-heartedness, the men nevertheless realize that his faults overshadow his good qualities."

The *Boston Herald* advocated a wait-and-see attitude. "Stars generally are temperamental, Frazee has carefully considered the Ruth angle and believes he has done the proper thing. Boston fans undoubtedly will be up in arms, but they should reserve judgment until they see how it works out."

And *Herald* columnist Bob Dunbar, while lamenting the loss of the slugger, pointed out that a contract was a contract. "Frazee believes he has not been squarely dealt with [although] the departure of Ruth is regretted by all," he wrote.

Seemingly, Ruth's lone defender in the daily press was Nick Flatley of the *Boston Evening American*, who blamed Barrow, claiming that former manager Bill Carrigan, who'd retired to Maine, had been able to tame wild man Ruth.

Not a single Red Sox player was quoted in any of Boston's nine daily newspapers after Ruth was sold.

One hundred eighty miles south of Boston, the *New York Times* praised the Yankees' newest acquisition. "The two Colonels—Ruppert and Huston—were praised on all sides for their aggressiveness and liberality in landing baseball's greatest attraction."

In 1920, Ruth's .376 batting average, 54 home runs and 137 RBIs generated an attendance of 1,289,422 fans at the Polo Grounds in his first year with the Yankees, the first time in baseball history that a team's home attendance exceeded one million. It also directly led to the construction of Yankee Stadium, "The House That Ruth Built," the building of which was hastened when the New York Giants unceremoniously ousted the tenant Yankees from their home field.

The balance of power had definitively shifted in the AL. The Yankees were en route to becoming the greatest dynasty in the annals of Major League Baseball.

5

NO, NO HARRY

Although the sale of Ruth certainly changed the course of history for the New York Yankees, the overall effect on Boston's franchise could have had a positive effect if only Ban Johnson had left Harry Frazee to his own devices.

There's no guarantee that Ruth would have become the hitting machine he did after joining the Yankees if he had stayed in Boston. The short right-field fences in both the Polo Grounds and Yankee Stadium were far more inviting targets for left-handed sluggers than cavernous right field at Fenway Park, and the "lively" ball with its extra oomph had yet to be introduced to Major League Baseball.

There's little question that Frazee intended to restock the Red Sox roster once he sold Ruth. But, pressed for players, he repeatedly sent Sox prospects to other teams—predominantly the Yankees—for proven veterans he felt could immediately strengthen his club. Unfortunately for Frazee and the Red Sox, the men he obtained fell flat while many of the players he traded away became stars.

Ban Johnson was not a man to be trifled with. And, although wounded through his loss of the court battle with the Yankees over

Carl Mays, he was still a formidable adversary—and Harry Frazee was dead center in his sights.

"Johnson ran his league like a private club and Frazee hadn't asked permission to join," wrote author Glenn Stout. "Over the next few years everything Frazee said and did went against the wishes of Johnson—among other things he wanted the league presidents replaced by a single commissioner—and everything Johnson did was designed to run Frazee from the game."

Johnson rallied his troops—the Boston press, the national media, and his privately funded supporters—in order to pressure Frazee to ultimately throw in the towel and give up his quest to maintain ownership of a Major League Baseball franchise.

Frazee was handicapped by Johnson: over the following seasons every American League team except for the New York Yankees refused to do business with him. His option was either to deal with New York or not to make any deals at all. Ultimately even Comiskey wouldn't swap players with the beleaguered Boston owner.

Richard Johnson, co-author of *Red Sox Century*, believed Frazee truly wanted to re-stock Boston's club after selling Ruth. "I think Frazee had every intention of obtaining some quality ballplayers for the Red Sox when he sold Ruth, but you have to understand how badly Ban Johnson poisoned the waters in Boston by implying that Frazee was a Jew. Boston was, and to a degree still is, incredibly parochial, and there was an extreme, pervasive prejudice against Jews."

Meanwhile, Ban Johnson had found an unlikely ally in Joe Lannin, Boston's former owner who had sold the club to Frazee. Lannin, who had purchased the Buffalo franchise of the International League, hadn't gotten along with Johnson while Lannin controlled the Red Sox, but now the men needed each other. Frazee still owed

Lannin a substantial amount of money, and Johnson figured Frazee was in a cash crunch. He viewed it as a means to pressure Frazee to unload the franchise, Johnson's fondest wish.

Lannin had a lien placed on Fenway Park on February 9, 1920, while the AL owners were jousting at the league meeting in Chicago. If he didn't get his money by March 3, Fenway would be auctioned off. Rumors abounded that Frazee was preparing to sell the club, so Lannin obtained an injunction that forbade further disposition of the team's players. Meanwhile, Johnson rushed to Boston to put together a group to buy the club, but Frazee wasn't selling.

Frazee and Lannin ultimately settled their dispute out-of-court, and *The Sporting News* reported "the matter was compromised and settled to the satisfaction of both parties."

|||||

Despite losing Ruth, Boston finished the 1920 season with a 72–81 mark, six games better than the year before. Still, the downward spiral continued. A spate of injuries decimated the Sox that year, but Frazee's hands were tied because the "Loyal Five" refused to deal with the three "Insurrectos." Johnson's power may have been on the wane, but most AL clubs still didn't want to incur his wrath.

Johnson also found other ways to rankle the Red Sox owner.

Boston had loaned a promising young third baseman, Harold "Pie" Traynor, to a minor league club with the unwritten stipulation that Traynor ultimately would be returned to the Red Sox, a common practice of the era. Instead, the minor league team sold Traynor to the Pittsburgh Pirates. When Boston appealed the matter to Johnson, the AL president refused to take any action. Traynor ended up enshrined in the Hall of Fame.

The American League president also found assistance in his campaign against Frazee from an unlikely source: auto magnate Henry Ford.

In a move to further his political aspirations, Ford had founded a weekly newspaper, the *Dearborn Independent*, which by 1920 was distributed on a national basis; circulation estimates ranged from 250,000–400,000. Its focus had changed by the 1920s, and not for the better, when Ford decided that all the world's ills could be traced to the Jews. According to the gospel of Ford "the International Jew" controlled the world's finances, politics and culture, including Major League Baseball.

In September 1921, an article blamed the Black Sox scandal on Jewish gamblers, completely ignoring the fact that a key figure in the scandal—perhaps its most instrumental actor—was Joseph "Sport" Sullivan, an Irish-American Bostonian who was indicted for his part in the travesty.

Another article, railing against Frazee's push for a single commissioner of baseball, charged the idea was a Jewish plot to subjugate the major leagues' hierarchy.

Aside from several attorneys, the only "Jews" specifically cited were Pittsburgh owner Barney Dreyfuss and Frazee. "Baseball was to be 'promoted' as Jewish managers promote Coney Island," asserted writer W. J. Cameron.

The *Independent*'s "exposé" mortally wounded Frazee in the press. For reasons still unknown, he never set the record straight, although it is thought that Frazee may have been preoccupied at the time with a nasty divorce case and the death of his father.

The *Sporting News* ran other demeaning articles about Frazee during the early days of 1922, no doubt at the bidding of Johnson, who had lost his battle against a single commissioner the previous November.

Frazee's final years as owner of the Red Sox weren't pleasant. Boston newspaper reporters had never been thrilled with him. Stripped of their perks shortly after Frazee bought the club, the *Independent*'s "revelations" hardened the reporters' resolve to back Johnson.

Although a big trade with New York in December 1920 was initially well received by the media, pitcher Waite Hoyt and catcher Wally Schang both became big stars in the Big Apple. All four players whom the Sox received in return spent two years or less in Boston, and only second baseman Del Pratt did well, hitting over .300 in both seasons he spent with the team.

The Boston press rejoined the fray when Frazee sold long-time outfielder Harry Hooper to the Chicago White Sox in March. "All Frazee wanted was the money," Hooper told author Peter Golenbock. "He was short on cash and he sold the whole team down the river to keep his dirty nose above water." Boston's newspapers then cut back their Red Sox coverage. Some barely covered the club at all during Frazee's last years of ownership.

The Red Sox finished 1921 in fifth place with a record of 75–79. Yet the team still made a profit. Meanwhile, the New York Yankees won the franchise's first pennant, although they lost the World Series to their Polo Grounds landlord, the Giants.

Frazee engineered yet another trade with New York during 1921, sending shortstop Everett Scott and pitchers Joe Bush and Sam Jones to the Yankees for shortstop Roger Peckinpaugh and three pitchers. Scott would be the Yankees' regular shortstop through 1926. Bush won twenty-six games for New York in 1922 while Jones won sixty-seven games during his stay in the "Big Apple."

Peckinpaugh, considered a better fielder than the younger Scott, was later traded to the Washington Senators as part of a three-team deal. He never appeared in a Red Sox uniform. In return, Boston received Joe Dugan from the Athletics and Frank O'Rourke from the Senators. Dugan would toil for the Sox for several months before he went to New York, where he became a fixture in the infield.

The media was in an uproar, with Burt Whitman of the *Herald* terming the trades "the rape of the Red Sox."

The team ended its 1922 season by taking two of three games from the Yankees, but Boston finished dead last. The Yankees repeated as AL pennant winners, although they again lost the World Series to the Giants.

Frazee redirected his attention to the stage, purchasing Boston's Arlington Street Theater and becoming more involved in his productions. Figuring that he'd no doubt end up selling the team to a Johnson ally, he also methodically began selling off the remainder of his better players.

Finally, on July 12, 1923, Frazee sold the club to a consortium headed by Bob Quinn, the business manager of the St. Louis Browns. The deal was held up after Frazee tried to hike his asking price—and after Quinn had trouble coming up with the 25 percent cash that Big Harry was demanding. Ban Johnson was thrilled—and Harry Frazee was history.

"Johnson is Elated That Frazee Is Finally Out of Baseball," blared a headline in *The Sporting News* a week after the sale, while the *Boston Post* declared the sale was the "Best Thing That Owner Ever Did for Team." Nick Flatley of the *Boston Evening American* chimed, "Red Sox fans were cheering loudly today, for the first time in years and years. The ball club has finally been sold. It's effectively in new hands . . . [with Quinn] displacing H. H. Frazee, who has been Boston's most unpopular temporary citizen, ever since he sold Babe Ruth four years ago."

In a final, parting gesture, Frazee held up the sale until August 1, thus preventing the new ownership from making any trades before the July 31 deadline.

After he sold the Red Sox, Frazee produced *No, No Nanette*, the biggest hit of his theatrical career, which toured worldwide and netted several million dollars.

Baseball historian Glenn Stout swears there is no truth whatsoever to the claim that Frazee funneled money from the Ruth sale into the reworked production of *My Lady Friends*. "*No, No Nanette* was spun off from another play but there were numerous *other* plays in between," Stout said. "There was a five- or six-year time period in between. How did Frazee [underwrite] those other plays in between? He made money in between those two productions. Frazee produced at least two other very successful plays in between."

Frazee died in 1929 of Bright's Disease, a kidney malady that was untreatable at the time. He left an estate of roughly $1.5 million.

|||||

Once he acquired the team, Quinn immediately went on a spending spree, shelling out a quarter-of-a-million dollars on seventeen minor leaguers. "Our big idea is to go out and get ballplayers," he announced.

Meanwhile, the 1923 world champion New York Yankees featured a roster that had virtually been stocked courtesy of the Red Sox. Besides starters Babe Ruth, catcher Wally Schang, third baseman Joe Dugan, and shortstop Everett Scott, infielder Mike McNally, and outfielder Elmer Smith served as reserves. Carl Mays, Waite Hoyt, Sam Jones, Herb Pennock, Joe Bush, and George Pipgras all were former Red Sox pitchers.

Boston's ineptitude became all too clear late in the season when outfielder Dick Reichle tottered under a towering Babe Ruth fly ball but lost it in the sun. Ruth scored on an inside-the-park home run. Remarked manager Frank Chance, "Pretty smart, Dick. It's late in the season, and I wouldn't want to get hit on the head either."

Despite Boston's newfound optimism, the Sox came in last place for the second consecutive year, posting a record of 61–91. Meanwhile the Yankees finally won the team's first-ever world championship.

The Sox got off to a hot start in 1924, bringing joy to the hearts of their fans and the press, who were smitten by Quinn, although, in fairness, they would have been smitten by anyone other than Harry Frazee. However, after reaching first place in early June, Boston collapsed, and wound up in seventh place. But attendance nearly doubled that year, thanks to the positive media coverage.

Then disaster. Again.

Quinn's primary backer, Palmer Winslow, a wealthy Indiana glass manufacturer, died without leaving any provisions to further fund club operations. For all intents and purposes, Quinn was broke, as were his remaining two partners.

Instead of selling the franchise , a logical move in the years prior to the stock market crash, Quinn grimly held on against all odds. The seventeen minor league stars he purchased were all busts, and he couldn't afford high-priced ballplayers. Young players were rushed to the majors before they were ready, and were sadly overmatched. Any hot prospects were traded in exchange for older players whom Quinn could afford.

In 1926, Quinn sent his premier pitcher, Howard Ehmke, who had won forty-eight games during three years with the club, to Philadelphia for pitchers Slim Harriss and Fred Heimach. Harriss and

Heimach combined for a record of 8–19 with the Sox, while Ehmke won twelve games for the A's. In five years, Ehmke went 40–25 for Philadelphia.

Then the Yankees made an offer that Quinn refused. Since the Yankees' Wally Pipp appeared firmly entrenched at first base, New York offered a twenty-one-year-old named Lou Gehrig in exchange for Sox first baseman Phil Todt. Boston declined. Todt played six more years for the Red Sox, batting .258 and hitting fifty-six home runs. Gehrig was arguably the greatest first baseman in baseball history. So much for Quinn's baseball acumen.

"He had all the right intentions," Glenn Stout said. "Quinn wanted to fulfill what [the new ownership group] intended to do. And I'm sure there was a lot of ego involved. He figured a successful franchise was simply one trade away, one prospect away. Yet he may well have recouped the money if he'd unloaded it during the Roaring Twenties. At the same time, we don't know if it was tied up in probate with Winslow's widow."

In 1925, the Sox sank even further, finishing in last place, with a record of 47–105. The club won one more game in 1926 than it had in 1925, but the Red Sox were mired again in the cellar. The Yankees, meanwhile, again won the AL pennant.

Boston's big news of 1926 didn't take place on the baseball diamond. A three-alarm fire destroyed Fenway's grandstand roof and left-field bleachers. It was the fourth fire in the same spot over two days, but the Boston Fire Department oddly chose to rule it accidental. The cash-strapped Red Sox used most of the insurance proceeds to cover payroll, leaving a vacant lot where the bleachers once stood. Repairs wouldn't be made for more than seven years.

On what was left of the field, Quinn fired manager Lee Fohl, and lured former manager Bill Carrigan out of retirement. But Carrigan had no better luck than Fohl, taking the team to a 51–103 mark in 1927. He remained through the 1929 season, with the club finishing in last place each year. As for the Yankees, they won world championships in both 1927 and 1928.

When the stock market crashed in October 1929 any chance that Quinn had to sell the club at a profit evaporated. Yet he still stubbornly hung on. Under former coach Heinie Wagner the team continued its losing ways in 1930, posting a 52–102 record. In 1931, the Sox improved to 62–90, with one tie. They sank even lower in 1932, losing 111 games, still a club record, despite the fact that outfielder Dale Alexander—hitting .372—became the first Red Sox in history to win a batting title.[9]

The Yankees, meanwhile, swept the Chicago Cubs in the World Series, the last championship New York would win with Babe Ruth.

Then Quinn finally found a savior—of sorts.

9 In an equally odd sidebar, hard-throwing right-hander Ed Morris was stabbed at a going-away party in Florida just prior to leaving for spring training in 1932. Morris jumped into the Perdido River, swimming across the state line into Alabama. He contracted an infection and later died.

6

THE BIG BANKROLL

The savior's name was Thomas Austin Yawkey.

He had just turned thirty years old when he appeared at a press conference hosted by Quinn on February 25, 1933. The media, used to Quinn's preening and posturing, fully expected the preseason press conference to be just another fête to curry favor with the media. To the reporters' surprise, Quinn had arranged to sell his hapless club to the husky young man flanking him at the head table.

"I haven't got the money to continue," said Quinn, announcing the sale of the franchise—including Fenway Park—for the very same $1.2 million he'd bought it for nearly ten years earlier.

Long-time Boston sportswriter Joe Cashman said the press was completely taken aback when Yawkey was introduced as the new owner. "Yawkey seemed too young to have that kind of money. This was just a kid."

A kid worth in excess of $40 million, as of his thirtieth birthday, four days earlier.

For his part, Yawkey said he would be thrilled to turn the franchise around. "The big kick comes from taking something that's down and seeing if you can put it up and across. That's what my daddy did. I want to see if I'm as good a man as he was."

"Daddy" was Bill Yawkey, whose Detroit Tigers won the American League pennant in 1907, four years after he'd acquired the team. Tom Yawkey would fail to match that feat, and fail badly.

Born Thomas Yawkey Austin, Yawkey was baseball royalty. Orphaned as a youth, he was adopted by his uncle, Bill Yawkey, a close friend of Ty Cobb, the infamous Tigers outfielder. Young, impressionable Tom quickly became a protégé of Cobb, under whose wing he stayed until early manhood. Tom was also influenced by Eddie Collins, a White Sox Hall of Famer and a graduate of the Irving School in Tarrytown, New York, the same tony school Yawkey attended. In fact, Yawkey was so star-struck by Collins, his greatest desire was to win the Edward T. Collins Medal as the school's top scholar-athlete. He never did.

After Bill Yawkey sold the Tigers, Tom moved to New York City. Ultimately he also inherited a 25,000-acre estate called South Island Plantation outside of Georgetown, South Carolina. That's where young Tom came under the influence of Cobb, "The Georgia Peach," who hunted and fished with the youth.

Most accounts assert that Collins introduced Yawkey to Quinn. Although some historians maintain that Ty Cobb introduced him to Collins, the best evidence indicates that Yawkey met Collins, an unblemished member of the infamous 1919 Black Sox, at a funeral. Either way, Cobb encouraged the young man to pursue his dream of buying a baseball team, but by the time Yawkey had the means to do so, he and Cobb had had a falling out.[10]

Quinn and Yawkey began negotiating the sale of the club by early 1933 and Yawkey initially asked Quinn to stay on and as-

10 Soon Tom Yawkey would also finance a whorehouse near the property—dubbed the Sunset Lodge—that would cater to a high-class clientele until 1969, when the authorities shut it down.

sist with operations. But Quinn declined, urging Yawkey to get Collins instead.

"I'll buy the club if you'll run it," Yawkey told Collins, who was reportedly next in line to manage the Philadelphia Athletics.

"I couldn't do that," Collins replied. "I couldn't leave [Connie] Mack. I've been with him all these years."

But when Mack heard about the offer, Mack forced his hand, telling Collins he'd fire him if Collins didn't accept the position with the Red Sox. (It was just as well that Collins didn't wait around to accept the reins from Connie Mack in Philadelphia. Mack managed the club through the 1950 season.)

Mack had an ulterior motive. Cash-strapped because he'd lost a fortune in the stock market crash, he wanted to sell many of his team's most valuable assets to the Red Sox after Collins took over club operations.

"We knew Connie was in financial trouble. He said, 'I have to break up the team.' He told us," recalled outfielder Roger "Doc" Cramer, one of the stars Mack sent to Boston.

Yawkey, a Yale graduate, came to be regarded as the last "gentleman owner" in the field of sports. In reality, however, he was a complex man who drank to excess and surrounded himself with yes-men, crippling the Red Sox franchise throughout his forty-four years of ownership and beyond. A petty man who alternately overpaid and mistreated his ballplayers, he played a central role in thwarting the integration of Major League Baseball in Boston, at least as it pertained to the city's American League franchise.

Although Yawkey publicly announced that Collins would rebuild the franchise from the ground up, his patience with that slow process lasted only until May 1933. "I don't believe that the Red Sox, having been the doormat of the American League, can be built

up overnight," Yawkey initially remarked. "It would be the height
of folly to dump a lot of money into the thing all at once in the hope
of quick and salutary results."

However, within several months Yawkey's mantra had changed
to: Let the spending begin! At the owners' meeting in May, Yawkey
simply announced, "Who has any really good players for sale? The
money is on the table."

He first acquired catcher Rick Ferrell and pitcher Lloyd Brown
from the St. Louis Browns in return for catcher Merv Shea and a
reported $50,000. He then snapped up former Sox pitcher George
Pipgras and infielder Billy Werber from the Yankees for $100,000,
the same sum Boston had received from New York for Ruth
in 1919.

Although Ferrell anchored Boston's catching corps for a number of years, Brown, who had won fifty-nine games between 1925-
33, went 8–11 in his single season with the Red Sox. Werber spent
four years in Boston, hitting .300 only once. Pipgras, whom the Sox
sent to New York in 1923, won ninety-three games for the Yankees, but subsequently went 9–9 for the Red Sox over three seasons.
Yawkey's initial deals reflected his later ones: over-pay for veterans
beyond their prime, sign untested youths who never realized their
potential, and obtain players whose character flaws offset their abilities to help the club.

Yawkey was so overanxious, he paid top dollar for Pipgras and
Werber when he could have picked them up off of waivers for pen-
nies on the dollar several days later. Other clubs simply salivated at
his naïveté. He truly was a babe in the woods.

Both Yawkey's primary home and office were located in New
York, although he'd later enter into a long-term rental agreement for
a suite at the Ritz Carlton Hotel in downtown Boston. While he ruled

the team from afar, Yawkey's club improved to 63–86 in 1933, but still finished in seventh place.

Baseball historian Glenn Stout said that Collins was a knowledgeable baseball executive for the most part. "I think Collins was a pretty astute baseball guy. He knew you had to get the best players. To a degree, Collins had to be influenced by Mack, who built up teams, tore them down, and then rebuilt them. . . . One of the problems Collins had was that he predominantly was a player from the dead ball era."

After his first year of ownership, Yawkey underwrote a major renovation of Fenway Park, rebuilding the bleachers and grandstand that had burned and adding a significant number of new seats. The renovations, which increased the available seating from 26,000 to 38,0000, cost more than $1.5 million.

Yawkey then hired Bucky Harris as manager, but without consulting general manager Collins beforehand. Harris, who managed the Washington Senators during their pennant-winning years of 1924 and 1925, had been a mortal enemy of Collins's since their playing days.

Collins tried every which way to get rid of Harris, another precursor of things to come. For years thereafter, many Red Sox general managers would work at cross-purposes against that of their field managers.

Collins had already become unpopular when he fired a large number of long-time Red Sox employees essentially because they were Irish-American Catholics (Collins professed to be an Episcopalian). Apparently Yawkey took little, if any, notice.

Going into the 1934 winter meetings, Yawkey continued to spend big bucks, buying pitchers Lefty Grove and Rube Walberg, plus second baseman Max Bishop from the Athletics. The cost was $250,000 and two marginal players.

Walberg, who'd compiled a record of 134–114 with Philadelphia, never won more than six games in a single season for the Sox.
He posted a 21–27 record while in Boston. Bishop, who'd excelled
while with the A's, spent two years with the Red Sox, appearing
in 157 games and batting .251. Getting Grove, considered one of
the best pitchers in baseball, was Yawkey's most successful player
move to that point. ("Lefty Grove could throw a lamb chop past a
wolf," declared one sportswriter.) In spite of a variety of afflictions
and injuries, Grove would win 105 games for Boston over eight seasons and finish his career with exactly 300 wins. The Hall of Fame
left-hander would have such a tough time physically in 1934 that
Mack offered Yawkey his money back. Yawkey refused.

The Boston media decided that the club had cornered the American League pennant for years to come, with both the *Globe* and the
Post awarding the championship to the Red Sox by default. Nothing
could have been further from the truth.

Grove disliked Harris almost as much as Collins did, and he helped
split the team into two camps: the veterans, who ran roughshod over
Harris, Collins, and Yawkey, and the bit players and rookies. The dissention that permeated the team reflected the same, tired blueprint that
would plague the Sox throughout most of Yawkey's reign.

Yawkey was so star-struck he continued to over-pay his ballplayers, and he refused to make any of the established stars toe *any* kind
of line. Most took full advantage, and the owner undercut his managers and general managers by failing to back them in issues involving
discipline. Players, managers, and general managers all had direct
pipelines to the owner, completely blurring any chain of command.
More often than not, the last person to get Yawkey's ear prevailed.

On January 5, 1934, a five-alarm fire ripped through Fenway's
new stands, causing $250,000 in damage. After Yawkey reiterated

his commitment to complete the construction prior to the season opener, a second, smaller fire tore through part of the reconstructed bleachers. This time the fire department deemed it arson.

The best the club could do in 1934 was break even, with a record of 76–76. That was in spite of the acquisition of suspended Cleveland hurler Wes Ferrell, Rick's brother and a fine pitcher, but another difficult character to manage. In an attempt to refute the charge that he couldn't manage his hard-drinking, high-priced veterans, Harris responded, "I would have fired the drinkers in five minutes but you don't fire high-priced name players." Then too, many of those hard-drinking players drank with Yawkey, who delighted in hobnobbing with his charges.

Toward the end of the year, Yawkey asked Collins to name the best ballplayer in the league. Spying an opportunity to get rid of Harris on the sly, Collins replied, "Joe Cronin."

Cronin, the player-manager of the Washington Senators, was beyond his prime. His bat speed had slowed, his legs were gone, and he was a liability in the field; the former All-Star shortstop had also suffered a broken wrist that drastically diminished his fielding prowess. He also was an egomaniac, perhaps the most selfish player in all baseball. Unbeknownst to Yawkey, Collins had set the stage to jettison Harris.

Yawkey paid Senators owner Clark Griffith $250,000 for Cronin, who was also Griffith's son-in-law. Boston threw in shortstop Lyn Lary to boot. Cronin received a raise to $35,000 per year as part of a five-year deal. And since Cronin had been Washington's manager, Yawkey wasn't about to demote him, so Harris was sent packing. Harris wound up back with the Senators.

Another factor in the quest to obtain Cronin's services was that he was Irish-Catholic, which counted for a lot in Boston. That Collins would push to hire the Irish-Catholic Cronin was indicative of his deep antipathy toward Harris.

Despite his inept fielding, Cronin held down the shortstop's job in Boston for seven seasons, although he missed much of 1936 after an injury. Though a feared power hitter, Cronin's obsession with remaining the starting shortstop, coupled with his refusal to move to third base, would have far-reaching ramifications upon the future fortunes of the franchise.

Lifelong Red Sox fan Don Chase, a native of Watertown, Massachusetts, said the fans recognized that Cronin was a liability in the field. "Cronin was a great pinch hitter, but he couldn't field a lick."

In 1935, the Sox barely improved, to 78–75, ending up in fourth place.

In another wintertime deal with Philadelphia, Yawkey purchased over-the-hill outfielder Bing Miller, forty years old, while he also snagged first baseman Babe Dahlgren from the Pacific Coast League. Miller would stay with the Sox for two seasons before retiring, although he did hit .304 and .298 in forty-seven games. Dahlgren would also last two years in Boston.

Expectations of the fans and the press were high, because, like today, they equated price tag with ability. Hopes soared even further when Yawkey bought A's first baseman Jimmie "The Beast" Foxx, a certified home run hitter who drove in scads of runs, and pitcher Johnny Marcum, for between $150,000 and $250,000 and two players.

Hall of Famer Lefty Gomez, who pitched for the Yankees, said Foxx instilled fear in the hearts of pitchers throughout the American League. "I was pitching one day when my glasses clouded up on me. I took them off to polish them. When I looked up at the plate, I saw Jimmie Foxx. The sight of him terrified me so much, I haven't been able to wear glasses since."

The Sox also obtained Doc Cramer, who was delighted. "I liked going to Boston because [the players] got more money. At Boston, Yawkey treated the players very well."

In addition, Boston acquired shortstop Eric McNair, over Cronin's vociferous objections. "We can certainly use Foxx and Roger [Doc] Cramer would be a star in any man's ball club," Cronin told the *Post*. "But I don't know what in the world we would use McNair for. I plan to play shortstop myself."

McNair would spend three frustrating seasons in Boston, ultimately ending up suicidal at the treatment he was afforded by Cronin, according to several teammates. Until he was hit in the head by a pitched ball in an off-season exhibition game, Foxx was, well, Foxx, the most feared home run hitter of his time.

Cronin continued to favor Catholics and players from the West Coast, and he intensely disliked the former Athletics on the club, of which there were many. In turn, the veterans resented him, especially the pitchers because he insisted on calling virtually every pitch.

"I can't recall one of the Philly players that he took to," remarked Cramer. "Once during a game I heard Grove tell him he couldn't play shortstop on a high school team."

"Lefty didn't like Cronin," agreed catcher Gene Desautels. "'Cronin isn't a good manager,' he would say. And Cronin couldn't do anything because Yawkey was instrumental in getting Lefty, and [Yawkey] was the one who liked him, just like he liked Jimmie Foxx and Cramer and Eric McNair and all those guys he got from Philadelphia."

As the team limped to a 74–80 mark in 1936, good enough for sixth place, both the fans and the media soured on the club.

The public, said the *Boston Globe*, had "leaped to the conclusion that the pennant was in the mail. When it was not delivered, their disappointment was as bitter as that of a boy who has not received the promised atomic peashooter for 1,000 cereal labels."

The Yankees proceeded to become world champions four seasons in a row, from 1936 through 1939, logging additional chapters in what would become the greatest dynasty in the history of professional sports.

Boston barely improved in 1937, raising its record to 78–75 and fifth place in the standings, although the season wasn't without its annual dramatics.

Harkening back to the days of Carl Mays, Wes Ferrell threw a couple of tantrums on the mound, berating teammates who made errors behind him and twice stalking off the field in the middle of a game. After the second incident Cronin blew up. "I'm all through with him," Cronin sputtered. "He's gonna be fined $1,000, suspended and sent home."

For his part, Eddie Collins seemingly backed his player-manager, asserting, "Anything Joe Cronin has done will be backed up by Tom Yawkey and myself to the limit."

Not hardly. First, Yawkey downplayed the brouhaha, telling the press, "The next fifteen months will see such upheaval on this club that the whole matter will be completely obliterated." Yawkey then reduced Ferrell's suspension to ten days and rescinded the $1,000 fine, whereupon the owner disappeared, not to be seen in Boston for six months.

In the off-season the Red Sox procured another malcontent, outfielder Ben Chapman, a notorious racist and all-round ill-tempered man. He, too, incessantly feuded with Cronin. "Let's just say that Cronin wasn't a good shortstop defensively," said Chapman. "[The ballplayers] wanted Eric McNair, who had led the American League in fielding for Connie Mack's A's, at shortstop."

This dissatisfaction with Cronin's play in the field was becoming universal. "He resorted to kneeling in front of the ball as an outfielder does—the [$250,000] squat," wrote Harold Kaese of the *Boston Globe*. "One day the ball hit the other knee and careened out to the right fielder."

On October 2, 1937, the Red Sox traded Red Kress, Buster Mills, and Bobo Newsom to the St. Louis Browns for outfielder Joe Vosmik. Although Vosmik did a solid job for Boston during the two years he played for the club—batting .324 in 1938—Newsom was a powerhouse hurler in the American League for years. He was a four-time All-Star who, after being traded to Detroit, won two games in the 1940 World Series and led the AL in strikeouts in 1942.

Around that time Yawkey did take a step that could have revolutionized the club's operations when he hired former major league umpire and Cleveland general manager Billy Evans to establish a farm system. Evans, widely recognized as one of the most astute judges of talent in baseball, immediately began cobbling together a minor league organization that would provide the Red Sox with homegrown talent. But, like many other aspects of the operation, ultimately Yawkey would allow the endeavor to be sabotaged. Yawkey, in his indifference, shortchanged the farm system, establishing or purchasing only eight clubs. In comparison, most other major league teams affiliated with many more minor league franchises. St. Louis alone underwrote twenty-eight.

"Boston's decision to change course was ill-conceived. For a fraction of what he'd spent on players," wrote Stout and Johnson in *Red Sox Century*, "Yawkey could have acquired nearly every premier prospect in the country and created the most productive and extensive farm system in baseball. Yet he missed a remarkable opportunity."

Year after year the franchise was always just short a player or two.

After the 1937 season Yawkey stood pat for the first time since he'd acquired the franchise. Eddie Collins signaled the sea change in an interview he gave to *Baseball Magazine*. "We have abandoned, definitely, the attempt to fight our way to a pennant by the purchase of ready-made stars." Yet the franchise persisted in allowing its minor league system to languish.

The Red Sox logged their best season thus far under the Yawkey regime in 1938, finishing second to the Yankees, and posting a record of 88–61. Boston led the American League in batting with a .299 mark and an on-base percentage of .378.

Jimmie Foxx won the batting crown with an average of .349, the RBI title with 175, and slugging average (.704). He hit fifty home runs, but missed out on the Triple Crown because of Hank Greenberg's Ruthian fifty-eight round-trippers for Detroit. Lefty Grove topped all American League pitchers with an ERA of 3.08.

In June 1936, general manager Collins made the one and only West Coast scouting foray of his career. He signed two promising ballplayers, a second baseman from Los Angeles named Bobby Doerr, and a slender teenager who pitched and played the outfield. His name was Ted Williams.

7

TEDDY BALLGAME
AND THE WAR YEARS

They called him "The Kid," "The Splendid Splinter," and "Teddy Ballgame," among other names. Many won't be listed here, but no matter, because what Theodore Samuel Williams was, in reality, the greatest pure hitter baseball has ever known.

When Eddie Collins discovered Williams, a skinny seventeen-year-old from San Diego, Ted had just signed his first professional baseball contract with his hometown Padres of the Triple A Pacific Coast League. The youngster was raw, brash and impetuous—but, boy, could he play baseball!

Bill Lane, the owner of the San Diego franchise, at first turned away Collins's overtures. Although Lane had signed Williams, he wasn't entirely sold on the teen's abilities, and he didn't want to ruin his prospects of selling other players to the Red Sox. But Collins, in one of his more astute moves, insisted upon taking an option on the young pitcher-outfielder.

Ever since Williams played on the sandlots of Southern California and practiced his swing night after night while home alone, he aspired to be a great hitter. "A kid copies what is good," Williams once said. "I remember the first time I saw [lifetime .349 major league hitter] Lefty O'Doul. I was looking through a knothole, and I saw the guy come to bat in batting practice. I said, 'Geez, does that guy look good.' And it was Lefty O'Doul, one of the greatest hitters ever."

Bobby Doerr, ultimately a Hall of Fame second baseman, remembered a tall, rawboned youth who came for a tryout in the middle of the 1936 season. "Ted had come in June for a tryout. San Diego liked him and signed him. At the time Collins came down, Ted wasn't playing, but Collins watched him hit, liked his swing, so he went to Bill Lane . . . and said he would like to buy Ted's contract."

The Sox purchased Doerr's contract, while Lane and Collins entered into a handshake agreement that guaranteed Boston the right to buy Ted's contract after the youngster acquired some seasoning.

Williams grew up in a one-parent household. His mother May, a dedicated Salvation Army worker who spent the bulk of her time spreading the Gospel, was widely known as the "Sweetheart of San Diego" and the "Angel of Tijuana." She and Ted's father separated when Ted was a youth, but they didn't divorce for twenty years. Although Sam Williams took no part in Ted's life, Williams said he didn't blame his father, a Spanish-American War veteran and photographer, for leaving. "I wouldn't have wanted to be married to a woman like that," wrote Williams in his autobiography, *My Turn at Bat*.

Even while playing ball at the North Park Playground, Ted earned notice. The New York Yankees tried to sign him while he was still in high school, but May Williams shunned the offer of $250-$400 per month made by Yankees West Coast scout Bill Essick. Had she *not* spurned the offer, Williams may very well have ended up playing alongside another West Coast phenom, "Jolting" Joe DiMaggio.

Despite having promised May that he'd keep Ted until the youngster was twenty-one, Lane sold Williams's contract to Boston for a reported $25,000 when Ted was only nineteen. Lane allegedly also promised May a piece of the purchase price, but reneged on the deal, although according to press reports, May did receive $2,500 from the Red Sox after Williams left for Boston.

The teenager traveled to Florida for spring training in 1938, where he immediately alienated his teammates as well as manager Joe Cronin, whom he allegedly called "Sport" when the two were introduced. "That didn't go over too big with Joe," recalled Doerr.

Williams had a big mouth and his on-the-field antics upset the others in camp. He refused to take fielding practice seriously, declaring, "They ain't paying me to field. I'm going to get paid for hitting."

Veteran center fielder Doc Cramer tried to teach Williams nuances of playing the outfield. "You couldn't do much with him," Cramer later said. "I did help him a little bit. He couldn't catch a ground ball. Used to go right between his legs. He wasn't getting ready to catch it—that was the main thing. But he got a lot better."

Instead of following the action while stationed in the outfield, Williams would swing an imaginary bat, which sent Cronin into orbit. The player-manager would shout at the youngster, urging him to pay attention and work on his fielding. But Williams would continue to goof around in the field, slapping himself on the butt with his glove and shouting, "Hi-ho Silver! Away!" while chasing fly balls.

Veterans told Williams, "Wait until you see Foxx hit." Ted retorted, "Wait until Foxx sees me hit."

"He really did say that," confirmed Cramer.

The notoriously thin-skinned Williams would sulk or throw tantrums when he felt he was being mistreated or snubbed, a pattern he would follow for years.

Even though Collins and Cronin recognized his raw talent, Williams was sent to Boston's Triple A club in Minneapolis. Cronin especially was incensed at Williams's behavior and weary of his immaturity. "Billy Evans and Eddie Collins said, 'Let's put him in that small bandbox in Minneapolis and get him some confidence,'" explained minor league first baseman Tony Lupien, who later spent three years with Williams in Boston. "It was well-planned what they were doing."

In a final, parting shot, Ted teed off on the starting outfield trio. "When Ted was leaving . . . after they farmed him out," recalled Ben Chapman, "I remember one remark he made to Doc Cramer, Joe Vosmik, and me [all .300 hitters]. He said, 'I'll be back, and I'll be making more money than the three of you put together.'" Although Chapman laughed at the idea, he knew in his bones that Williams would back up his words. "When he said what he did about the three of us, I thought, 'He may be right.'"

Ultimately, Williams was.

Williams tore up the Triple A American Association while in Minnesota, winning the league's Most Valuable Player Award and the Triple Crown by hitting .366, slamming 43 home runs and knocking in 142 runs. There was no keeping him off the Sox in 1939.

Yet his addition to the Red Sox made little difference even though Williams batted .327, with 31 home runs and a whopping 145 RBIs in his rookie season. Cronin remained a liability at shortstop, committing thirty-two errors for an abysmal .959 fielding average. Although there was an answer in the wings, the player-manager stubbornly remained intent upon keeping his starting job—and refused to move to third base, which was then occupied by the hard-hitting Jim Tabor.

Sox minor league director Billy Evans had engineered the purchase of the Triple A franchise in Louisville for about $200,000, and which featured a slick-fielding shortstop named Harold "Pee Wee" Reese. Evans was absolutely convinced that Reese was the Red Sox shortstop of the future. Cronin had other ideas.

Williams's rookie year, 1939, was full of drama and angst, as the youngster's antics and declarations to the media constantly attracted attention. When he arrived for spring training, Cronin told him, "You've got a lot of ability and have had enough schooling. This is serious business and there's no place for clowning."

According to Stout and Johnson, Williams was a cornucopia of quotes for the press. "Williams was a verbal inspiration, a player whose personality equaled his talent. He had opinions on everything and wasn't yet wary of the printed word . . . In another time, the club would have helped shield their young star, but there was already enough resentment over Williams that he was left to learn his own way around the press. Williams didn't disappoint anyone that spring, with either his bat or his tongue."

Indeed, Williams threw a fit in Atlanta when, during an exhibition, he badly misjudged a foul fly ball. After picking up the ball, he heaved it over the roof of the right-field grandstand. Cronin pulled him immediately. "I've got to take the busher out of him," declared the exasperated manager.

But nothing could intimidate the youngster. He remarked to the *Boston Transcript*, "I haven't seen any pitching from these big leaguers that scares me."

Williams was able to deflect criticism when, after committing an error or making a fool out of himself, he would proceed to hit a towering home run, or perform another such superhuman feat. Yet Ted's lapses in the field continued to plague the team, and drove Cronin to distraction. On one occasion, the player-manager yanked Williams from a game after he made two glaring errors. "He was taken out because he didn't hustle on the fly[ball], because he had not been hustling all afternoon, and because he had not been hustling for about a week," Cronin told the press.

The team's lack of pitching depth and poor fielding doomed Boston's hopes in 1939. In addition to Cronin's thirty-two miscues, Williams committed nineteen errors, and third baseman Tabor racked up an astounding forty miscues of his own.[11]

Farm director Evans was convinced a big part of the answer was playing in Louisville: shortstop Pee Wee Reese. But Reese had performed badly in an exhibition game against the parent club during spring training, and Cronin, ever mindful of the threat Reese posed to his own job security, lobbied to dump the diminutive infielder. In July, the player-manager realized his fondest wish, as the Sox sold Reese to the Brooklyn Dodgers.

"He was totally into turf protection," said Glenn Stout. "That's my interpretation. Cronin hurt them for a lot of years. He was lacking as a manager. Longevity in baseball doesn't mean you've accumulated the instantaneous repository of wisdom you need to be a successful manager."

Beginning in 1940, Reese, as anchor of the Dodgers' infield, led Brooklyn to seven National League pennants and made the NL All-Star team ten times. Although Cronin was elected to the American League All-Stars twice more during his career (1939, 1941), he committed eighty-one more errors before he retired in 1945.

In 1939, the Sox again cruised to a second place finish, seventeen games behind the Yankees.

The franchise sold off more players than they acquired. The only player of note they obtained during that period was outfielder

---

11 Tabor was a hard-drinking, hard-hitting ballplayer who'd once threatened Williams after a particularly lackadaisical play in the field by Ted while the two men were in Minneapolis. Tabor would ultimately drink his way out of baseball, dying at age thirty-six.

Dominic DiMaggio, the youngest brother of the New York icon. With the addition of DiMaggio as center fielder and the 1939 acquisition of Lou Finney from—where else—Connie Mack's A's—Ted moved from right to left. The Red Sox also tailored right field for the left-handed Williams, placing both bullpens in the vast right-field power alley, thus lowering the distance from 405 feet to 382 feet while bringing in the right field stands from 325 feet to 302 feet.

The 1940 season brought even more heartache to Red Sox fans when Foxx slumped badly and DiMaggio got hurt. The fans resented the trades management made during the off-season, and Ted's indifferent defensive play. And the media began taking a much more critical look at the young star's behavior on the field. Grove threatened Williams, and Cramer had a fistfight with Ted over Williams's nonchalant play on the diamond.

When Williams continued his nonsense, Cronin threatened to bench him. "I didn't want to do this," explained Cronin. "I don't want Williams to get this kind of reputation, but there's no other way." But then Cronin reversed himself.

Nevertheless, Williams demanded to be traded, declaring, "I don't like the town, I don't like the people and the newspapermen have been on my back all year long." After the quote was printed, Williams denied saying it.

And with that, Williams declared open war on the press, a war that would last twenty years. If he only had simply let his bat do his talking, things might have been entirely different, but that just wasn't his nature. Williams would feud with the media and snub Red Sox fans all the way through his retirement in 1960 and beyond.

Inciting the fans didn't bother Williams. "The boos stir me up," remarked Teddy Ballgame. Yet he was a fan magnet. The constant focus on Williams deflected attention from the other aspects of the Red Sox operation.

The press failed to take critical looks at Cronin's management, Collins' administration and Yawkey's record as an owner—apparently just the way the front office liked it.

Williams seemed to have a blind spot when it came to self-analysis, always blaming someone else for problems of his own making. In fact, it was in 1940 following his move to left field that Ted decided he'd never again tip his cap to the fans in Fenway Park.

"There can be 30,000 people cheering me," Ted once said, "but up in the back row will be one guy booing, and I'll hear him."

Reflected general manager Collins, "If he'd just tip his cap once, he could be elected mayor of Boston."

Doc Cramer related one specific incident that proved indicative of Williams's contempt for the press. "I was sitting on the bench one time before a game, talking to Jack Malaney [of the *Boston Post*], and Ted came out. He said, 'Hiya, Doc. You smell anything?' Ted was talking about Malaney." Cramer added that, embarrassed, he didn't know what to do.

Detroit won the 1940 pennant, overtaking the slumping Yankees. Boston finished fourth, with a record of 82–72, another golden opportunity wasted.

Williams hit .344, with 23 home runs and 113 RBIs, and second baseman Bobby Doerr emerged as a star in his own right.

Following the club's disappointing showing, came a plethora of nonsensical trades, dumping three starting pitchers, perennial .300 hitter Doc Cramer, and catcher Gene Desautels. After trading Cramer, who'd led the AL in 1940 with 200 hits, to Washington for outfielder Gee Walker, a lifetime .294 hitter, they sent the "Madman from Mississippi," along with Desautels and pitcher Jim Bagby, to

Cleveland. The Red Sox got back three players, including young pitcher Joe Dobson.

The 1941 season got off to an inauspicious start when Williams chipped a bone in his ankle during an exhibition game. He was limited to pinch-hitting until April 29. When he returned to the starting lineup, Williams went on a legendary tear; his remarkable season was eclipsed only by Joe DiMaggio, who hit in fifty-six consecutive games and became a national obsession that year.

By July 1, the Sox had fallen further and further behind the soaring Yankees, despite the fact that Williams was batting over .400. In one of the most dramatic performance of his career, Ted rapped a three-run homer in the top of the ninth inning to win the 1941 All-Star game.

Again, the Red Sox faded badly, finishing in second place behind New York. And again the Yankees became world champs.

Williams, meanwhile, hit .406, a batting feat most experts assert will never be matched. With his average technically at .400, he insisted on playing in the season-ending doubleheader in Philadelphia. He responded with six hits. "If I was being paid $30,000 a year, the very least I could do was hit .400," he cracked.

After the season, Collins traded Stan Spence and Jack Wilson to the Washington Senators for Ken Chase and Johnny Wela. A pitcher, Chase appeared infrequently over two seasons, while Wela never played for the parent club. Spence became an All-Star outfielder for Washington in 1942, 1944, 1946, and 1947.

On December 7, 1941, the Japanese Imperial Navy attacked Pearl Harbor, plunging the United States into the Second World War. It would have an indelible effect on the fortunes of the Boston Red Sox. Although the franchise would lose a number of players to the service during the 1942 season, Ted Williams wasn't one of them.

Williams provided the sole support of his mother, and therefore was entitled to a military deferment. If the media hadn't universally disliked him, he may have been able to play through the war years, but the press made such a stink over his deferment that Ted felt forced to join. Williams enlisted in the Naval Air Corps in the fall of 1942, and served for three years as a flight instructor at the Pensacola Naval Air Station.

But before Williams enlisted, he continued his stellar career in 1942, hitting .356, with 37 home runs and 137 RBIs. The Sox, however, were again stymied by the Yankees, finishing in second place with a record of 93–59. During the season, the club released Jimmie Foxx, who became gun shy at the plate and washed up at age thirty-four due to the beaning he sustained. It was the second legendary player the Sox had parted ways with in a few months: Lefty Grove had thrown his last game in the majors for Boston at the close of the 1941 season.

Tom Yawkey's first marriage was in tatters, a combination of his indifference to his wife of seventeen years, his alcohol-fueled rants, and his underwriting of the Sunset Lodge brothel. Yawkey's drinking had grown markedly worse, and it cost him the man he entrusted with building his fledgling minor league organization.

After accepting a one-year contract to continue his employment with the franchise in 1941, Billy Evans was dispatched to run the Triple A farm club in Louisville. Then, according to an unpublished interview, Evans received a telephone call from a drunken Tom Yawkey in September. "Billy, we think it will be in the best interest of the Red Sox if you were to sever your connection with the club," Yawkey slurred.

"That was all," Evans told Harold Kaese. "It was a rough deal. I was fired over the telephone and without reason. If I had been out that night or asked Yawkey to reconsider, I honestly think I'd still be working for the Red Sox."

Yawkey became even more erratic. He would go to the ballpark before any of the players and have the batboys throw batting practice to him. Then, as the players arrived, he would retire to his office, only to return to his box seat with Collins and drink his way through the game.

His adopted daughter, Julia, never really knew her father. "He's a strange man," she told a reporter in the early seventies.

Two new impact players joined the club in 1942: pitcher Tex Hughson and infielder Johnny Pesky, who replaced the aging and slow afoot Joe Cronin at shortstop, two years after Cronin surreptitiously engineered Reese's sale.

During the war years the Red Sox lost virtually the entire starting lineup, except for first baseman Tony Lupien. Not surprisingly, Boston was mediocre, finishing 68–84 in 1943, and an even 77–77 in 1944. (Despite losing the 1942 World Series, the Yankees were world champs in 1941 and 1943.)

The Sox slumped even further in 1945, the year they passed on a chance to sign Jackie Robinson. Boston finished seventh with a record of 71–83. The year proved to be the worst of the club's war years, and the franchise completely blew an opportunity to rewrite history by taking a chance on Robinson. The team's shortsightedness would haunt them for decades.

8

THE GREAT SCAM

O ne hundred ninety-one days before Jackie Roosevelt Robinson signed a minor league contract with the Brooklyn Dodgers on October 23, 1945, he had a tryout with the Boston Red Sox.

Unfortunately for Robinson, his Negro League compatriots, and countless Red Sox fans, the tryout was nothing more than a hoax perpetrated on crusading journalists, one uncompromising Boston politician, and the millions of African-Americans who longed to see their brethren compete at the major league level. African-Americans had been banned from Major League Baseball since Moses "Fleet-wood" Walker played for Toledo in the American Association, considered a major league at the time. By the end of the decade, in 1887, an unofficial "gentlemen's agreement" throughout organized baseball effectively kept the major leagues lily-white.[12]

---

12 John McGraw of the New York Giants tried to sign a black man in 1901 by passing him off as an American Indian, but the powers that be wouldn't have it.

According to Art Rust, Jr. in *Get that Nigger off the Field*, McGraw met a Cincinnati native named Charlie Grant while training his Giants at Hot Springs, Arkansas. Grant was a gifted ballplayer, having played second base for a top Negro League club. Choosing an odd-sounding name he found on a map, McGraw hatched a plot to foist Grant off . . . as an American Indian.

"There's a creek on this map called Tokahama," McGraw allegedly declared to the flattered Grant. "As far as anyone else is concerned, you're a full-blooded Cherokee."

But sly Charlie Comiskey wasn't fooled, exposing the plot. Grant never took the field.

Part of the problem stemmed from Kenesaw Mountain Landis, baseball's commissioner, an avowed racist, who staunchly opposed integrating the majors despite the world war that was raging. Though the military was also segregated, many African-Americans saw combat and others were on the front lines in support roles. African-Americans could fight and die for the supposed cause of freedom, but not play Major League Baseball.[13]

Then Landis died, and former U.S. Senator "Happy" Chandler was appointed commissioner. Chandler had a more benign view than the heavy-handed Landis.

After a year of intense lobbying and the threat of flexing political muscle, Boston City Councilor Isadore H. Y. Muchnick finally forced the Bosox to give a few African-American ballplayers a tryout.

Muchnick, the forgotten man in the saga, ultimately joined forces with two influential black sports journalists, Wendell Smith of the *Pittsburgh Courier* and sports editor Mabrey "Doc" Kountze of the *Boston Guardian* in an attempt to procure tryouts for African-American ballplayers with both the Red Sox and the Braves.[14] Kountze had tried to exert pressure concerning integration on Major League Baseball since the 1930s.

Muchnick enlisted Smith to line up some talented African-American ballplayers for tryouts with the two clubs. Smith delivered Robinson, who was playing for the Kansas City Monarchs, along with Sam Jethroe of the Cleveland Buckeyes and Marvin Williams of the Philadelphia Stars.

According to Howard Bryant, author of *Shut Out*, Muchnick had hit upon what he perceived as the perfect means to force the city's

---

13 Ironically, Landis was so-named because his father, a surgeon, saw service at the Battle of Kennesaw Mountain, Tennessee with the 35th Ohio Volunteer Infantry Regiment, although Abraham Landis misspelled the name of the mountain.

14 Robinson did have a brief tryout with the Chicago White Sox in 1942. Chicago's failure to sign him wasn't as egregious as Boston's because the White Sox integrated in 1951. The Red Sox "welcomed" their first black ballplayer in 1959.

two major league franchises to at least grant tryouts to talented black ballplayers in 1944: the threat to rescind the suspension of Boston's so-called Blue Laws, which allowed Sunday baseball in the city. For years the law had forbidden playing professional baseball in Boston on that day of the week. Fenway Park, because of its proximity to a church, did not host a Sunday game until 1932, when the law was changed. (Prior to that, the Red Sox had played selected Sunday games at Braves Field following the suspension of the Blue Law in 1929.) The rescission of the annual vote required a single "nay" vote, so Muchnick had it within his power without any additional support.[15] When Muchnick originally put both Boston clubs on notice in 1944, Sox general manager Eddie Collins quickly and decisively tried to deflect the question. "We have never had a single request for a tryout by a colored applicant."

The season was near at hand, so Muchnick dropped the matter, but then revived it in the spring of 1945, again threatening to withhold the waiver. "I cannot understand how baseball, which claims to be the national sport and which in my opinion received special favors and dispensations [i.e., anti-trust exemptions] from the Federal Government because of alleged moral value, can continue a pre–Civil War attitude toward American citizens because of the color of their skin," he wrote.

Collins responded in a letter to the councilman, "I have been connected with the Red Sox twelve years and during that time we have never had a request for a tryout by a colored applicant. . . . It is beyond my

---

15 Muchnick never received the credit he deserved for his part in trying to break the color-line. Instead, he was portrayed as an opportunistic politician attempting to curry favor with black voters.

understanding how anyone can insinuate or believe that 'all ballplayers regardless of race color or creed, have not been treated in the American Way' so far as having equal opportunity to play for the Red Sox."

Collins's claim that black ballplayers weren't interested in playing Major League Baseball because they made more money in the Negro Leagues was laughable, as most Negro League teams barely scraped by. However, Collins added that the Red Sox would be agreeable to offer tryouts to black ballplayers if asked.

"Here are three men who want a tryout," Muchnick immediately proffered.

Effectively cornered, Collins agreed to schedule a tryout for April 12, 1945. The three ballplayers arrived in Boston the day before.

The tryouts didn't take place that day. Collins would later claim that they were cancelled due to the death of President Franklin Roosevelt, but Roosevelt's death wasn't made public until early evening after he'd suffered a cerebral hemorrhage shortly before 5 PM.

Wendell Smith was outraged, declaring, "[The Red Sox] are not fooling me" and charging the Sox with scamming the African-American ballplayers. "These boys came here for a tryout and if they don't get one it will be simply another mark against the undemocratic practices of major league owners and officials," he wrote in the *Pittsburgh Courier*. "We are not going to stop fighting no matter how much they duck and hide and try to evade the facts."

Robinson and the other two players were disturbed at the delay. "Even if they don't accept us, we are at least doing our part and if possible making the way clear for those who follow," he said. "Some day some Negro player or players will get a break. We want to help make that day a reality."

Smith invoked the name of Crispus Attucks into another of his columns concerning the injustice of the situation. Attucks was the second man killed in the Boston Massacre in 1770—an escaped slave, free for twenty years at the time of his death. Smith began with the words, "This is Boston, cradle of America's democracy . . . "

The mainstream press picked up the story, forcing Collins's hand. The *Boston Daily Record*'s Dave Egan—of Ted-Williams-bashing fame—wrote, "Here are two 'believe-it-or-not items,' exclusively for the personal enlightenment of Mr. Edward Trowbridge Collins, general manager of the Boston Red Sox. He is living in . . . 1945, and not in the dust covered year 1865. He is residing in the city of Boston, and not in the city of Mobile, Alabama . . . therefore we feel obliged to inform you that since Wednesday last three citizens of the United States have been attempting vainly to get a tryout with his ball team."

Citing Collins's earlier assertion that black ballplayers were welcome to tryout if they wanted, Egan went on to say, "Every other method having failed, these three young men will present themselves at Mr. Collins's gate this afternoon, to inquire whether or not those words were written in good faith, to ask an opportunity, if not with the Red Sox, then with the worst and the weakest of its farm clubs."

Although Egan's story apparently broke a previously agreed upon embargo of the matter between Muchnick and Collins, the Sox were finally forced to allow the trio a chance to show their stuff. While the mainstream press had been silent, the Sox had stalled and stalled and stalled. The media would virtually ignore the tryout once it was held.

The tryout was scheduled for 10:30 AM, and the Sox were slated to take a train to New York City at 1 PM.

Only manager Joe Cronin sat in the stands with Muchnick and Smith. Coach Hugh Duffy ran the tryout. Since Collins was the team's general manager, he would have been the club official responsible for signing ballplayers, not Cronin. Collins allegedly met with the three Negro League players before the tryouts but then left.

After watching the trio hit, field, and throw, members of the media and club officials alike spoke highly of the three African-American athletes, primarily about Robinson's prowess. Muchnick later bragged about how hard Robinson tattooed the Green Monster.

The daily papers picked up the story after a fashion, but most played it down. The newspapers that circulated within the black community at large initially expressed optimism, but then became increasingly bitter, with Kountze later terming the affair, "one of the biggest letdowns the author ever experienced in his entire career of sportswriting."

Globe reporter Clif Keane subsequently wrote that someone up in the back of the grandstand hollered, "Get those niggers off the field!" near the conclusion of the "tryouts." The voice was never identified. Many speculated it belonged to either Collins or Tom Yawkey, and decades later Keane asserted it was Yawkey's voice.

Jethroe, wrote Howard Bryant in *Shut Out*, told a friend that Cronin "was just up in the stands with his back turned most of the time. He just sent some of his men out there and told them to throw some balls, hit some balls to us, and then come back and say we had ability."

Red Sox Vice President Dick Bresciani, who joined the franchise in 1972 and later oversaw its publications and press relations, insisted that the abortive Robinson tryout was misconstrued. "I know there are so many stories about that famous tryout, and there's nobody around who was there. They're all gone. I know that there was one man, a serviceman, and his son contacted me a few years ago, and talked about his father. And his father had brought in some young players that day. They had had a sandlot tryout before they had Jackie and [Jethroe and Williams]. And they asked those kids to shag balls [during the Negro League players' tryout]. And he claims his father said he never heard anything derogatory said by anyone."

Author Glenn Stout, however, remained dubious.

"Why would you say something derogatory in front of an eighteen-year-old kid at a tryout?" posed Stout. "You can't say for sure. But certainly [anything out-of-line] would have stayed in Jackie Robinson's mind and he held it against [the Red Sox] until the end of his life."

"To be honest," Sam Jethroe later remarked, "I never wondered if we were going to be offered contracts." The three didn't bother to try the Braves.

Sportswriter Joe Cashman, later claimed, "[Red Sox Hall of Famer Hugh Duffy] liked Robinson very much, and he told the Sox to keep him. But Yawkey wanted no part of it. He didn't want to be the one to break the color line."

The slim few newspaper reporters attempting to gain clarity as to why the Red Sox seemed to show such little interest in African-Americans were met icily and sometimes with outright hostility.

Cronin broke a leg the first week of the 1945 season, which he later offered as an excuse in defending why the team never pursued the three black players. Team officials also claimed that the only minor league clubs available were south of the Mason-Dixon line, precluding the presence of black ballplayers because of "Jim Crow" laws.

In the wake of Cronin's injury, Collins wrote Wendell Smith, claiming Cronin's broken leg "threw everything out of gear," as if Collins—the general manager of the club—had no say-so over whom to sign.

In the fifties, Cronin—by then the Sox president—asserted,

"They weren't ready for the majors." After he became American League president, Cronin admitted the Sox were mistaken in not signing Robinson, claiming, "I didn't do the hiring anyway. I was just the manager."

Robinson became the NL Rookie of the Year in 1947 as a first baseman, and was the National League's Most Valuable Player in 1949 (at second base). He also led the NL in batting in 1949, and was elected to the Hall of Fame in 1962. Jethroe was named National League Rookie of the Year in 1950—with the Boston Braves.

"They engaged in racial discrimination for many years," maintained seventy-eight-year-old Don Chase, "and it all went back to Yawkey. They definitely didn't want black players. There's no question they didn't have the right attitude. It hurt them for years."

Cronin snubbed Robinson when Jackie was honored at the 1972 All-Star game. Instead, the league president munched on a hot dog beneath the grandstand as Commissioner Bowie Kuhn and National League President Chub Feeney appeared with the ailing former star, who died within days of the occasion.

Monte Irvin, a Negro League star who later played for the New York Giants, and served in the commissioner's office in public relations, told Kuhn that Cronin refused to take the field with Robinson. "What I figured," Irvin later said, "if you remember, Jackie had had a tryout with Boston, and Jackie had said some things about [Cronin], and this was a holdover from that. Joe didn't want to have any part of that ceremony."

The inept handling of the tryouts earned the franchise the enmity of the African-American community; to this day team officials are still trying to win African-Americans over, in spite of the evenhandedness of the new ownership under John Henry.

Boston also blew the opportunity to sign another great major leaguer, Willie Mays, five years after the club passed on Robinson.

Mays joined the Birmingham Black Barons, a Negro League team, at age 17 in 1948. By 1950, he was widely recognized as a certifiable "five-tool" player, one with the ability to hit, hit with power, throw, field, and run.

A Red Sox Double A minor league team shared the field with the Black Barons in Alabama and had options on any of their ballplayers. A scout, probably Larry Woodall, was dispatched to Alabama to check out Mays. But when a storm front rolled in and rained out the games, Woodall wired Boston to tell them he wasn't going to sit around waiting for the storm to subside. "I'm not going to waste my time waiting for a bunch of niggers," the Texan declared, and franchise officials apparently concurred.

Another account has Red Sox scout George Digby scouting the young phenom. Despite a glowing report to the Boston front office, general manager Joe Cronin supposedly remarked, "We have no use for the boy at this time."

The young Mays was crestfallen. Nearly fifty years later, he speculated, "There's no telling what I would have been able to do in Boston . . . I really thought I was going to Boston . . . But for that Yawkey. Everyone knew he was a racist. He didn't want me."

Mays became the National League Rookie of the Year in 1951 with the New York Giants, making him the third African-American player spurned by Boston to win the award in five years. He was named the NL's Most Valuable Player in 1954 and again in 1965. He hit 660 home runs despite never playing in what would be termed a true hitter's park. Mays was elected to the Hall of Fame in 1979, his first year of eligibility.

Instead, in 1950, Boston signed thirty-one-year-old Lorenzo "Piper" Davis, an infielder, who was clearly beyond his prime. In fact, Davis was player-manager of the Birmingham Black Barons during Boston's scouting trip to see Willie Mays in action.

Jules Tygiel, in *Baseball's Great Experiment: Jackie Robinson and His Legacy*, wrote, "Davis could have played in the major leagues right away, but the Red Sox sent him to Class A in Scranton . . . and if they kept him beyond May 15, they had to pay the Barons another $7,500 [in addition to the initial $7,500 purchase price]. Davis started the season in Scranton leading the team in batting average, home runs, runs scored, stolen bases. He just tore the league apart. After all, here was a major league player in A-ball.

"And on May 13, they call him into the office. He said he thought he might be getting promoted up to [Triple A] Louisville. But they told him, 'We're sorry, we have to let you go for economic reasons.' Obviously, they didn't want to pay the rest of the money."

While changing trains in Washington, D.C., Davis ran into Joe Cronin, who stuck to the party line by reiterating that Boston released him because of money problems. Piper Davis was the one and only black player the Red Sox signed until Earl Wilson and Pumpsie Green in 1953.

Davis's brief stay did, however, serve a purpose: Critics could no longer claim that the Red Sox never signed a African-American ballplayer. In fact, management began claiming that they'd simply be delighted to sign *more* black ballplayers if only they could find some that could help the club.

Davis was dubious. "Tom Yawkey had as much money as anyone on the East Coast," he said. "I don't talk about it that much. It wouldn't help. Sometimes I just sit there and a tear drops from my eye. I wonder why it all had to happen, why we had to have so much hate."

There's little question that the addition to Boston's roster of Robinson, Jethroe, and/or Mays could have made a huge difference in the club's fortunes throughout the late forties and early fifties.

Had Earl Wilson not been drafted into the Marines, Bresciani said, the entire matter might be moot. "Unfortunately, the Red Sox were the last [team to integrate], and that's the albatross that's always been around this franchise's neck. So, if we'd beaten out the Phillies by a year, or if Earl Wilson—who was an outstanding pitching prospect—hadn't gone into the service, we might've brought him up the year before, who knows? And then nobody would care because we'd have been the next-to-last one, and nobody ever cares who the next-to-last one was."

IIIIII

With the return of many key players following the end of World War II, the Sox won the American League championship. Ted Williams, Johnny Pesky, Bobby Doerr, and Dom DiMaggio rejoined the fold, and the team had strong, effective pitching. Boston had also traded shortstop Eddie Lake to Detroit for hard-hitting first baseman Rudy York.

For the first time, Tom Yawkey became a target of the press. Previously a media darling because of his free spending ways, the Red Sox owner found himself under fire for sticking with Joe Cronin as manager, even though his team led the league.

Like Harry Frazee thirty years previous, Yawkey had lost the support of the press—although journalists insisted it was fully justified.

In an article in the *Saturday Evening Post* titled, "What's the Matter with the Red Sox?" the *Globe*'s Harold Kaese skewered Yawkey. "How has Cronin stayed in the saddle? He has stayed because

Yawkey wanted him. Yawkey, like innumerable others, idolized him as a player. Yawkey is stubborn, wealthy and loyal. When he signed [Cronin] to a three-year contract in 1944, Yawkey said, 'I'm perfectly satisfied with Joe. He can manage as long as he likes.' When Cronin was being [criticized for his play in the field] as a shortstop, it was Yawkey who said, 'Instead of a better shortstop helping the pitchers, don't you think better pitchers would help the shortstop?'"

The team reached first place on April 28, 1946, and never relinquished it. They cruised all summer, although the Tigers did give the Red Sox a slight scare late in the season when the Sox endured a seven-game losing streak.

After the Sox took the title, word leaked out that they were planning to trade Williams, who'd been hurt in an exhibition game. He'd been hit on the right elbow by Washington hurler Mickey Haefner in a meaningless exhibition staged by the Sox just prior to the World Series. Many journalists believed the negative impact the injury had on Williams cost the Red Sox the world championship. He went 5-for-25 in the Series, batting a meager .200, with a single RBI.

Nobody from the club would refute the trade rumors, not Collins, Cronin, or Yawkey. Asked point-blank by Kaese whether there was any truth to the rumors, Yawkey simply snapped, "No comment." When pressed, he sneered, "Double no comment."

Whatever the rumors, the truth was that Boston was headed to the World Series for the first time in twenty-eight years. They would play the St. Louis Cardinals, a team that had won the National League pennant four times in the last five seasons.

The Sox took Game One, 3–2, with Rudy York hitting a home run in the tenth inning. Cardinals pitcher Harry "The Cat" Brecheen shut out Boston in the second game, 3–0, tying the Series and sending it to Fenway.

Right-hander Dave "Boo" Ferris repaid the Cards in Game Three with a 4–0 shutout of his own, to give the Sox a two-games-to-one lead. St. Louis roared back in Game Four to drub the Sox, 12–3.

The Red Sox beat St. Louis in Game Five, 6–3. Joe Dobson threw a complete game, with Ted Williams collecting his lone RBI of the series.

The Sox needed one of two games at Sportsman's Park in St. Louis to win the Series. However they simply couldn't close the deal, dropping Game Six—again to Brecheen—by the score of 4–1. Although Ferris was well rested, Cronin opted to start hurler Mickey Harris instead. Then, while coaching third base, Cronin inexplicitly waved Bobby Doerr home on a short single to left field on a hit by Pinky Higgins. Predictably, Doerr was easily erased at home.

After the Sox fell behind the Cards 3–0 in the fourth inning, Cronin called upon hurler Tex Hughson, thus eliminating utilizing the very effective but fragile Hughson from pitching in Game Seven.

Managerial errors ultimately doomed Boston in Game Seven, primarily due to Cronin's handling of the pitching staff and his shuttling of fielders. The game was decided when speedy Cardinals outfielder Enos "Country" Slaughter scored from first base on a hit in the eighth inning. To this day, folklore has it that shortstop Johnny Pesky "held the ball," allowing Slaughter to round third base and score. But center fielder Leon Culberson, subbing for the injured Dom DiMaggio, hesitated before throwing the ball to Pesky.

Author and researcher John B. Holway stated there wasn't any hesitation on Pesky's part, asserting, "I have played the tape again, in slow motion and in stop action. I have timed it with a stopwatch. The verdict: If Pesky held the ball, the camera didn't see him do it. . . . The camera shows Pesky taking the throw, whirling to the left, and throwing home in one continuous motion. Catch, wheel, throw."

Be that as it may, in their first World Series appearance since 1918 the Sox had lost the Fall Classic. They wouldn't appear in another World Series for another twenty-one years, and Yawkey would never live to see a world championship banner fly over Fenway Park.

|||||

As bad as the loss of the Series was, the ensuing years would bring even more misery upon the Red Sox and their loyal fans. At least they had Ted Williams, but even that could have turned out differently.

Following the World Series debacle, Yawkey announced that Ted Williams wasn't going anywhere, declaring, "We very definitely will not trade Williams before or during the 1947 season."

That season proved to be a mess. The club's pitching fell apart, DiMaggio played injured all year, and nobody but Williams and Pesky hit. And Yawkey nearly reneged on his word not to trade Williams.

Yawkey was drinking with Yankees owner Dan Topping one evening in early April when the two agreed to exchange stars: Williams for Joe DiMaggio. The deal would have been a travesty, as DiMaggio was four years Ted's senior, and was injured while Williams was still in his prime. Fortunately for the Sox, after Yawkey sobered up, he asked the Yankees to sweeten the deal by throwing in a young catcher named Yogi Berra, and New York backed out of it.

By that time Cronin had completely lost the club, with his players stubbornly insisting he didn't know how to handle his pitching staff.

The Sox limped into the end of the '47 season in third place, sporting a record of 83–71. Williams, who won the Triple Crown, provided the lone bright spot, but his surly attitude with the press no doubt cost him the American League's Most Valuable Player Award.

Meanwhile, in the National League, the Brooklyn Dodgers nabbed the pennant, with Jackie Robinson at first base. Robinson would continue to play first base until 1948, when he moved over to second, the position at which he is best known. In the 1947 Fall Classic the Dodgers fell to—who else?—the New York Yankees.

Eddie Collins retired after the 1947 season, and Cronin, who succeeded him as general manager, immediately hired former Yankees manager Joe McCarthy in spite of McCarthy's prodigious drinking problem.

In the words of Stout and Johnson, "[Yawkey] wasn't put off by McCarthy's alcoholism. Men who knew how to take a drink impressed him. Drunken tirades had never disqualified anybody from working [in] Boston's front office."

Despite McCarthy's record of 1,460–867 with the Yankees, the new Sox manager had his foibles, quirks, and prejudices, and was widely criticized as a "push button manager." With New York that had been easy enough. Boston, however, wasn't New York.

With the taste of near victory in 1946 remaining in his mouth, Yawkey was persuaded to again open his wallet after the lackluster '47 season. In a trade so big it required two separate transactions, Yawkey paid $375,000 and traded nine minor players to the St. Louis Browns for shortstop Vern Stephens and pitchers Ellis Kinder and Jack Kramer.

Although the media tabbed Stephens as the new Red Sox third baseman, McCarthy petulantly left him at short, instead moving Johnny Pesky. Both had been perennial All-Stars.

At first, the sixty-one-year-old McCarthy was highly thought of by many of the Red Sox players in spite of his idiosyncrasies, though others had trouble getting used to his ways. McCarthy was not particularly adept at handling his pitching staffs, and he was prone to overusing his starting position players.

Pitcher Tex Hughson was no fan of the new skipper. After returning to Boston following an injury rehab stint in 1948, he clashed with McCarthy, who was repeatedly appearing drunk. "I could tell you stories about how he mistreated players on the club," Hughson recalled. "I saw Bobby Doerr, a hell of a ballplayer. McCarthy was sitting in the dugout when he was drunk and all, and he was trying to move Bobby over [in the field] . . . He finally got up and waved the white towel [and swore at Doerr] . . . I didn't appreciate that. Bobby Doerr was a hell of a good man, and a good friend of mine."

After a slow start in 1948—Williams again seemed to be the only player hitting the ball—the Red Sox began to respond. But in a three-way battle with New York and the Cleveland Indians, they never could firmly secure first place.

Ultimately Cleveland dropped its last two regular season games, while Boston swept the Yanks, setting up a one-game playoff. Cleveland manager Lou Boudreau elected to go with pitcher Gene Bearden, the club's hottest pitcher, but McCarthy inexplicably selected journeyman right-hander Denny Galehouse.

It was simply one of those head-scratcher mysteries that Red Sox fans question to this day. By choosing Galehouse, McCarthy passed over a well-rested and very effective Ellis Kinder and rookie sensation Mel Parnell. Moreover, Galehouse had warmed up for *six innings* during the regular season finale against the Yankees.

Predictably, Galehouse was shelled, and the Indians thrashed the Sox, 8–3, to win the pennant. If they'd won the game, the Red Sox would've gone to the World Series against the cross-town Braves, who won their first National League pennant since 1914.

Still, Red Sox management felt good about the club's showing, essentially standing pat during the off-season. But the Sox pitching again fell into disrepair, with Kramer, Dobson and Tex Hughson all succumbing to arm problems for most of the '49 season. And again only Williams provided any firepower at the plate. McCarthy's handling of both the pitching staff and the part-time players was comical.

The Sox got things straightened out after the 1949 All-Star break because they had an easy schedule and took advantage of it.

Ellis Kinder and Mel Parnell pitched exceptionally well down the stretch, so as the season wound down, McCarthy began using the two hurlers, to the exclusion of his other pitchers. He even employed Parnell and Kinder in relief when they weren't starting, a sure recipe for disaster.

The season came down to the final two games of the season against the Yankees in New York, with the Sox holding onto a precarious one-game lead. But again, it wasn't to be.

In the first game, after staking Boston to a 4–0 lead, the Yankees came back with two runs. Then Parnell, who'd thrown nearly 300 innings during the season, tired, gave up a third run, and McCarthy was forced to summon the seldom-used Joe Dobson, who clearly wasn't up to the task. But McCarthy had to hold Kinder out to start the season finale if the Sox lost. They did.

Dobson gave up the tying run, and Yankees reliever Joe Page shut down Boston. Then, Dobson gave up a line drive home run to New York outfielder Johnny Lindell in the bottom of the eighth to lose the game, 5–4.

Lindell's homer set up what amounted to a repeat of the climax of 1948: a winner-take-all, one-game playoff.

The Yankees drew first blood in the first inning on a triple by shortstop Phil Rizzuto, who scored on a ground out off the bat of

Tommy Heinrich. The run stood up. In the top of the eighth with one out, McCarthy pulled Kinder, a good-hitting pitcher who been throwing well, and sent up a rookie, left-handed hitting Tom Wright, who drew a walk, but Dom DiMaggio hit into a double play. Then McCarthy called upon Parnell, who imploded. In spite of three late Boston runs, the Sox lost, 5–3.

Devastating losses in the last game in three out of four consecutive seasons. One of those African-American ballplayers the Sox passed up certainly could've helped.

And things were about to get even gloomier for the Red Sox.

BENIGN NEGLECT

9

The 1950 Red Sox were limping along with an overall record of 31–28 when McCarthy was finally forced to throw in the towel on June 23.

Approaching sixty-three years of age, he'd been drinking excessively as the club foundered, and in the words of Stout and Johnson, "was viewed with increasing skepticism, yet Cronin and Yawkey chose to retain him."

But McCarthy went on a bender after the team lost a Father's Day game to the Detroit Tigers, and when the Red Sox arrived in Chicago to face the White Sox a day later, he was still drunk. Cronin sent McCarthy home for a couple of days, but apparently all the team executives privately agreed that he was through. "McCarthy was having trouble on the road, getting real drunk," Red Sox catcher Matt Batts, who was a McCarthy man, told author Pete Golenbock. "For several days they looked for him in Detroit. They found him in the gutter, skid row. He was in real bad shape."

Boston coach Steve O'Neill, a former catcher, was named as the new manager. Under O'Neill the Sox went on to a 63–32 skein to finish the season. But it was too little, too late. The Yankees won the pennant; Boston finished four games back.

Another black mark on McCarthy occurred when Ted Williams pitched a fit after misplaying a fly ball. After the Sox dropped the opening game of the doubleheader May 11 against Detroit, 13–4, they proceeded to lose the second game of the twin bill when Williams misplayed a bases-loaded single, blowing an Ellis Kinder shutout in the process. Termed "the greatest tantrum of his career," Williams then extended his middle finger to the crowd after hitting a grand slam.

The Red Sox issued a perfunctory apology on behalf of Williams, but Gerry Hern of the *Boston Post* derided the so-called apology, correctly discerning that it didn't really emanate from Williams.

Ironically, Williams—so sensitive to criticism—would, according to teammate Dom DiMaggio, devour the newspapers. "You buy every newspaper you can get your hands on," DiMaggio chided Ted, "and spend half your time reading them—just to find someone to get mad at!"

Two days after McCarthy "resigned," North Korea invaded her southern neighbor to begin the Korean Conflict. The war would have far-reaching effects upon Major League Baseball, especially the Red Sox. As the war continued to escalate, Boston went on a tear under manager Steve O'Neill, whom the players regarded as a harmless sort with a penchant for dozing on the bench. After having to deal with such a strong-willed field manager as McCarthy, Yawkey and Cronin found it more to their liking to employ compliant ones who wouldn't rock the boat, a blueprint the team would follow through the mid-sixties.

The Sox batting order, featuring Williams, Stephens, DiMaggio, and Doerr, along with newcomers Walt Dropo and Billy Goodman, were firing on all cylinders. Every starting position player was flirting with a .300 average. Williams, Stephens, DiMaggio, and Dropo all were named to the American League All-Star team.

Then everything fell apart.

In the All-Star game at Comiskey Park, Ted Williams severely injured his left elbow while going after a ball, slamming into the scoreboard. "[Ralph] Kiner got up and hit a long, high arching fly," Dropo recalled. "Ted ran back after it, and, after he caught it, he put his gloved left hand up to brace himself as he ran into the wall, and broke his elbow."

"We had been right in the middle of the pennant race," he lamented. "With Ted, we could have won the thing."

Williams, who still batted four times in Chicago after being hurt, had his elbow checked when the four teammates arrived back in Boston. He discovered he'd be sidelined for two months while recuperating from surgery. He went under the knife two days later, and the Red Sox's best chances for a dynasty had passed them by for yet another generation.

Billy Goodman, who'd ultimately play every field position except catcher during a sixteen-year career in the majors, took Williams's place in left field. Although he hit .354 in 1950, he didn't produce the RBIs or homers like Williams.

Ted was back in the lineup by Labor Day, but Boston couldn't catch the Tigers *or* the Yankees. At the season's end, in spite of missing sixty-five games Williams hit .317, Dropo hit .322, DiMaggio batted .328, Pesky hit .312, Stephens .295 (with thirty-four home runs), and Doerr batted .294. The Red Sox hit .302 as a team, leading the AL, and had four players with twenty-seven or more home runs. Dropo and Stephens each amassed a phenomenal 144 RBIs.

However, the pitching, as often was Boston's problem, was in disarray. Dave "Boo" Feriss, who went an enviable 21–10 in 1945, and 25-6 in 1947, sank to 12–11 in 1948. He was at the end of his career, appearing in only one game for Boston in 1950.

Ellis Kinder went 14–12 on the year and, although he threw eleven complete games, his ERA ballooned to 4.26. A year earlier, Kinder had posted a credible 3.36 ERA and a sterling record of 23–6. He pulled double duty in 1950, leading the team with nine saves. Mel Parnell led the Red Sox with an 18–10 mark, but his ERA was an unimpressive 3.61.

Meanwhile, the Yankees would reel off four consecutive world championships starting in 1950.

Boston continued its slide in 1951, finishing third again, its record slipping to 87–67. After the season, O'Neill was replaced by Cleveland Indians player-manager Lou Boudreau. Yawkey had long lusted after Boudreau, who had compiled a Hall-of-Fame career as shortstop and manager of the Indians. Boudreau played during parts of two seasons for the Sox before he assumed the sole mantle of field manager.

Dom DiMaggio called ex-manager O'Neill a harmless sort. "Steve was an affable sort of guy, but as a strategist, I would have selected a guy like Cronin or McCarthy." The younger DiMaggio would sorely regret the change in management. It cost him his career.

Thinking he'd hit upon a means of restocking his club with young, ready talent, instead of pursuing trades for proven ballplayers, Yawkey ordered team management to sign every decent prospect available. But once Yawkey shelled out nearly $800,000 for seventeen young, unproven players, he found that approach wasn't the panacea he'd originally believed.

As if the Red Sox didn't have enough problems, Ted Williams was recalled into the Marines and was ordered to report for duty in

May 1952. Williams left after the April 30 game, playing in only six contests, bound for combat duty in Korea as a fighter pilot, where he served as the wingman for John Glenn, later an astronaut and U.S. senator.

Meanwhile, Boudreau put the team on notice that he wasn't a manager to be trifled with. "My primary job is to inject speed, spirit, and the will to win into a ballclub which has seriously suffered from a lack of all three ingredients," Boudreau told the *Saturday Evening Post*. "They just haven't wanted to win badly enough." The new boss criticized his veteran players, accusing them of being overpaid and pampered. "The combination is a little too much to resist for the kind of men who are easily impressed by outside influences. If we don't change them, we'll get rid of them."

Which is exactly what Boudreau did, as he proceeded to gut virtually the entire starting lineup.

Stalwart second baseman Bobby Doerr retired after the 1951 season, and Boudreau engineered a massive trade with the Tigers. The Sox sent Dropo (who had a horrendous sophomore season in 1951), Johnny Pesky, Bill Wright, Don Lenhardt, and Fred Hatfield to Detroit. In return, Boston received George Kell, an All-Star third baseman, along with pitcher Dizzy Trout, infielder Johnny Lipon and outfielder Hoot Evers. None ended up playing as a regular, except for Kell, the key acquisition in the deal. Even at that, Kell was gone by mid-1954.

Boston's youth movement welcomed a bevy of rookie ballplayers, most who weren't prepared to play at the major league level. Second baseman Ted Lepcio, outfielder Jimmy Piersall, shortstop Milt Bolling, infielder Gene Stephens, catcher Sammy White, and first baseman Dick Gernert all joined the club. Only White was ready, hitting .281 with ten home runs and 49 RBIs in 115 games.

The new skipper wanted to convert Piersall to shortstop, publicly announcing his intentions without notifying Piersall. The youth, a high-strung, hyperactive sort, was shaken to the core, but once he began working out at that position during spring training in 1952, he reconciled himself to the change. Ultimately, Boudreau switched Piersall back to the outfield after Boston acquired Lipon in June, a move that convinced the youngster that the manager simply wanted to get rid of him. Instead of sitting Piersall down and explaining his motives, Boudreau simply issued his mandate.

Piersall was again rattled, and he began to act erratically, aping opponents and teammates alike, and giving up deliberate, nonchalant strikeouts at the plate.

The team sent Piersall to the minors at mid-season, but he continued to grow more irrational. Piersall's mother had suffered from mental problems during his youth, and he had a brittle psyche due to the pressure his father put on him to be a professional ballplayer. When his father became disabled after Piersall graduated high school, the young man was forced to forego college and instead pursue a professional baseball career.

In addition, Piersall's wife, Mary, had suffered a miscarriage before the 1952 season. It was the final straw, and Piersall snapped in the middle of the year after he was reassigned to Birmingham.

As he later wrote in his autobiography, *Fear Strikes Out*,[16] the young ballplayer suffered a severe nervous breakdown, ending up in a mental institution in Westborough, Massachusetts, where he underwent electro-shock treatments.

The ugly affair was indicative of the way Boudreau managed the club. He delighted in switching the lineup around at will, causing *Boston Post* columnist Bill Cunningham to charge that Boudreau

---

16 Later a movie starring Tony Perkins.

"was like a kid playing with blocks." Indeed, only five Red Sox players appeared in 100 games or more during the 1952 season. Goodman took top honors, appearing in 138, while DiMaggio was second with 128 appearances.

All told, the team hit 113 home runs for the entire season, a good number by league standards but not for the park the Red Sox played in. Gernert led the squad with nineteen. Not a single ballplayer collected 100 RBIs. The pitching was abysmal as well: only McDermott and Parnell recorded ten or more wins.

Miraculously, the team stayed a contender until September before folding under pressure. It ended up in sixth place, with a sub-par record of 76–78.

The National League's Braves then took the city aback by bolting to Milwaukee in an effort to offset massive losses in annual attendance; crowds had dropped off by more than 40 percent since 1948, when the Braves won the pennant. Yet the Red Sox failed to capitalize on their newfound monopoly in Boston and its environs. "It was stupid," said longtime fan Don Chase. "It seemed the people liked the Red Sox more than the Braves to start with."

There was no sense of urgency to win. Boudreau continued to tinker with his lineup and overplay his young and inexperienced players, to both their detriment and to the team's.

Boudreau remained committed to the "youth movement," pressuring the ultra-loyal Dom DiMaggio to retire after batting only three times in 1953. DiMaggio left the club a bitter man after Boudreau awarded the starting center-field job to twenty-three-year-old Tommy Umphlett, who hit a respectable .283 in 1953 (the Sox then sent Umphlett to the Washington Senators, where he played two more years, barely hitting his weight).

DiMaggio walked. "I suppose Boudreau had a five-year rebuilding program going when he brought up all the young fellows and got rid of all the old-timers," the outfielder said. "But he hurt the parent club and destroyed the minor league system. He set the Red Sox back thirteen years."

Walt Dropo, for one, was happy to go to Detroit. "Two years later it wasn't even a challenge to beat the Red Sox. Boudreau can say whatever he wants about it. He was a failure."

A weary Ted Williams returned from Korea in July after flying thirty-nine combat missions (and once crash landing his jet aircraft). He was safe and sound, although he'd suffered inner ear problems due to flying at high altitudes. Williams, who missed nearly five full seasons from his military service during the two wars, came back with a vengeance. He outshone the rest of the American League, hammering thirteen home runs, knocking in thirty-four runs, and hitting .407 in thirty-seven games. He collected thirty-seven hits in only ninety-one at bats.

Williams was back, but the team was a shell of the club he'd left. Only Billy Goodman and Vern Stephens remained from the powerhouse teams of the mid-century. (Al Zarilla had also rejoined the club after spending two years in exile with Chicago and St. Louis.)

The pitching was decent, but the Sox lacked a back end to their starting rotation. Parnell won twenty-one games, while Mickey McDermott went 18–10. Aside from them, only pitcher Hal Brown won in double digits, going 11–6 in his lone year as a starting pitcher. Kinder did bounce back as a reliever, posting a record of 10–6 with a sparkling 1.85 ERA and recording twenty-seven saves.

The franchise's 1953 record of 84–69 earned it a fourth place finish behind the Yankees, Indians, and the White Sox.

|||||

Finally, in 1953, the Red Sox signed two additional black ball-players, descendants in a way of the disillusioned Piper Davis.

The two were infielder Elijah "Pumpsie" Green, a product of Oakland, California, and a hulking catcher named Earl Wilson from Ponchatoula, Louisiana. The front office liked Wilson's right arm and converted him to a pitcher. He would remain a feared batter, often utilized as a pinch hitter.

The two slowly made their way through the Red Sox farm system. Wilson signed at eighteen years of age, and Green, brother of future Dallas Cowboys All-Pro defensive back Cornell Green, at age nineteen. Wilson was drafted into the Marines in 1957, interrupting his career for two years.

The team treaded water through the fifties, finishing fourth in 1954, 1955, and 1956; and improving to third place in 1957 and 1958. Again, the Yankees won the American League pennant for four consecutive seasons, from 1955–58, twice emerging as world champions.

Boudreau was fired in 1954 after the team posted a 69–85 mark. His replacement was Pinky Higgins, a close drinking buddy of Yawkey's—and an avowed racist who made no bones about it. By that time, Cronin had left, replaced by former Red Sox manager Bucky Harris, another malleable front office official for Yawkey to dominate.

Yawkey blew off questions concerning bringing up a black player—when he deigned to answer such questions at all. "The Red Sox will bring up a Negro when he meets our standards," he'd declare.

The year 1955 was marred by yet another incident that fit seamlessly within the club's star-crossed history.

Aristotle George "Harry" Agganis was a hometown boy known to all as the "Golden Greek." A native of Lynn, Massachusetts, Agganis was a schoolboy baseball and football icon; even in high school Agganis had his own fan club. At Boston University, he starred as an All-American quarterback, a defensive back and punter.

Paul Brown, founder of the Cleveland Browns, offered the young New Englander $100,000, an unheard of sum in those days, to play professional football, but Agganis, who'd spent time in the Marines during his years at BU, wanted to stay close to his widowed mother.

Agganis declined Brown's offer and signed with the Red Sox. True to form, the club placed him on their major league roster, following just a single season in the minors. Although he struggled during his rookie year of 1954, hitting only .251, the lefty managed to hit eleven home runs and collected 57 RBIs.

Agganis was poised to have a breakout year in 1955. He was hitting .313 in limited service under Higgins when he came down with what was diagnosed as pleurisy on May 16.

"Agganis was with us in Kansas City, when he started spitting up blood," said Red Sox pitcher Mel Parnell. "When I got back to Boston, I talked to the team doctor, and he told me, 'Agganis will never get out of the hospital.' And he didn't." The twenty-six-year-old died on June 27, 1955 of a blood clot in his lung.

Boston finally sank under its own dead weight in 1959. The next time the Sox would finish in the top half of the AL would be 1967.

With rare exception, in spite of Red Sox claims that the media was "out to get them," the press ignored the franchise's warts and blemishes that were all too apparent to any objective observer. One journalist who did try to hold the Red Sox accountable for their refusal to field African-American ballplayers was Bud Collins, a young reporter for the *Boston Herald*, who had an infamous public confrontation with Higgins at an annual Boston Baseball Writers' Association dinner. Higgins became incensed at Collins's repeated questions about integrating the club and purposely dumped a plateful of beef stroganoff into the reporter's lap.

IIIIII

Pumpsie Green had a tremendous spring training in 1959, but ultimately was given a ticket to the Sox farm team in Minneapolis. After he was cut from the parent club at the end of spring training, all hell broke loose. Incensed, Jackie Robinson, who had already been retired for three years, finally spoke out about his abortive tryout. Asserting Yawkey was the primary problem, he told the *Chicago Defender* that if Yawkey had signed some African-American ballplayers "maybe he would have won another pennant or two."

"In one simple sentence he cut through the obfuscation and convoluted logic the Red Sox used for years to defend their actions," wrote Glenn Stout. "Robinson blamed the man at the top: Tom Yawkey. The buck stopped there; for once Robinson made the charge, scrutiny of the Red Sox's racial attitudes increased, especially of Yawkey's views."

Green's abrupt return to the minor leagues triggered more than moral outrage. It spurred an investigation on charges of racism.

The NAACP pressured the Massachusetts Commission Against Discrimination to investigate the club's practices. Incredibly, the MCAD accepted the franchise's claim that the team employed a total of eight African-Americans, but only one at Fenway Park. However, the commission did force the club to sign a written guarantee pledging that the Red Sox would henceforth make "every effort to end segregation," a tacit admission that the club hadn't done so in the past.

Record American sports columnist Larry Claflin drew Higgins's ire when he asked whether Green, who was batting over .300 and fielding superbly in the International League, would be recalled to the Sox. Higgins's response was to call Claflin a "nigger lover" and spit tobacco juice on him.

Higgins was the prototypical evil cartoon character. Asserted Stout, "You couldn't make up a character like Higgins—that a person like him was in an organization for so long and wielded so much power. He sort of represents the last nail regarding the question of racism and cronyism because he embodied both."

With the team in last place on July 3, 1959, Higgins was fired and replaced by coach Billy Jurges.

Green was recalled to the Red Sox eighteen days later. In a twisted way Higgins kept his word: "There'll be no niggers on this ballclub as long as I have anything to say about it."

Higgins, meanwhile, remained with the club as a scout, yet another drinking buddy Tom Yawkey refused to sever his connections with. Interestingly enough, the other two teams that were the last to integrate, the Detroit Tigers and the Philadelphia Phillies, had distinct ties to the Red Sox. Author Howard Bryant aptly described Boston's operational blueprints.

"Even in a whites-only environment, the Red Sox would hire some of the game's worst racists. [General manager Eddie] Collins hired Herb Pennock . . . to be his scouting director in 1935."

Years later, serving as the Phillies' general manager, Pennock would vociferously oppose Robinson's appearances in that city. Pennock convinced Collins to sign Ben Chapman, another notorious racist, and Chapman later took over as Philadelphia's field manager. Chapman was widely acknowledged as one of the worst tormentors of Robinson, and the Phillies were recognized as the most racist franchise in the National League. Then too, another player Pennock prevailed upon Collins to acquire for the Red Sox was Pinky Higgins.

As for the Tigers, Yawkey's adoptive father had owned the Tigers, which likewise dragged its feet on integrating. And starring for and later managing that team was Ty Cobb, who was prosecuted a number of times for assaults he launched upon helpless African-Americans, both men and women.

Although Ted Williams remained silent about Green, he made a point to warm up with the rookie before every game. Green never forgot Williams's kindness.

The *Boston Globe* cautioned the public not to get its hopes up too high. "Pumpsie Green can only hope he is given as much opportunity to prove himself as Don Buddin."

But Green, who had hit .325 in Minneapolis, wasn't given a real opportunity to win a starting job. The Sox previously gave Buddin, the young, incumbent shortstop, three years to prove he could play shortstop at the major league level. Green never was given a chance to play regularly, getting 260 at-bats in his most active season in Boston. By 1963 he was out of baseball and back in Oakland.

The Sox closed out the season at 75–79, in fifth place. The descent continued.

10

GENERAL
MISMANAGEMENT

The Red Sox changed strategic direction starting in the late forties, eschewing the franchise's previously failed methods of
attempting to field a championship baseball club.

Buying big-name players hadn't worked. The concept of building a farm system from the ground up was discarded before a broad
enough foundation was constructed. So Tom Yawkey proceeded to
buy young, unproven ballplayers—in droves.

"I don't think he really had any idea what he was doing," charged
baseball historian Glenn Stout. "Yawkey was in awe of baseball players, past and present. Whoever had his ear at the time, or whoever
was most important within the management scheme of things, that's
whom he listened to, or whose approach he adopted. It depended
upon whom he socialized with at the time. There was a distinct lack
of any consistent approach, and he didn't have any confidence in his
own personal knowledge of baseball operations."

Into the fifties, Yawkey shelled out big bucks for a myriad of youngsters, including Frank Baumann, Ike Delock, Jerry Casale, Wilbur
Wood, Ted Lepcio, Frank Sullivan, Don Buddin, Billy Consolo, Tom

Brewer, Jerry Stephenson, Dave Morehead, Stu McDonald, and Harry Agganis. None would become an impact player with the Red Sox.

Times were different then. The scientific aspects of the game were completely ignored. The Bill James method of statistical analysis was unheard of. Nobody looked at percentages. It was hunch baseball, pure and simple.

Field managers and coaches associated with the Red Sox simply assumed that when a player reached the major leagues, he was a finished product and was polished enough to play at that level. Plus, management never ascertained whether or not any given player was attuned to the nuances of the game, such as throwing to the correct base, or hitting the right cutoff man. Making matters worse, Boston's coaching staff never took an active role in teaching those finer points.

The franchise rushed some players up to the parent club too quickly. Others, who were ready to contribute to Boston's efforts, were left to languish in the minor leagues. It was a pattern that would persist through the mid-sixties.

Al Hirshberg cited two young prospects, Ted Lepcio and Gene Stephens, as prime examples. "Lepcio was years away from the big leagues when the Red Sox brought him up in 1952," Hirshberg wrote in the *Saturday Evening Post*. "Instead of sending him back for seasoning, they kept him around, fighting for a job he wasn't ready for. After the Sox gave up on Lepcio, he never did attain his promise.

"It was just the opposite with Stephens," continued Hirshberg. "He first came around in 1952, then went to the minors, where he belonged at the time. When he came up to stay in 1955, he was ready, but the Red Sox had no room for him."

After spending several years as Ted Williams's designated caddy, Stephens's skills had eroded so badly that he never realized his potential.

Another youngster who waited in the wings for years was future All-Star third baseman Frank Malzone. Malzone signed without a bonus in 1948. He wouldn't see appreciable time in Boston until 1957, long after he was ready for the "Bigs." Yet, even after tearing the cover off the ball and helping Triple A Louisville win the Junior World Series, Malzone was sent back to the minors after but a single spring training game in 1955.

"It was ridiculous," Malzone recalled. "I knew all along I was going back to the minor leagues. I just wasn't getting the chance."

After another abortive attempt to make the club in 1956, Malzone finally made the Red Sox in 1957. "It's funny," he said, "years later the scouts would tell me stories, about how they fought for me. Like one day, [scouts] Eddie Popowski and Charlie Wagner were sitting at a meeting with Cronin and Higgins, and everybody was talking about who was going to play third. Wagner and Popowski swore that they said, 'We don't have to find anybody. We got a kid, and right now he's at Louisville. Frank Malzone.' And they told me they didn't get too good a reaction from the rest of the people at the meeting. Wagner and Popowski thought they both were going to get fired the next day. Who knows why? Maybe politics."

Malzone theorized that the Red Sox may have simply been focused on getting a reasonable return from their bonus babies. "It's like that today in college. One kid gets a scholarship and the other one doesn't, and the coach says, 'He's got to get a chance to satisfy the athletic director.'"

However, another reason that Malzone wasted away in the minors for all those years might have been prejudice. The last minor league team on which he spent time, the Triple A San Francisco Seals, had a host of Italian-Americans on the club: Billy Consolo, Ken Aspromonte, Sal Teremino, Bob DiPietro, and several others.

Former Boston pitcher Jerry Casale voiced that conjecture. "When I went out to the San Francisco Seals in 1956, the first cuts [during spring training] were Malzone, Aspromonte, Larry DePitbo, Bob DiPietro, Sal Teremino, and Bill Renna. Seems funny, all those nice Italian boys on one team. They talk about prejudice today. There was prejudice in those days, too."

|||||

Among the prospects prematurely rushed to the major leagues before he was ready, and ultimately overwhelmed by the level of play, was a youngster named Don Buddin.

Buddin, who came from South Carolina, was heavily touted after his high school won the state championship in 1953. Scouts flocked to his hometown of Olanta, vying for his services. Each had thirty minutes to make his pitch. Boston's Mace Brown was the one who persuaded Buddin and his father to sign.

The media estimated that Tom Yawkey paid about a $50,000 bonus to acquire Buddin. Yawkey himself crowed loudly about the boy's potential. "I think the kid has a chance of being a great ballplayer," Yawkey said. "Don Buddin—if nothing ill befalls him—could become one of the top ballplayers of his time," agreed the *Boston Globe* in 1954.

Buddin, who joined the parent club in 1956, clearly wasn't ready for the pressures of Major League Baseball. Just shy of twenty-two, he failed to both hit *and* field. After spending a year in the U.S. Army, Buddin returned, holding down the starting shortstop job from 1958 through 1961.

Leading the league in both double plays and errors in 1958 and 1959, Buddin earned the moniker, "Bootin' Buddin." The Sox finally sent him to the fledgling Houston Colt .45s (now the Astros) following the 1961 season in exchange for veteran shortstop Eddie Bressoud.

Bressoud, who originally signed with the Giants, was dumb-founded at the way the Red Sox treated their youngsters. "The Giants organization, where I came from, as well as the Dodgers, were known as very good teaching organizations," Bressoud noted. "It appeared that the players in the Giants organization were more fundamentally sound when they got to the big leagues than the players with the Red Sox."

Billy Consolo was a bonus baby who reportedly received a $24,000 bonus to sign with the Sox. He vainly sat on Boston's bench for seven long, wasted seasons. Consolo never got to bat more than 190 times in a single season during the seven years he spent with the team. He hit .270 *that* season. "They didn't let Billy Consolo play," said Jerry Casale. "Higgins hated Consolo, but he had to keep him because [Consolo] signed [for] a bonus . . . It was terrible . . . One time I saw [Higgins] on the train, bombed bad. He didn't even know who I was."

As for Casale, he spent part of three fruitless seasons with the Sox (1958–60). In 1959, he started twenty-six games for Boston, ending up 13–8, with an ERA of 4.31. He was out of baseball by 1963.

Casale's plight was indicative of how the Red Sox handled their young pitchers. Either the team rushed them to the majors, where the young hurlers would be cuffed around, never to recover, or else management allowed them to molt in the minors until they were beyond their prime. Some of the young hurlers were overused until they were hurt to the extent that they never threw well again.

Don Schwall won the American League Rookie of the Year Award in 1961, posting a 15–7 record, with ten complete games and an ERA of 3.22. He was twenty-five. In 1962, after a sub-par record of 9–15, the Red Sox unceremoniously shipped him off to the Pittsburgh Pirates. He never bounced back, and was out of baseball by the age of thirty-one.

In four seasons, pitcher Wilbur Wood went 0–5 for the Sox in limited duty. After two years, he was likewise sent to the Pirates, then went to the Chicago White Sox, where he became a knuckleballer. He had a 163–148 record over twelve years, and posted a sparkling lifetime earned run average of 3.24. From 1971 through 1974, he won at least twenty games a year for the White Sox.

Both Jerry Stephenson and Dave Morehead, two of Boston's highest paid bonus babies, were among those who were ruined because they were rushed to the parent club and then misused. Although both sustained serious arm injuries, the Red Sox nevertheless persisted on sending them to the mound, and neither ever recovered.

Former *Boston Herald* beat writer George Kimball called it a sign of the times. "I think a lot of teams mishandled pitchers, young and old, back then," said Kimball. "This was an age in which 'sore arm' was a common medical diagnosis. Given today's understanding of physiology we know that every situation is different."

|||||

Former players said Billy Jurges simply wasn't cut out to be a major league manager. "Billy Jurges was basically a good coach," said Frank Malzone. "But he couldn't handle men. He got nervous. He was very high-strung . . . he was not manager material, that's all."

Any team unity that may once have existed devolved into an "every man for himself" mode. Each player was preoccupied with his own statistics. And, no matter what, everyone knew that Tom Yawkey, as star-struck of major leaguers as ever, would continue to overpay every player on the roster.

The Sox finished 1959 in fifth place with a record of 75–79, nineteen games behind the pennant-winning Chicago White Sox.

Jurges remained as field manager in 1960, with Higgins lying in wait. Indeed, Higgins soon got his chance to help throw the rudderless Jurges overboard. Frustrated by knowing he couldn't win with the roster he had been saddled with, Jurges finally popped off to the press. "I know what's wrong with this club," Jurges told writer Clif Keane, "but I can't do anything about it. My hands are tied." That proved to be Jurges's epitaph, as nobody dared talk outside of school under the benevolent dictatorship of Thomas A. Yawkey. Ten days later Jurges was gone, allegedly for "health reasons."

Pinky was back, again managing the club, this time through 1962, when he was elevated to serve as general manager. After a great deal of infighting, he prevailed over nemesis Bucky Harris, who had been instrumental in finally integrating the club (Harris had also engineered a trade for outfielder Willie Tasby, the first black position player Boston acquired via trade).

||||||

The 1960 season achieved notice for one reason, and one reason alone—it was Ted Williams's last hurrah. The Splendid Splinter retired after hitting a home run in his final at bat in late September.

He took the occasion to berate the media during the pre-game festivities. Gesturing toward the press box, he said, "Despite the fact of the disagreeable things have been said about me—and I can't help thinking about it—by the Knights of the Keyboard out there, baseball has been the most wonderful thing in my life. If I [was] starting over again and someone asked me where is the one place I would like to play, I would want it to be Boston, with the greatest owner in baseball and the greatest fans in America."

Even with that, Williams still steadfastly refused to tip his cap after hitting the ball into the right-field stands during his final at bat. It would be more than thirty years before he would tip his cap at Fenway Park.

In the wake of Williams's swan song, author Ed Linn noted, "Now Boston knows how England felt when it lost India."

Boston posted the sorry record of 65–89 in 1960, finishing in seventh place. That year was the last time Fenway Park saw more than one million fans pass through its turnstiles for seven years. Conversely, the Yankees would win five consecutive pennants, from 1960 to 1964.

Without Williams, the franchise was in shambles. Higgins would manage the club into mediocrity during the 1961 season, with record of 76–86, and through the 1962 season when the Sox wound up in eighth place. The team would trade away or lose many of its mainstays, including catcher Sammy White, outfielder Jackie Jensen, and pitchers Don Schwall, Tom Brewer, and Mike Fornieles.

Poor coaching and management would also consign the careers of many promising ballplayers to obscurity. Second baseman Chuck Schilling, and pitchers Bill Monbouquette, Ike Delock, and Dick Radatz, were among the casualties.

Yet individual players showed flashes of brilliance during the 1962 season. Veteran infielder Pete Runnels won his second batting title in three years, hitting .326. Earl Wilson, who joined the Sox in 1959 one week after Pumpsie Green, became the first African-American pitcher in American League history to throw a no-hitter when he blanked the Los Angeles Angels on June 26; Wilson even hit a home run to provide his own margin of victory. Bill Monbouquette threw a no-hitter of his own on August 1. And hulking closer Dick "The Monster" Radatz led the American League both in appearances, with sixty-two, and saves, with twenty-four.

Radatz served as a perfect example of how the Red Sox routinely burned out young players through overuse.

The club had signed the six-foot, five-inch, 240-pound right-hander as a free agent in 1959, and he spent several seasons in the minor leagues, honing his craft. After serving as a starter with the Sox farm team in Raleigh, North Carolina, Radatz joined the Triple A club in Minneapolis. He regularly threw in excess of ninety miles-per-hour and, at first, resisted the move to convert him to a relief pitcher.

During spring training in 1961, minor league manager Johnny Pesky informed Radatz that he would be going to Seattle to be trained as a relief pitcher. Radatz initially declined. "Back then, if you weren't good enough to be a starter, you were shipped to the bullpen," he said. "Relief pitchers were not nurtured or trained in the minor leagues."

Pesky assured the hurler that he would school Radatz in relief pitching. "As it turned out," Radatz said, "it was the best thing that ever happened to me." Radatz didn't have a varied repertoire of pitches, which might have doomed him as a starting pitcher anyway. The former baseball All-American at Michigan State said he discovered that he enjoyed seeing a lot of action.

Radatz made the Red Sox squad in 1962 as a non-roster spring training invitee, and debuted on April 10 at age twenty-five.

He posted a 9–6 record with twenty-four saves and an ERA of 2.24. For the next four years he was the most dominant reliever in baseball.

The 1962 season wasn't without its comic relief. At center stage was Gene Conley, a big, right-handed pitcher who simultaneously played Major League Baseball and professional basketball with the Boston Celtics. "I didn't stop," he admitted to *Boston Globe* writer Stan Grossfeld. "I had to wear a jockstrap year-round."

Conley played center and forward for three consecutive Celtics' world championship squads (1958–61), pitched for the 1957 world champion Milwaukee Braves, and was the winning pitcher in the 1955 All-Star game. He appeared in three All-Star games, and in 1959, he struck out Ted Williams on an overhand curveball.

"He missed it by this wide," Conley said in January 2008, holding his hands two feet apart. "I saw him twenty-five years later at a Jimmy Fund tournament. And I said to him, 'I'm Gene Conley.' He said, 'I know who you are, for crying out loud, Conley. And I also remember that dinky curveball you threw to strike me out with.' I said, 'Dinky curveball? You missed it by that far.'"

However Conley is best remembered for a stunt he pulled in 1962. After a tough loss he sustained in mid-July against the Yankees, the Red Sox were stuck in wall-to-wall Bronx traffic on a bus—without air conditioning. Conley suffered a meltdown.

He had been cuffed around during the game and started drinking after being knocked out of the box. "I was disgusted from the game," Conley recalled. "I was tired from sports. Because of the All-Star game, we had four, five days off. In the clubhouse, I started drinking beer. By the time the game ended, I was pretty well smashed. And I could care less."

Conley announced that he needed to use a rest room, and urged Pumpsie Green to join him in leaving the bus, which was stuck near the Lincoln Tunnel. After they got off and went into a little club off the highway, the traffic jam eased and the bus left.

"We didn't stay and have a beer or nothing," said Conley. "We just went in to go to the bathroom."

Conley and Green were stranded.

With four days off ahead, they opted to do some partying and spent the night in New York City. Following an evening at Toot Shor's celebrated bar, they got a room at the Commodore Hotel. And after some additional drinking Conley decided he would fly to Jerusalem.

Green bailed out, returning to the team, which was in Washington, D.C. by then. But Conley bought himself a plane ticket to Israel before returning to Shor's for a few more drinks. "I told everyone, 'Hey, I'm gonna go to Jerusalem. I'm going to Bethlehem. I'm going to the Promised Land. I'm gonna get everything straightened out between me and my Savior.' And they looked at me like I had three eyes." (Ironically, Conley's wife, Kathryn, and their children were at a church camp at the time he decided to make his peace with God.)

Word got out, and reporters and photographers were waiting when Conley went to LaGuardia Airport. The only hang-up was that Conley didn't have a passport. He wasn't going anywhere. But he *was* starting to sober up a bit.

He called his parents, who told him about the brouhaha he had caused. He then contacted his wife and took a train to Providence to meet her there, in order to avoid the media. But reporters staked out his suburban Boston home, so Conley tried to explain himself. Then he called Tom Yawkey, who fined him for show but returned the money at the end of the season.

Conley told the *Globe* it didn't bother him that mention of the abortive trip to Israel would probably appear in his obituary. "I don't care, because I played with some of the best ballplayers in the history of the game," he said.

The team sank once more in 1962, registering a 76–84 record. Stout and Johnson described the team as "a dull, nearly faceless, collection of players mostly on their way to oblivion."

Yawkey maintained an absentee ownership under the influence of his second wife, the former Jean Hiller. She *did* persuade him to curb his drinking, although he stuck with his old cronies to run the club, Higgins in particular.

Higgins's continued connection with the team perpetuated its racist reputation, and the players they persisted in signing were big-name high school or college stars, most of whom never made it to the majors. They also continued to sign hefty, right-handed hitters, mostly white.

"The Plantation" had become "the Country Club."

THE COUNTRY CLUB

Cronyism, poor management, racism, and downright stupidity all continued to be hallmarks of the Tom Yawkey regime. The decade of the sixties began with the Red Sox aptly earning the sobriquet, "The Country Club."

Yawkey overpaid his ballplayers no matter where the club finished, and no matter how badly a player performed. He remained enthralled by his charges, even though he'd once again distanced himself from the team.

Constantly carping about his decaying ballpark, Yawkey began lobbying for a taxpayer-underwritten stadium, like the ones that were in the works in other cities. Yawkey even implied that he might move the franchise if Massachusetts politicians didn't fund a new one. On the field, meanwhile, the Red Sox had a player who provided a glint of hope for the future of Boston baseball.

Carl Yastrzemski became one of the very few Red Sox bonus babies who actually panned out. The son of a Long Island potato farmer, Yastrzemski had his sights set on Yankee Stadium. While he was growing up, Yaz wanted to be part of the Bronx lineage that began with Babe Ruth, and continued through "Jolting" Joe DiMaggio and Mickey Mantle. But it wasn't in the cards. Yastrzemski's father, a semi-pro ballplayer of some renown, was intent upon Carl's getting a college education. Not just any college education, but one at a notable Jesuit institution. The younger Yastrzemski spent his freshman year at Notre Dame.

Although he had visited Yankee Stadium for a tryout the following summer and hit four balls out of the ballpark, young Yastrzemski was offered only a $40,000 bonus to sign. His father said, "No," over the teenager's objections. The family priest had insisted Carl was worth a six-figure bonus, which Carl's father accepted as gospel.

Yankees scout Ray Garland traveled to Long Island with a contract in his pocket to try to seal the deal. He was authorized to raise the offer to $45,000. But when the elder Yastrzemski dug in his heels and flashed a sheet of paper with "$100,000" penciled on it, Garland responded by picking up sundry items off the table, hurling them into the air. "The Yankees never offered that kind of money to anybody, and they won't give it to your boy," he thundered.

"Then they won't get him," retorted Yaz's father. And they didn't.

Instead, after the family fielded substantial offers from Los Angeles, Philadelphia, Cincinnati and Boston, Red Sox scout Bots Nekola closed the deal with the Yastrzemskis. It cost Boston $108,000, a two-year Triple A contract at $5,000 a year, and the remainder of Carl's college tuition. It was perhaps the best money Yawkey ever spent, even though Joe Cronin was unimpressed. "He doesn't seem very big," he remarked concerning Yastrzemski's slight five-foot, eleven-inch, 170-pound frame.

Yaz had huge shoes to fill—the Sox fully expected him to be Ted Williams's successor, and in 1961, Yastrzemski took Teddy Ballgame's hallowed spot in left field. He batted .266 as a rookie and was second on the team in RBIs, with eighty. Those numbers increased to .296 and ninety-four the following year. The Red Sox won seventy-six games both seasons and even lost two fewer games in '62 because of rainouts, but the club dropped two positions in the standings, finishing eighth.

Following the 1962 season, Pinky Higgins was elevated to general manager. Courtly Johnny Pesky replaced him, although, again, it was Yawkey—not Higgins—who tabbed Pesky as the new skipper. That, in itself, didn't bode well for Pesky's job security. Again, true to form, the general manager of the club would work at cross-purposes against the field manager.

The 1963 edition of the Red Sox had a great deal of potential: solid hitting, outstanding relief pitching, and a corps of starters poised to win big and establish itself as a power to be reckoned with.

In his third year in the majors, Yastrzemski posted his first signature season when he hit .321 to lead the American League in batting. Frank Malzone had the second-highest average among the starting position players at .291. Malzone was such an underrated player, the irrepressible Leo "The Lip" Durocher once cracked, "The guy's got a fault? Dandruff, maybe."

Newcomer Dick Stuart, a "good hit, no field" acquisition from Pittsburgh, led the team with forty-two home runs and 118 RBIs.

Four pitchers ended the year in double digits, including three starters—Bill Monbouquette (20–10), Earl Wilson (11–16), and Dave Morehead (10–13), while Dick Radatz picked up fifteen wins and saved twenty-five games.

Nevertheless, the team finished the season below .500, placing seventh in the recently expanded, ten-team American League. The only teams they outpaced were the hapless Washington Senators, the Kansas City Athletics, and the expansion Los Angeles Angels.

The franchise was torn by dissension, and Pesky had trouble adjusting to his new role as a major league manager. Although Pesky had earned a reputation as a teaching manager while in the minors, he had scuttled that approach in the major leagues. "When he went to Boston, he wasn't the same kind of manager," noted pitcher Dave Morehead, who played under Pesky in the minors. "He stopped teaching."

For all of his determination and enthusiasm, Pesky was fighting an uphill battle with Higgins. Without the support of the general manager he was a dead man walking. The players knew it, and many took full advantage of it.

To a large extent, Pesky lost Yastrzemski's support during spring training when he moved Yaz to center field. The experiment fizzled, and Carl was moved back to left.

The biggest problem, however, could be laid at the feet of the first baseman, Dick Stuart. Stuart flatly refused to work on his fielding, which was so atrocious he was known as "Dr. Strangleglove." He showed up to games extremely hung over and shunned training. He was interested in hitting, and hitting alone. To call Stuart "defensively challenged" is much too charitable, wrote Brendan C. Boyd and Fred C. Harris. "He charted new dimensions in defensive ineptitude. He dropped foul pop-ups, misplayed grounders, bobbled bunts. He missed pick-off throws, dropped relays, messed up force plays. He fell down while covering the bag on easy rollers, knocked his teammates down while circling under flies. Every ball hit his way was an adventure, the most routine play a fresh challenge to his artlessness. It is hard to describe this to anyone who has not seen it."

Stuart once speared a hot dog wrapper blowing across the field, prompting the Fenway crowd to give him a standing ovation.

In addition to alienating his teammates by his play, Stuart went out of his way to harass Pesky, who repeatedly made the mistake of trying to verbally spar with the quick-witted first baseman. At the beginning of the 1963 season, Pesky announced the fines for curfew violations: $500 for the first offense, $1,000 for the second, and so forth.

Stuart immediately raised his hand and asked, "Is that tax deductible?" The players collapsed, issuing gales of laughter.

Shortstop Eddie Bressoud and second baseman Chuck Schilling once converged at the first base bag chasing a pop-up because Stuart hadn't budged an inch. They collided and the ball fell in for a double, scoring two runs.

"God, did you guys look funny," crowed Stuart.

Stuart and Minnesota's Harmon Killebrew were in a neck-and-neck race for the 1963 AL home run title, with the two teams slated to face each other at the end of the season. Both had forty round-trippers going into the three-game set. Stuart hit two round-trippers; Killebrew hit five.

Complaining about losing the home run crown to Killebrew, Stuart announced to the newspapers, "Killebrew had a distinct advantage. If I could have hit against our pitching staff, I'd have hit ten."

Former *Herald* reporter George Kimball was there—as a young fan. "I remember being at Fenway the last day of the 1963 season," reminisced Kimball. "Nobody was there, so I moved down and watched almost the whole game from behind the screen. Whenever Killebrew came to bat, [pitcher Earl] Wilson served up pitches *I* could have hit out of the park. Killebrew hit three homers that day and overtook 'Strangleglove' for the home run title."

Even Yaz, who had become disenchanted with Pesky, questioned why the manager didn't crack down on the out-of-control Stuart.

"I could never understand why Pesky took it," said Yastrzemski. "I thought he could have shut Stuart up by taking away some of [Stuart's] $40,000 salary in fines."

Perhaps Pesky knew that disciplining Stuart was hopeless because Higgins wouldn't back him up. Or, perhaps Pesky was simply out of his element managing at the major league level. The Sox finished the season in seventh place with a 76–85 record, twenty-eight games behind the Yankees.

Instead of gaining ground in 1964, the Red Sox fell further back from the pack, compiling a 72–90 record for an eighth place finish.

Coming off his twenty-win season, Monbouquette posted a mediocre record of 13–14. Wilson's record was 11–12, and Morehead was 8–15. On the mound only Radatz was his usual, dependable self, racking up a 16–9 won-loss record while saving twenty-nine games, posting a sterling earned run average of 2.29.

Rookie right fielder Tony Conigliaro, just nineteen years old, hit .290 to top the team while connecting for twenty-four home runs and 52 RBIs in 111 games. Stuart again led the team with thirty-three home runs and 114 RBIs.

Conigliaro, a North Shore native, quickly became a local hero when he homered into the screen on his first pitch he saw at Fenway in 1964.[17]

Stuart committed twenty-four errors and sported a fielding percentage of .981, fielding that was so atrocious it once precipitated a fight with Earl Wilson. While on the mound, Wilson induced a batter to hit a pop fly along the first base line. Distrusting both Stuart's fielding and his resolve, Wilson ran over to the foul line near the base, lunging—and missing—the ball. Stuart spiked Wilson in the process, sending the big hurler into a rage. They fought under the stands after the game. The outcome of the fistfight was never divulged.

17 Conigliaro established six separate records in 1964 that still stand as the best ever as a teenaged major leaguer—batting average, slugging average, homeruns, runs, total bases, and bases on balls.

Pesky lost control of the team that year to the extent that the unofficial team leader, Carl Yastrzemski, became irritated at the manager after Carl's best buddy, second baseman Chuck Schilling, remained benched after recovering from a broken hand. Schilling appeared in only forty-seven games that year. Yaz stopped talking to Pesky in July.

Yastrzemski had become Yawkey's latest darling. Although never proven, he may have campaigned for Pesky's ouster. Whatever the reason, with two games left in the 1963 season, Higgins fired Pesky. Named to succeed Pesky was former National League infielder Billy Herman, who had served as a coach under both Higgins and Pesky. And he was Higgins's friend.

Lifelong Red Sox fan Dennis Burke, a Connecticut native, says playing favorites hurt the club. "The players always seemed to come and go as you pleased. Yawkey always had his favorites, who could do anything they liked. Yaz was one of his boys, [Ted] Williams was one of his boys. And Yawkey was responsible for [the decline of] Fenway Park, and ordered bad trades."

Herman immediately made it clear that he preferred veterans to youngsters; as his logic went, veteran ballplayers didn't make as many mistakes as younger ones. However, Herman was powerless when it came to benching Conigliaro and rookie shortstop Rico Petrocelli, so he treated both with the utmost contempt.

Bressoud and Malzone maintain that Conigliaro was so green that the only thing he had going for him was his innate ability to hit the ball a long, long way. However, the two veteran infielders said Conigliaro didn't know which cutoff man to throw to on hits to the outfield.

Herman couldn't comprehend where Conigliaro was coming from—the generation gap was simply too great. But truthfully, Herman never really tried to bridge the gap between himself and his young ballplayers.

Conigliaro traveled with a portable record player on the team's road trips. The first-year Sox manager took umbrage with the music while on one trip, grousing, "I wonder how that thing would sound on a bus between Toronto and Toledo." He then benched the young slugger.

"It looks like somebody's trying to get rid of me," Conigliaro told a reporter.

When Conigliaro reported for a six-month stint in the Army Reserve, Herman snidely declared, "If any of you writers have any pull with the army, see if you can get them to take Tony for two years instead of six months."

Rico Petrocelli was poised to have a breakout year in 1965, but instead of nurturing the twenty-year-old, Herman delighted in hassling the youngster. The only time Herman spoke to the shortstop was to criticize him. All season Petrocelli was in and out of the lineup and his confidence was badly shaken.

"I can't make it," a supremely discouraged Petrocelli told Yastrzemski. "I'm going to quit."

Yaz tried to buck up the crestfallen shortstop, and resented the way Herman treated him. "Of all the Red Sox ballplayers," Yaz noted, "the one Herman disliked the most was Rico Petrocelli."

The manager fined the rookie $1,000 because Petrocelli left the ballpark without permission during a game after Rico had a premonition that something was wrong at home. Petrocelli's wife had been ill and, sure enough, he had to rush her to a hospital. The fine was roughly one-ninth of Petrocelli's salary.

The one supremely positive step general manager Higgins took in the wake of the 1964 season was to get rid of Dick Stuart. The Sox

October 3, 1903. Fans scale the wall at the Huntington Avenue Grounds prior to Game Three of the 1903 World Series between the (then) Boston Americans and the Pittsburgh Pirates. *Courtesy of the Boston Public Library/McGreevey Collection*

Harry Frazee (left) confers with Boston's field manager Jack Barry prior to a game in 1917. Barry would enter the U.S. Navy a year later. *Courtesy of the Boston Public Library*

Ed Barrow, who managed the Boston Red Sox from 1918–1920. Like Babe Ruth and numerous other budding stars, Barrow would travel south to New York City, where he made his name as general manager of the Yankees.
Courtesy of the Boston Public Library

Red Sox pitchers Babe Ruth (left) and Ernie Shore perch in front of the dugout during their 1915 rookie season. Ruth would spend most of the season in the minors. *Courtesy of the Boston Public Library*

Baseball's Highest Price for Babe Ruth, King of Home Run

THINK OF THE BASEBALLS FRAZEE WILL SAVE :: :: :: By Collier

Cartoon in the *Boston Herald* in the wake of Babe Ruth's sale to the New York Yankees, depicting other Boston landmarks for sale—including the Boston Public Library.
Courtesy of the Boston Public Library

American League President Ban Johnson (fourth from right, front row) watches a Red Sox game with *Boston Globe* owner General Charles Taylor (second from right, with moustache). Taylor purchased the club for his playboy son, John.
Courtesy of the Boston Public Library/McGreevey Collection

Mounted Boston Police battle Royal Rooters during the 1912 World Series. Police and patrons failed to clear the field, and any balls hit into the crowd were automatic ground-rule doubles. *Courtesy of the Boston Public Library/McGreevey Collection*

July 30, 1937. Red Sox third baseman "Pinky" Higgins takes a late throw from catcher Gene Desautels as Detroit's Charlie Gehringer successfully steals third. Higgins would also serve as a scout, field manager, and general manager of the club. *Courtesy of the Boston Public Library*

Newspaper reporters interview Ted Williams in the Red Sox locker room following a game, circa 1940. Williams' relationship with the press always proved problematic. *Courtesy of the Boston Public Library/Leslie Jones Collection*

Jackie Robinson of the Brooklyn Dodgers reads the *Boston Traveler* while in Boston to face the Braves in 1949. Robinson was one of three Negro League players who received a sham tryout from the Red Sox in 1945. *Courtesy of the Boston Public Library/Leslie Jones Collection*

Pitcher Earl Wilson (left) and infielder "Pumpsie" Green talk before the August 30, 1959 game at Fenway Park. Wilson and Green were the first two African-American players on the Red Sox. *Courtesy of the Boston Public Library/Leslie Jones Collection*

Red Sox owner Tom Yawkey during a meeting in September 1971. The years of chain smoking and heavy drinking are clearly etched on his face. His failure to stick to a comprehensive plan to build a good club would doom Boston's championship hopes for decades. *Courtesy of the Boston Public Library Sports Collection*

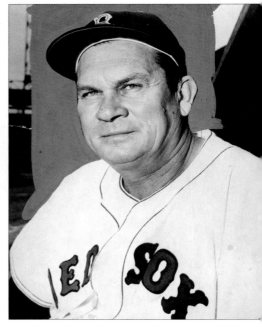

Red Sox manager Mike "Pinky" Higgins in 1959. Higgins swore that no African-American would play for the club while he was managing. Green and Wilson joined the team after Higgins was fired mid-season. *Courtesy of the Boston Public Library*

Carl Yastrzemski is congratulated by third base coach Eddie Popowski after hitting a home run during Boston's "Impossible Dream" pennant-winning year of 1967. Yaz would win the Triple Crown that golden season. *Courtesy of the Boston Red Sox*

Yastrzemski hits against the Kansas City Athletics at Fenway Park in 1967. The Sox would battle to the wire with the Tigers, Twins, and White Sox in their quest for the pennant. *Courtesy of the Boston Red Sox*

Boston outfielder Tommy Harper at the plate in 1972. Harper would set an all-time record for base stealing while with the Sox. He also blew the whistle on the club's tacit approval of a segregated club in Florida. *Courtesy of the Boston Red Sox*

July 26, 1965. Ted Williams gives Tony Conigliaro some pointers. Tony C.—one of Boston's most promising young hitters—had his career tragically cut short after he was severely beaned in August 1967. He would be dead at age 45. *Courtesy of the Boston Public Library/Boston Globe*

Tommy Harper is congratulated while crossing home plate after hitting a home run during the 1972 season. *Courtesy of the Boston Red Sox*

Luis Tiant, along with Curt Schilling and Josh Beckett, must be considered one of the greatest "money pitchers" in Red Sox history. He pitched a 163-pitch complete game in the 1975 World Series. *Courtesy of the Boston Red Sox*

The incomparable Luis Tiant pitching for the BoSox in 1974. Tiant was signed for a song while he was reinventing himself as a finesse pitcher after throwing his arm out. El Tiante would win 134 games for the Sox. *Courtesy of the Boston Red Sox*

Hall of Fame catcher Carlton Fisk anchored the Red Sox defense behind the plate through the 1970s. Failure to mail him a new contract in a timely manner in December 1980 allowed Fisk to become a free agent. *Courtesy of the Boston Red Sox*

Carlton Fisk slams his game-winning, twelfth-inning home run against the Cincinnati Reds in Game Six of the 1975 World Series. *TV Guide* termed it the single greatest televised sports highlight in history. *Courtesy of the Boston Red Sox*

Sox slugger David Ortiz bats against the Detroit Tigers in April 2008. "Big Papi" has been one of general manager Theo Epstein's prized acquisitions, anchoring the Red Sox offense. *Steve Babineau/Boston Red Sox*

Manny Ramirez, a bulwark of Boston's offense for six years, hits against Tampa Bay in June 2008. Over the next two months Ramirez would become anathema to the club, prompting the Red Sox to dump him at the trading deadline. *Megan LaBella/Boston Red Sox*

Originally Red Sox property, pitcher Curt Schilling played for Baltimore, Philadelphia, and Arizona before returning to Boston and playing a key role in the team's two most recent world championships. *Brita Meng Outzen/Boston Red Sox*

Boston first baseman Kevin Youkilis tees off on a pitch from a Tigers' hurler early in the 2008 season. Youkilis' solid defense and stellar hitting made him a legitimate candidate for the 2008 American League MVP Award. *Brian Babineau/Boston Red Sox*

Red Sox second baseman Dustin Pedroia turns a double play against Detroit in April 2008. In addition to his tremendous fielding, Pedroia's uncanny and timely hitting would win him the 2008 American League Most Valuable Player Award. *Michael Ivins/Boston Red Sox*

Right-handed starter Josh Beckett delivers a pitch in a game against Milwaukee on May 18, 2008. Beckett was a shell of his former self throughout the 2008 season primarily due to a string of injuries that hampered his performance. *Michael Ivins/Boston Red Sox*

packed the malcontent off to Philadelphia for pitcher Dennis Bennett. But even that backfired on the Sox.

The high point of 1965 was a no-hitter thrown by twenty-two-year-old Dave Morehead on September 16 at Fenway Park. The public had become so sickened with the ongoing soap opera that only 1,247 fans were in attendance that Thursday afternoon to see him make history.

Boston's management actually upstaged the no-hitter, summoning the press following the game. The news was that Pinky Higgins was out as general manager, fired because his drinking had gotten out of control.[18] Taking Higgins's place was Dick O'Connell, a college-educated World War II veteran who had worked for the organization for nearly twenty years. He would be the first—and last—of Tom Yawkey's general managers who wasn't a toady to the Sox owner.

Red Sox vice president Dick Bresciani said O'Connell knew how to use the knowledge of those who worked with him. "Dick O'Connell was a sharp, all-round intelligent person. He paid his dues in the Red Sox system beginning in the minor league system in 1947 [and] worked his way up in a variety of management positions, so he was around for a number of years before he was named general manager. Dick never believed he had all the answers. He utilized a lot of people. He utilized the scouts. He utilized his farm director. He utilized his scouting director. He gathered information from a lot of people to make his decisions."

Broadcaster Clark Booth agreed. "When O'Connell took over everything changed. He was probably the most important [front office] person in Red Sox history [up until the John Henry era]. In two years he turned that racial record around and . . . won a pennant. It

---

18 In another twist of fate, Higgins, while driving drunk, killed a black highway worker and was sentenced to prison. Two days after his release, Higgins dropped dead of a heart attack in Dallas.

was Dick O'Connell and [farm system director] Neil Mahoney who changed the history and fortunes of the team."

In 1965 the team's fortunes sank to new lows. For the first time since 1932 the Red Sox lost 100 games, mired in ninth place. There were a few bright spots. Yastrzemski hit .312 with twenty home runs and 72 RBIs, and Conigliaro led the American League with thirty-two home runs.

Unfortunately, the pitching continued to decline. Wilson was the staff ace, if you could call 13–14 the mark of an ace, while Radatz struggled at 9–11 with twenty-two saves. His ERA ballooned to 3.91 at a time when the AL average was 3.46. The '65 Red Sox led the league in numerous offensive categories, including home runs and walks, but it was offset by a pitching staff that tied with the lowly A's for worst in baseball at 4.24. Even the National League's hideous 112-loss Mets had a better mark.

O'Connell then put his imprimatur on the club.

"He was very shrewd in how he did it," Bresciani said. "The other thing was he had Mr. Yawkey's money and complete loyalty. That helps, when you have ownership willing to give you the resources to make things happen . . . and you don't have divisive situations."

Hopes were therefore high when the Red Sox assembled in Winter Haven, Florida, to open the 1966 spring training

The pitching staff looked more solid than it had in years. In addition to starters Earl Wilson, Jim Lonborg, Dave Morehead, and Dennis Bennett, the Sox had acquired Jose Santiago and Bucky Brandon, and everyone hoped that bonus baby Jerry Stephenson would be ready to step into the rotation and shine. The club had also shored up its relief pitching. Dick Radatz's production had drastically worsened, and he was traded to Cleveland for pitchers Lee Stange and Don McMahon.

Offensively, the two most promising additions were minor leaguers George Scott and Joe Foy. Scott was a gifted fielder, equally adept at third base and first, while Foy played third.

Spring training was predictably uneventful until racism again raised its ugly head. The victim was Earl Wilson. After a long day of training, Wilson and fellow pitchers Morehead and Bennett left the complex for a beer at a watering hole in Lakeland called the Cloud Nine. "The bartender asked Dave what he wanted and asked me what I wanted," Bennett said, "and looked at Earl and said, 'We ain't serving you. We don't serve niggers in here.'"

Stunned, the three men left. At first Wilson never publicly spoke about the incident, but Bennett was profoundly affected.

"Earl was upset, because he had never been refused service before," remarked Bennett.

Wilson then went to club officials, who downplayed the affair. Wrote Howard Bryant in *Shut Out*, "The Red Sox, as a valuable spring training tenant, held significant economic clout in the region. With the weight of a powerful baseball franchise behind him, perhaps the rigid customs of the region would begin to change. All he knew is that he didn't expect to hear what he was told."

Billy Herman told Wilson to forget the matter. Other team officials also instructed Wilson not to breathe a word to the media. Long-time Boston reporter Clark Booth maintained that the three pitchers were in the wrong simply for going to the Cloud Nine. "The Cloud Nine was supposed to be off-limits," Booth said. "They weren't supposed to be there. It was a little tricky. I don't see it as one of the most egregious racial incidents in the sorry history of the team. I would portray it as being a complex issue."

Knowing that bad publicity would hurt his standing with the team, Wilson tried to keep quiet about the incident. but the matter grated on him and he ended up sharing the story with the press.

Before Wilson's untimely death in 2005, he told Bryant, "Having that happen and then being told not to say anything about it was the most humiliating experience of my life."

Wilson was a marked man, and he knew it. It was just a matter of time.

When Boston acquired two black players from Kansas City, reliever John Wyatt, and speedy outfielder Jose Tartabull in June, Wilson and his roommate, outfielder Lenny Green, another African-American, joked that there were too many African-Americans on the team. Somebody had to go. "There was no doubt in my mind about that," Wilson once said.

The next morning when the telephone rang, Green refused to answer. Wilson picked it up to find Billy Herman on the other end. Wilson had been traded to Detroit for an aging outfielder, Don Demeter.

It's deliciously ironic that Wilson would hit more home runs than Demeter during the remaining time in their respective careers. Wilson, whose pitching record was 5–5 at the time of the deal, went on to win thirteen games for the Tigers in 1966, outpacing the best any of his former teammates would do (Jose Santiago won the most games for the Sox, with twelve).

During Boston's miraculous pennant run in 1967, Wilson won twenty-two games for Detroit, matching former teammate Jim Lonborg. There's little question that if the Sox had kept Wilson, they might have had enough pitching firepower to prevail over the St. Louis Cardinals in the 1967 World Series.

None of the newspapers that reported on the Wilson trade mentioned the Cloud Nine incident, and Wilson, himself declared, "I was completely surprised by the trade. I didn't have any idea they'd trade me."

Dick Johnson, Sports Museum curator, said he believed O'Connell was forced to dump the disillusioned hurler. "You've got to look at the circumstances. The club failed to mollify Wilson in the wake of his ejection from the Cloud Nine. Management's insistence that he simply disregard the injustice of the situation and go on with his life bothered him so much that ultimately he went to the media. He embarrassed the club. Read between the lines."

Meanwhile, Morehead, who was poised to bloom into a star, hurt his arm and never was the same again. The Sox insisted upon continuing to send him to the mound, until he literally couldn't lift his arm.

Adding to their woes, the Red Sox had learned that Dennis Bennett, the lefty they'd received from the Phillies in return for Dick Stuart, also had a bad arm. Once a pure power pitcher, Bennett had injured his arm before the Stuart trade, and was never effective again.

To its credit, Philadelphia offered to nullify the deal, but Higgins had inexplicably declined, instead letting the trade stand.

"The only reason they kept me was to save face over the trade," Bennett said. He underwent shoulder surgery during the 1966 season, but he never regained his effectiveness. (Bennett was also known for the arsenal he carried in his briefcase. The hard-drinking hurler once shot out the light in a hotel room after a dispute with roommate Lee Thomas.)

True to form, the 1966 season proved to be another washout.

Santiago led the club by posting a 12–13 record, and Lonborg broke even with a 10–10 mark. Veteran right-hander Don McMahon led the team in saves with nine. In the batting department, Boston again proved it had a lot of pop in its bats. Tony Conigliaro slammed twenty-eight home runs, followed by rookie George Scott with twenty-seven. Petrocelli hit eighteen, Yaz sixteen, and Foy hit fifteen.

O'Connell fired manager Billy Herman with sixteen games remaining. Interim manager Pete Runnels guided the club to eight wins, ensuring that—finally!—the Sox outpaced the crumbling Yankees in the standings for the first time since 1946.

But Boston finished the season in ninth place, with a record of 72–90, twenty-six games behind pennant-winning Baltimore. Only New York trailed them, and only by a half-game in the standings.

THE IMPOSSIBLE DREAM

A predominantly youthful Red Sox squad may very well have saved Major League Baseball in New England with its miraculous 1967 season.

Mired in ninth place in 1966, the Sox roared out of their doldrums in 1967, not only to contend for the American League title, but to win it, and win it on the last day of the season in one of the tightest pennant races in history.

Sox owner Tom Yawkey, who for years had groused, bullied and lobbied local politicians for a new ballpark, once again raised the issue before the season. Like his fellow owners he wanted the taxpayers to underwrite it. Yet Boston remained mired in the standings, and Fenway Park hadn't seen more than a million fans during a single season since 1960, Ted Williams's last year with the club.

Yawkey stated his case in *The Sporting News*. "You ask me how I feel about [Fenway Park] and I ask you what has changed about the stadium since I left here last fall? As far as I can see, nothing has happened. My position is the same as it was six months ago. I feel [a new] stadium is necessary for Boston, this state, and all of New England."

One key element *had* changed during the off-season, however. General manager O'Connell had selected Triple A manager Dick Williams as the team's field manager.

Rookie outfielder Reggie Smith, who previously had played for Dick Williams at Toronto, credited O'Connell with redirecting the club's stance on minority players. In fact, both O'Connell and Williams were colorblind. They didn't care about the color of a man's skin, nor about his ethnicity or background. All they cared about was winning ball games. And it paid off.

"Obviously, Dick O'Connell was there when the number of African-American players that came into the Boston organization [increased]," Smith said. "Him being the general manager, you would have to give him credit."

Sox vice president Dick Bresciani insisted that O'Connell had his finger firmly on the pulse of the ballclub. "The good thing was [our] minor league system was just starting to flourish," Bresciani said. "So Dick came in at the right time. He caught a wave of good, young players who had come up to the team . . . [and] I know how fully he utilized his scouts. . . . They had said, 'Jerry Adair would be a good pick up.' 'John Wyatt would be a great bullpen guy for you.' 'Jose Tartabull can be a good outfielder, pinch runner.' He did all those kind of things and they paid off. And he really got the farm system going."

Williams, an alumnus of the Brooklyn Dodgers, was a taskmaster. Former players called him a drill sergeant, and he was.

Wrote Bill Reynolds of the *Providence Journal*, "In retrospect, it was a baseball version of the perfect storm, a young team coming into its own, superstar seasons from Jim Lonborg and Carl Yastrzemski, and a young manager in his first job who seemed to have stepped out of the pages of adolescent fiction."

Two of the first steps the new manager took during spring training were to curtail the kibitzing between his players and former stars, most notably Ted Williams, and to strip Carl Yastrzemski of his team captaincy because Dick Williams "wanted everybody to play as an equal."

Although Ted Williams stomped off, Yaz quietly acquiesced to the rookie manager's wishes.

Another change Dick Williams made that sent Ted Williams "over the edge" was employing volleyball to augment baseball practice. "It kept us from standing around," said rookie pitcher Gary Waslewski. "Too often in spring training you're standing around doing nothing, shagging fly balls. That's a complete waste of time. To be moving and doing things was different."

The manager was creating a new culture. According to Rico Petrocelli, "[Williams] didn't say we would win a pennant, but he did say we would win. He said if we did things the right way, which was his way, we would be a better team. If you missed a cutoff, you heard about it. If you didn't move a guy over with a sacrifice [fly or bunt], you heard about it . . . Dick made us accountable. I really believe the fans fell in love with our style of play . . . and the winning. That was all Dick."

The Sox featured a core of young position players to build around Yastrzemski, Conigliaro, Scott, Foy, and Petrocelli. Williams brought second baseman Mike Andrews and center fielder Smith from Triple A.

Andrews previously had spent time with the parent club, and contrasted the changed attitude. "I remember Billy Herman coming into the clubhouse one day and saying, 'I'm sick and tired of all this [non-baseball] stuff. There's going to be no more golf talk' because we had a lot of golfers at that time. The next day I saw him in the clubhouse showing his new putter to Dave Morehead. I'm thinking, 'Oh, that [policy] went over big.'"

Under Dick Williams the golf clubs were kept under wraps.

Reflecting back, Williams made no apologies for his "take no prisoners" approach. "My style of managing goes back to Branch Rickey baseball with the Brooklyn Dodgers," he said. "You execute, you move runners along, you hit the cutoff man, you throw to the right base, you don't make mental mistakes."

Las Vegas oddsmaker Jimmy "the Greek" Snyder made the perennial cellar-dwelling Sox hundred-to-one underdogs, and most preseason publications discounted the Red Sox chances, picking them to finish either ninth or tenth in a ten-team league. *Sports Illustrated* was the lone exception: "If [manager Dick Williams] can find some pitching, too, the 1967 Sox may revive baseball in Boston."

Williams simply asserted, "We'll win more than we lose."

Williams promoted Billy Rohr, a young left-handed pitcher from the Toronto Maple Leafs when he took his new post. Rohr, who had won fourteen games for the Leafs in 1966, made his Red Sox debut at Yankee Stadium on April 14, 1967.

Although New York was no longer the fearsome Bronx Bombers of previous decades, they still fielded a potent team with the likes of Mickey Mantle, Tom Tresh, Joe Pepitone, and Elston Howard.

"Jim Lonborg was my roommate," Rohr recalled. "We went out to dinner the night before, and he spent a good part of the night going over the Yankees hitters with me—probably above and beyond any call of duty that he signed up for. Frankly, I don't have a recollection of ever feeling terribly comfortable. We scored a run in the first inning and it was 1–0 until the eighth. So there wasn't a lot of comfort there."

Yankee Bill Robinson lined a shot off Rohr's shin in the sixth inning and the ball deflected to third baseman Joe Foy, who threw out Robinson. The pitcher remained on the mound despite the pain. "As long as the bone stayed in place, I was going to stay out there," Rohr cracked later. He had a no-hitter going for him.

The formidable Mickey Mantle prepared to pinch-hit against him in the eighth inning. "What happened was the preceding hitter hit a pop-up, a fly ball to somebody, I think left field," Rohr said. "I turned around to watch it, and then I began to hear this ovation. So I turn around and there's Number Seven swinging about fifteen bats on deck. I thought, 'Okay, kid, this is it. Here he comes.'"

Rohr retired Mantle on a fly ball to right field.

Opening the bottom of the ninth, Tresh sent a hard liner to left field. Carl Yastrzemski snagged the line drive at his feet, fully extending his body before somersaulting head-over-heels. "It was the greatest catch I ever saw in my life," Rohr declared.

Joe Pepitone followed with a fly ball out to right. That's when Howard hit a hanging curveball down the right field line to break up the no-hitter. Rohr described the pitch as a "tennis serve." Ironically, Howard would join Boston late in the year, and appear in his final World Series as a member of the Red Sox.

"[Rohr's] curveball was really good that day," Petrocelli said. "You really didn't see that same curveball in later starts. It would be more of a lazy curveball, and he got hit hard."

The 3–0 win at Yankee Stadium was the young pitcher's moment in the sun. He had but two more major league victories, his curveball lost its bite, and he was out of organized baseball by the close of 1972.

To diehard Red Sox fans the victory provided the first inkling that something special was afoot.

In May, first base coach Bobby Doerr, a mainstay of the powerhouse 1940 Red Sox squads, helped reinvigorate a slumping Yastrzemski by suggesting that the slugger lift his hands and adjust his batting stance. Yaz, who had undergone a strenuous off-season workout regimen, came alive.

The day that Doerr gave Yastrzemski the advice, the club swept a doubleheader from Detroit, with Yaz turning in a three-for-eight performance that included two home runs. At the end of May the Sox sported a 22–20 record, but Williams had higher hopes.

And they were realized. Jim Lonborg was settling in, proving nearly unhittable, and Jose Santiago established himself as the solid second starter in the rotation.

General manager O'Connell made a trade for infielder Jerry Adair on June 3. A day later, he sent aged outfielder Don Demeter and expendable first baseman Tony Horton to the Indians for right-handed starter Gary Bell, an All-Star in 1966.

The move left an unhappy Rohr as the odd man out. "I was trying to steer the ball, which you can't do," he explained. "You have to just throw it. Then I went in the Army [Reserve] for two weeks for summer camp and I think the day I went in, they traded for Gary Bell. When I got out, there wasn't any room in the rotation."

Bell joined Lonborg, Santiago and right-hander Lee Stange in the rotation for the duration of the season.

"This is one of those years when it looks like the pennant is up for grabs," O'Connell told the press. "We've bolstered our starting pitching with experience and ability."

Adair and Bell both shone in their debut on June 8 against the White Sox, with the resilient infielder collecting three hits, and Bell beating Chicago, 7–3. Williams declared that Adair was "the Red Sox secret weapon."

Chicago manager Eddie Stanky then opened his mouth by slamming the surging Yastrzemski, calling him, "an All-Star from the neck down."

Stanky lived to regret his words, because Yaz and his teammates promptly unleashed a veritable reign of terror against Chicago.

He bombarded the White Sox with a six-for-nine showing in a Fenway doubleheader split with first-place Chicago. After hammering a home run, Yaz tipped his cap toward the White Sox manager while rounding third base. A night later, the Red Sox pulled a gutsy tenth inning comeback against Chicago on a two-run Conigliaro home run to defeat them, 2–1.

The victory prompted the *Boston Globe* to appropriate the song title "The Impossible Dream" from the musical *Man of La Mancha*, a catch phrase that caught on.

The Sox were two games over .500 and in fifth place by the All-Star break, but the entire league was bunched up, with no clear favorite for the pennant.

Then Boston reeled off a ten-game winning streak following the All-Star game. More than 10,000 screaming fans greeted the team at Logan International Airport on July 23. Many trace the roots of the Red Sox Nation to that steamy Sunday evening. The scene at the airport was simply mayhem. "I'll never forget the young kids on the shoulders of their fathers, waving," recalled Rico Petrocelli. "'Here comes Yaz! Yeah!' The place went nuts. 'Here comes Joe Foy!' We just couldn't believe it. I'd never seen anything like that. That really inspired us."

The Red Sox were stunned. Lee Stange later said he feared the fans would become so rowdy they'd tip over the team bus. "I felt the franchise was practically reborn that night we arrived at Logan," Dick Williams declared.

"Before '67 there wasn't a Red Sox Nation, I'll tell you that," Yastrzemski reflected years later. "The Red Sox became winners in '67. We brought back baseball [to Boston]. I know."

Don Chase echoed Yastrzemski's thoughts. "The 1967 season revitalized the Sox," said Chase. "The fans had become apathetic until then."

Fenway attendance, which had been just 8,324 on opening day, would go on to exceed the previous year by almost one million fans.

After a successful home stand during which Boston engineered several dramatic comeback victories, the team began a nine-game road trip that got off to a horrendous start. The club lost three straight contests to the Twins, 3–0, 2–1, and 2–0. They then took two-out-of-three from the A's in Kansas City, but again faltered on the West Coast, dropping three games to the California Angels, 1–0, 2–1, and 3–2. The reliable Red Sox bats suddenly were silent.

Returning to Fenway after the 2–7 trip, the team took two of three from the Tigers, but on August 18 the focus changed. Angels hurler Jack Hamilton threw a pitch that hit twenty-two-year-old Tony Conigliaro on his left cheekbone. California left fielder Rick Reichardt said he could hear the crack from 100 yards away.

"The pitch sailed toward Tony's head," remembered Yaz. "He threw his hands up, but that didn't help. The whole park must've heard the crack the ball made as it hit Tony under the left eye. We all ran out as he collapsed in a heap at the plate."

Conigliaro lay still; the ballpark fell hushed. Conigliaro then began thrashing his legs.

Petrocelli, the on-deck batter, rushed to Conigliaro's side, followed by Dick Williams. Petrocelli murmured, "Everything's going to be okay."

If only there had been a shard of truth in those words of comfort. The youngest player in the majors (at the time) to hit 100 home runs was seriously hurt, never to be the same. Though he would be

Comeback Player of the Year in 1969 and hit thirty-six home runs a year later, Tony C.'s vision problems eventually returned and his career was ruined. He suffered a heart attack and stroke before dying at the age of forty-five.

For his part, Hamilton was fortunate to escape with his life, as the angry and stunned crowd turned on him with a vengeance. He disavowed any notion that he was deliberately throwing at the young star. "I was just trying to get the ball over," Hamilton insisted. "Tony stands right on top of the plate."

The following day the Sox defeated California, 12–11. They then swept the Angels in a doubleheader, 12–2, and 9–8. In the first game, the switch-hitting Reggie Smith became the first Red Sox player in history to homer from both sides of the plate in a single game. In the nightcap, Boston fell behind 8–1 before rallying to edge California when Jerry Adair sent a ball into the net above the Green Monster, Fenway Park's thirty-seven-foot-high left field wall. Adair went five-for-seven on the day.

The Sox were one and a half games behind the league-leading Twins, and a single game behind the second-place White Sox.

Finally, Tom Yawkey reopened his billfold, paying $150,000 for Kansas City A's first baseman Ken "Hawk" Harrelson. Harrelson was engaged in a spat with A's owner Charles O. Finley, publicly terming the cantankerous owner "a menace to baseball," whereupon the cantankerous Finley promptly released him. The Sox immediately tabbed Harrelson, a legitimate power hitter, as their new right fielder. He arrived in the city on August 24, the day Conigliaro was released from the hospital.

Several days later, the Red Sox occupied first place in the American League, the first time in nearly twenty years that Boston found itself in such a position in late August.

With the exception of Conigliaro's beaning, it was a glorious summer for Boston's long-suffering fans.

Traveling to Chicago, the Red Sox managed a miraculous victory over the stubborn White Sox in the first game of a Sunday doubleheader. After taking a 4–1 lead, Boston faltered, and the White Sox pushed across two runs, making the score 4–3. In the bottom of the ninth, Red Sox starter Gary Bell gave up a leadoff double to the speedy Ken Berry. Against closer John Wyatt with one out, catcher Duane Josephson lifted a soft line drive to weak-armed Jose Tartabull in right field. Tartabull came up throwing, pegging the ball to catcher Elston Howard. Although the ball was off to the side, Howard expertly blocked home plate with his foot, placing a sweeping tag on Berry to end the game with a smart double play.

A thirteen-year major league veteran—and former American League MVP—Howard broke the color barrier with the Yankees in 1955. "There was a powerful symbolism in Elston Howard coming to Boston," Yastrzemski later remarked. "Maybe it would help reverse all those down years."

The pennant race remained in a state of flux throughout September, with the Red Sox sparring with Chicago, Detroit, and Minnesota. Uncharacteristically Yastrzemski then plunged into a slump. Williams benched him, the only game Yaz would miss during the entire campaign and, as the team left on a road trip, Yastrzemski remained at Fenway Park to take extra batting practice, with owner Yawkey in attendance.

Yawkey's increased presence irked manager Williams. After a decade or more of benign neglect on the part of the millionaire owner, his constant appearances in the Red Sox clubhouse smacked of front running.

"You'd have thought he was one of the . . . players," groused

Williams in his autobiography, *No More Mr. Nice Guy.* "He was in the clubhouse, around the batting cage, on the field until the last possible moment . . . Where had he been when we got our [butts] kicked earlier in the season?"

The tantrum Yawkey threw early in the 1967 season concerning his inability to secure a new stadium at the cost of Massachusetts taxpayers made matters even worse. His venom alienated many officials and fans and the relationship between Williams and Yawkey became more strained.

Yaz finally broke out of his slump in Washington on September 5, slamming two home runs and propelling the Sox into a virtual four-way tie with Detroit, Chicago, and Minnesota. With the Red Sox having the next day off and the White Sox winning, the Tigers sweeping a doubleheader, and the Twins losing, the four contenders were separated by a miniscule .001 of a percentage point.

On September 10 the Red Sox won their eighty-second game of the year, ensuring at the minimum, a break-even season—their first winning season since 1958. And Lonborg secured his twentieth win two days later, becoming Boston's first twenty-game winner since Bill Monbouquette in 1963.

The Sox then hit a serious speed bump, dropping a three-game set to the defending world champion Baltimore Orioles. Boston departed for an eight-game road trip, and the amazing Yastrzemski again became a hitting machine, dominating the squad's remaining twelve games as no one ever had.

Boston went on a roll starting with a series against Detroit. In the initial game, Yaz tied the score in the top of the ninth with a moonshot homer. Utility infielder Dalton Jones won the game with another home run in the top of the tenth. A night later, the Sox rallied late to eke out a 3–2 victory.

The Red Sox went on to take two from Cleveland, and split a four-game set against Baltimore. Then it was back to Boston for the final four games of the season, the first two against the Indians followed by a two-game series against the contending Minnesota Twins.

The two games against Cleveland proved to be a disaster. The Sox dropped the first by a 6–3 score against pitcher Luis Tiant. The next afternoon Lonborg and the Sox were shut out 6–0 by Sonny Siebert and two Tribe relievers.

So the season came down to the two games against the powerful Twins. With top hurlers Jim Kaat (16–13) and Dean Chance (20–14), and heavy hitters Harmon Killebrew, Tony Oliva, Rod Carew, Cesar Tovar, and Bob Allison, Minnesota presented a formidable lineup. All the Twins needed was to split the series to win their second pennant in three years.

The tension throughout New England was palpable. Fenway was jammed on the sun-splashed afternoon of Saturday, September 30. Right-hander Jose Santiago, sporting an 11–4 record, took the mound for Boston, facing the veteran Kaat, who was en route to 283 career victories.

Both teams came out of the box with the jitters. Santiago surrendered one run in the top of the first inning. The Sox however, got a huge break in the bottom of the third when Kaat left the game after straining his left elbow. In came Twins starter Jim Perry, sporting a 2.95 ERA.

With two men aboard, Jerry Adair singled to right to tie the game. Yaz then hit a grounder toward Ron Carew at second base as first baseman Killebrew lunged in vain for the ball. Inexplicably, Perry failed to cover first and the other runner scored, putting the Sox ahead, 2–1. Minnesota evened the score the next inning, but Yastrzemski snapped the tie with a three-run dinger in the bottom of the seventh. On in relief, Bell allowed a two-run home run to Kille-brew with two outs in the ninth before getting Oliva to line out. Final score: Red Sox 5, Twins 4.

After 161 grueling games, the season came down to one last contest pitting Boston ace Jim Lonborg against Minnesota's Dean Chance. The prospects proved so alluring that NBC bumped its American Football League TV coverage in favor of broadcasting the game coast-to-coast.

Lonborg had been ineffective against the Twins all year; in fact, he had never beaten Minnesota in his entire career and had lost to the Twins three times that year.

The Twins drew first blood, scoring two runs through poor field-ing on the part of Gold Glovers Yastrzemski and first baseman Scott. Still down 2–0 leading off the bottom of the sixth inning, Lonborg dropped a surprise bunt and beat it out. Adair and Jones followed with solid singles to load the bases, bringing Yaz to the plate. The left fielder smacked Chance's second pitch into center, to tie the score. That brought Harrelson to bat, and he hit the ball to shortstop Zoilo Versalles, who threw home too late to catch Jones.

Minnesota manager Cal Ermer pulled Chance, bringing in re-lief specialist Al Worthington, who promptly threw two consecutive wild pitches, allowing Yastrzemski to score. Smith, followed with a chopper to first that Killebrew failed to field. Boston now led, 5–2.

The Twins were determined not to go quietly into the night. Killebrew and Oliva hit back-to-back singles in the top of the eighth inning. Allison slammed a Lonborg pitch to deep left. Off at the crack of the bat, Yaz dove for the sinking liner, and came up with the ball on one bounce. Although the single drove in Killebrew with Minnesota's third run, Yastrzemski gunned down Allison trying to stretch the hit into a double.

Following a leadoff single in the top of the ninth, Minnesota's speedy Carew bounced into a double play. Pinch hitter Rich Rollins then hit a soft line drive to Petrocelli at short, who caught the ball for the final out.

"All I could think of was, 'Oh, my God! I can't believe it! We might have won the pennant!'" Petrocelli later said. "Might have" because Detroit had defeated the California Angels in the first game of a doubleheader. If the Tigers could sweep, they would face the Sox in a single-game, winner-take-all elimination tilt.

The Fenway faithful stormed the field, stripping Lonborg of his glove, his cap, his shirt, his tee shirt, and even his shoelaces.

The pitcher, wrote the *Globe*'s Bud Collins, "was sucked into the crowd as though it [was] a whirlpool, grabbed, mauled, patted, petted, pounded, and kissed."

While the Red Sox players waited and listened in the clubhouse, management huddled around the radio in Tom Yawkey's office. Then the Tigers' Dick McAuliffe hit into his first double play of the year—and ended Detroit's season.

For the first time since 1946, Boston had won the pennant. Sox fans went absolutely bananas. One man painted the words, "Red Sox Thanks" in four-foot high letters on the side of his suburban home. Another diehard fan stationed in Vietnam extended his tour for another year to qualify for a furlough so he could attend the World Series (the *Globe* provided him with tickets).

Almost lost in all the excitement was Yaz winning the Triple Crown: batting .326, with forty-four home runs and 121 runs batted in. Coming a year after Frank Robinson had done it for the Orioles made the feat seem slightly less extraordinary, but no player in either league has won titles in batting, home runs, and RBIs in the same year since.

After a two-day hiatus, the Sox faced off against the National League champion St. Louis Cardinals at Fenway Park.

The Cards still boasted much of the formidable lineup with which they had bested the Yankees three years earlier. With center fielder Curt Flood, speedy Lou Brock in left, third baseman Mike Shannon, second baseman Julian Javier, and Tim McCarver at catcher, as well as newcomers Orlando "Baby Bull" Cepeda at first base and the ever-dangerous ex-Yankee Roger Maris in right, St. Louis won 101 games and captured the National League by a double-digit margin.

Starting on the mound for the Cards was the fierce Bob Gibson, who had suffered an abbreviated season after his leg was broken by a line shot off the bat of the Pirates' Roberto Clemente. But he still went 13–7 with an ERA of 2.98. "Bob Gibson is the luckiest pitcher I ever saw," declared McCarver. "He always pitches when the other team doesn't score any runs."

The rest of the Cardinals' starting rotation was likewise formidable: Nelson Briles, Dick Hughes, Ray Washburn, and a young Steve Carlton. The bullpen was also solid, with lefty Joe Hoerner (2.59 ERA), and righty Ron Willis (2.67 ERA), closing out fifty-six of the 122 games they appeared in.

For Boston facing the Cards would prove to be an insurmountable battle.

With Lonborg having pitched the final game of the season three days earlier, Game One pitted Red Sox righty Jose Santiago against Gibson. Santiago homered for Boston's lone tally. Gibson was simply overpowering, shutting down Boston on six hits while striking out ten.

Jim Lonborg was the entire story in Game Two, also at Fenway, taking a no-hitter into the eighth inning, ultimately defeating the Cards, 5–0, behind a one-hit effort. Yaz teed off with two home runs after going hitless in Game One.

In Game Three at St. Louis, Briles threw a seven-hitter as the Cardinals soundly beat the Sox, 5–2. Boston's bats also remained quiet in Game Four, with Gibson hurling a 6–0, complete game shut-out, to extend the Cards' lead to three-games-to-one.

Lonborg took the mound in Game Five, and again he was superb, besting St. Louis on only three hits, 3–1. Remarkably, Lonnie had given up only four hits during his two complete game victories.

Back in Boston, Williams played a hunch by starting rookie right-hander Gary Waslewski in Game Six. Waslewski teamed with nominal starter Gary Bell to even the series at three games apiece. The Sox bats had come alive again, with the club rapping twelve hits, including two home runs by Petrocelli and solo shots by Yaz and Reggie Smith.

Following the game, Williams announced his starter in the rubber game would be "Lonborg and champagne," a declaration that comprised the *Boston Record-American*'s front-page.

It was indeed Lonborg on two days rest, but Jim finally ran out of gas. The big right-hander started strong, but gave up two runs in the third inning, a home run to Gibson in the top of the fifth, and another run before the inning ended. In the sixth, Lonborg gave up three more runs.

The final score was 7–2, St. Louis.

There was no pot of gold at the end of the rainbow for the '67 "Impossible Dream" Red Sox. The impossible dream had proven impossible after all.

AIMLESSLY WANDERING TILL '75

The euphoria following Boston's miraculous 1967 pennant run lasted for all of ten weeks—until Christmas Eve, when pitching ace Jim Lonborg tore up his knee skiing in Lake Tahoe.

According to media reports, he was chasing actress Jill St. John down a slope when he caught a ski edge, and tore ligaments in his knee. The Cy Young Award winner had shrugged off warnings when he announced he was going skiing over the holidays, including one from Red Sox general manager Dick O'Connell.

Lonborg made his way off the mountain and drove himself to San Francisco, where the leg was put into a cast. Then he flew to Boston for a medical evaluation. Everybody tried to minimize the injury. "I'm not angry with Jim," said manager Dick Williams. "I'm just relieved it's not as bad as we first thought."

Lonborg underwent knee surgery, but such procedures in those days were a far cry from today. By the time the Sox gathered in Winter Haven for spring training, he could hardy walk, much less throw. He was supposed to be the linchpin of the pitching staff. Suddenly he was an afterthought.

The injury effectively ruined Lonborg's baseball career, at least in Boston. Although he had some winning seasons after he left the franchise—Lonborg logged eight post-Sox seasons in the major leagues (mostly with Philadelphia)—he would never again be anywhere near as dominating as he was during the "Impossible Dream" season. He retired in June 1979, with a lifetime record of 157–137.

Also during the 1967 off-season, many of the club mainstays became complaisant, lazy, and distracted. Carl Yastrzemski was everywhere—except at Gene Berde's gym where he had formerly trained so diligently. Years later, when asked why he didn't return to his off-season training regimen, Yastrzemski simply said, "It was too hard."

Everywhere the players went they were feted like the overnight celebrities they'd become. Even newcomer Ken Harrelson cut a deal to host his own television show. Potential sponsors swarmed Boston's ballplayers, who received numerous endorsement deals. Baseball had become less important to them.

Tony Conigliaro made a vain attempt at a comeback during spring training, but his eyesight failed him.

Although Dick Williams and Dick O'Connell had agreed in principle to a three-year contract extension, Tom Yawkey had suddenly misplaced his magnanimity, calling for a two-year deal instead. Williams, who had rented an expensive apartment and wanted to relocate his wife and kids to metropolitan Boston, was concerned about job security. He wanted to purchase a home, so he fought for a third year. Ultimately, Williams got his way, signing a three-year contract at an estimated $50,000 per season, but he also earned Yawkey's undying enmity. (Williams later revealed that he had suspected that Yawkey had one of his cronies in mind for the manager's post.)

"Maybe he'd decided on another steambath buddy for the job," posed Williams, voice dripping with sarcasm.

After making the deal, Williams was strolling around Fenway Park when he saw members of the grounds crew digging up the turf in left field. Yawkey had ordered that the sod be dug up to transplant to Carl Yastrzemski's backyard. Williams was so upset, he was halfway home before he realized that he left his son at the ballpark.

Another rude awakening came at spring training when George Scott, who had hit .303, with nineteen home runs and 82 RBIs in 1967, reported for camp grossly overweight. (In 1968, Boomer would hit an anemic .171, with three homers and twenty-five runs-batted-in.) Scott was noted for referring to his long home runs as "taters." Grumbled Williams, "It looks like he ate them all."

Success *had* spoiled the Red Sox. No matter how much Williams ranted and raved, the team was now out of its element.

Fans flocked to Fenway Park because in the wake of their "Impossible Dream" pennant, the team was expected to win, or at the very least, contend. It wasn't in the cards. By midseason, the Sox were mired at .500. Just as Lonborg tried to make a comeback, righty Jose Santiago got injured, never to win another major league game. Although Ray Culp, a right-hander Boston had gotten from Philadelphia, went 16–6, lefty Dick Ellsworth posted a 16–7 record, and Gary Bell broke even at 11–11, the loss of both Lonborg and Santiago crippled the Red Sox pitching.

Plus, nobody hit that year. And not just in Boston. Yastrzemski won the batting crown again with an average of .301, but he was the only American Leaguer to bat over .300. Every Sox hitter's average dropped, with the exception of Harrelson, who batted .275, hit thirty-five homers and drove in 109 runs.

It took a late-season surge starting in August for the Sox to somewhat right themselves, finishing the year in fourth place with a record of 86–76. Players and fans alike looked toward 1969 as "The Year of the Comeback."

Tony Conigliaro, his eyesight at least temporarily restored, again manned his post in right field. Boston retained most of its starting lineup, and the club hit well, leading the league in home runs with 197. Yastrzemski and Petrocelli each hit forty, Reggie Smith twenty-five, and Tony C. twenty. Scott hit sixteen and Andrews hammered fifteen. But, as often happened, a dearth of quality pitching did the team in. Culp went 17–8, and the newly acquired Sonny Siebert posted a 14–10 mark, but other than rookie Mike Nagy's 12–2, the rest of the staff was horrible. Lonborg went 7–11.

Then, too, the team had become disenchanted with Dick Williams's dictatorial manner. Asked to rate Williams, Tom Yawkey responded, "Good," which Williams found insulting.

By the end of the summer, Williams had completely lost his players. He became convinced they weren't motivated enough. He alienated Yastrzemski, Smith, Scott, and Stange, as well as the recently traded Hawk Harrelson and relief ace John Wyatt. Young outfielder Joe Lahoud, who had found a mentor in Yaz, also became a favorite target of the abrasive manager.

Losing Carl Yastrzemski's support may very well have been Williams's death knell, as Yaz remained a Yawkey favorite. On September 23, Yawkey ordered general manager O'Connell to fire Williams and his coaching staff. Although O'Connell vehemently disagreed with the move, he obediently did Yawkey's bidding.

"No question that Dick Williams was the right man for us in 1967," Yastrzemski later declared. "His attitude helped turn around a team and brought the Sox a sense of accountability. He was wrong, though, in ripping guys in public and in keeping them in his doghouse."

As soon as Yawkey issued his edict, he left for his South Carolina estate to avoid the fallout. It was a pattern Yawkey followed throughout his ownership: delegate authority, then distance himself.

Wrote *Globe* columnist Ray Fitzgerald, "The days of wine and roses didn't last long, which should have been predictable. The one thing Thomas A. Yawkey cannot abide, even more than a losing ball team, is an unhappy one."

Minor league manager Eddie Kasko was named as Williams's replacement. Kasko was the exact opposite of Dick Williams, a laid back, easygoing man who instituted "Fun Days" as part of the club's spring training routine the following year. The Sox played out the 1969 season under coach Eddie Popowski, finishing with an 87–75 record, while the 109-win Orioles ran off with the first American League East title (with the addition of two clubs in each league in '69, both leagues were split into two six-team divisions). Baltimore would be knocked off by the Miracle Mets in the World Series that October, but the O's would rule the AL East with few exceptions through the first half of the coming decade.

|||||

The Sox quickly fell out of contention in 1970. At first it looked like Lonborg was returning to his 1967 form. He won four consecutive games, but then he hurt his arm, and was sent down to Louisville.

One of the bright spots was the resurgence of Tony Conigliaro, who hit thirty-six home runs and amassed 116 RBIs. Another was Yastrzemski who hit .329, with forty home runs and 102 RBIs. But Boston fans, eager for a scapegoat, irrationally turned on their former darling.

"Quicker than it takes to say, 'Yaz Sir, that's my Baby,' the fans have turned on the producer, director, and star of The Impossible Dream," declared Tim Horgan of the *Herald*.

The Sox repeated as also-rans, with a record of 87–75, finishing third in the Eastern Division. The Orioles cruised to another championship, this time winning the World Series to boot, and Sox attendance started dropping off.

Despite Tom Yawkey's previous pledge never to trade Tony Conigliaro, the Sox owner instructed O'Connell to dump the Boston icon. Conigliaro and Yastrzemski didn't get along—and *Yaz* was Yawkey's baby. "There was a lot of dissension between Tony C. and Yaz," Dennis Bennett said. "You could see it in the clubhouse and in some ways on the field."

Under Kasko, the rifts in the Red Sox locker room continued. Conigliaro's younger brother, Billy, who had joined the club in 1970, openly feuded with Yastrzemski, Smith, and Joe Lahoud. All four played the outfield, and Lahoud was the younger Conigliaro's competition for the starting job in right field.

"When [Harrelson] was traded to Cleveland, there was a new rivalry," Lahoud later claimed. "It was then that everything started cooking."

A joint meeting with Kasko quieted things down but only for a while. In July, Billy accused Yaz and Smith of conspiring against him to keep him out of the starting lineup. The press egged on the feud, with writers misquoting Smith and Yastrzemski to make it sound as if they were criticizing Conigliaro. One story alleged that Billy played too deep, causing the Sox to lose a game at Yankee Stadium. In another, the younger Conigliaro charged that Yaz and Smith were the reason his big brother had been traded.

Smith, who had an explosive temper, erupted in rage. "Billy Conigliaro is not a mature player. What he said was not so much an emotional outburst because of his brother. It was malice afore-thought. And I don't want to play with him again."

The atmosphere in Boston's clubhouse remained incendiary, and the players openly criticized Kasko's managing. Boston again came in third place in 1971, eighteen games behind the Orioles, with an 85–77 record.

After the season both Billy Conigliaro and Lahoud were sent to the Milwaukee Brewers, along with Lonborg, Scott, pitcher Ken Brett and catcher Don Pavletich. In return, the Sox received pitchers Marty Pattin and Lew Krausse, and outfielders Tommy Harper and Pat Skrable.

In what was arguably the best player move of his career, Dick O'Connell had signed an arm weary right-handed pitcher named Luis Tiant. Nobody took note at the time because Tiant, who had begun his career with Cleveland as a fireballing starter, (posting an otherworldly ERA of 1.60, and striking out a remarkable 264 batters during a twenty-one-win season in 1968) had thrown out his arm, only to resurrect himself as a "junk ball" pitcher.

Tiant was admittedly little more than a mediocre relief pitcher in 1971, going 1–7 after being called up from Boston's Triple A team. But between 1972 and 1978 he won 134 games for the Red Sox.

"His repertoire begins with an exaggerated mid-windup pivot, during which he turns his back on the batter and seems to exam-ine the infield directly behind the mound for signs of crabgrass," wrote author Roger Angell. "With men on base, his stretch con-sists of a succession of minute downward waggles and pauses of the glove, and a menacing sidewise, slit-eyed, Valentino-like gaze over his shoulder at the base runner. The full flower of his art, however, comes during the actual delivery, which is executed with a perfect variety show of accompanying gestures and impersonations."

Echoed the inimitable Reggie Jackson, "Tiant is the Fred Astaire of baseball."

Tiant and Boston's fans bonded, an interesting occurrence considering the volatile racial unrest simmering in the city, and Tiant said joining the Red Sox spawned his happiest years in organized baseball.

"It was good, and that's why I'm here [as a roving pitching coach in 2008]," said Tiant. "They gave me the opportunity to be who I am today. The town, the people and the team loved me, and that's why I'm here today. I've been all over the United States and there's no place like Boston for me."

Dick Bresciani said the acquisition of Luis Tiant may have been Dick O'Connell's single greatest accomplishment aside from the 1967 "Impossible Dream" team.

"Here's a guy who had been injured and let go by Minnesota and Atlanta, down in the minor leagues at Richmond, and some of our people had seen him and called Dick and said, 'Give this guy a look . . . because [we] think he's still got something left.'

"So [Tiant] ended up in the bullpen. He was pitching middle relief and in '71 he didn't do that well, but he was getting healthier," Bresciani opined. "And when I joined the team in '72 he was still relieving and serving as a spot starter. By the end of June we'd had an injury and we said 'Luis, you've got to start [regularly],' and he won and kept winning and went 15–5 and led the league in ERA [1.91 in 179 innings]. And off we went. He was terrific. It would be hard to top Dick's signing of Luis Tiant."

Aside from Tiant, the most important addition to the team at the time was a New Englander, Carlton Fisk. The rookie catcher hit .293

with twenty-two homers and 61 RBIs in 1972. He was voted the American League Rookie of the Year.

Eddie Kasko was retained despite the turmoil that wracked the club. Team unity was further torn apart when players split over whether to go on strike. A few—most notably Yastrzemski, who was making in excess of $125,000—were dead set against it. Although the Major League Baseball Players Association did call a strike, the work stoppage lasted only twelve days. An unequal number of games were canceled, based on each team's schedule, a factor that would come back to haunt the Sox.

Dick O'Connell, an astute trader when owner Yawkey wasn't issuing whimsical mandates, crafted one of his most incomprehensible deals when he sent relief pitcher Sparky Lyle to the Yankees for first baseman Danny Cater and infielder Mario Guerrero on March 22. Cater stayed with Boston for three years, hitting .262, playing on a part-time basis. Guerrero served as a reserve for two seasons.

Meanwhile, Lyle set the standard for relief pitching while in New York, posting a 57–40 record with a 2.41 ERA, saving 141 games. He pitched in three World Series, made the All-Star team three times, and became the first relief pitcher to win the American League Cy Young Award.

The 1972 season opened badly. Veteran shortstop Luis Aparicio, obtained in a trade with the White Sox for Mike Andrews, tripped over third base on a base hit by Yastrzemski. Yaz, running with his head down, barreled into third, not realizing that Luis had scrambled back to the bag. Yaz was out. The Sox lost to Detroit, 3–2.

Boston got off to a sluggish start, but righted itself around the All-Star break. Tiant emerged from the bullpen and began winning, joining pitchers Siebert, Pattin, Bill Lee, and rookies Lynn McGlothen and John Curtis.

The season went down to the wire, as Boston traveled to Detroit to face the Tigers, who trailed the Sox in the AL East by a half a game, for a season-ending three-game set.

Trailing 1–0 in the first game, Tommy Harper and Luis Aparicio singled, and Yaz hit a rocket over the center fielder's head. Harper easily scored from third as Aparicio raced around the bases, closely followed by Yastrzemski. Then the unthinkable happened. Aparicio stumbled over the third base bag, a near carbon copy of his fall at the beginning of the season. He dove back to the base, while Yaz tore into third. Yastrzemski was out because of his Little League–style base-running blunder—again. And Aparicio got the blame—again.

The players' strike had caused Boston to play one fewer game than Detroit, so the season came down to the middle game of the series. Luis Tiant gave up seven hits and three runs and the Tigers carried the day, 3–1, rendering the series finale meaningless.

The Tigers went on to play Oakland in the American League Championship Series. Boston went home.

Many Red Sox players openly wept in the clubhouse. Yaz called losing the 1972 AL East crown "the greatest disappointment in my life." For Boston fans it generated the most predictable of Red Sox mantras: Wait Till Next Year.

||||||

In preparing for the upcoming 1973 season, which would usher in the American League's designated hitter rule, O'Connell signed future Hall-of-Famer Orlando Cepeda, who at that point had hit .300 nine times and hammered 356 career home runs.

The turmoil in the clubhouse continued. Center fielder Reggie Smith continued to carry a chip on his shoulder, fighting with his teammates and accusing *everybody* of racism. Smith claimed that white players received different treatment than African-American players, at the hands of the Red Sox and the press. He blasted the media, asserting, "I feel there are guys in the press who are racist," and he struck at the fans with, "There are a lot of sick people up there [in the stands], and I'm getting pretty fed up with it."

There *was* a lot of racial strife in Boston to be sure, especially in South Boston, and no doubt some of it spilled over into Fenway Park. A federal court order to bus students in order to integrate the public schools sparked huge protests and widespread violence.

The Sox obtained shortstop Dick McAuliffe from Detroit in 1973 in return for young outfielder Ben Oglivie. The light-hitting McAuliffe, just shy of thirty-four, was clearly beyond his prime, and served as a part-time infielder for Boston for less than two seasons. Oglivie, twenty-four, spent thirteen productive years with the Tigers and Milwaukee. He appeared in three All-Star games, and led the AL in home runs in 1980.

Outfielder Tommy Harper led the American League in stolen bases with fifty-four, a Red Sox record, and designated hitter Cepeda hit twenty home runs. Despite his unhappiness Smith hit .303, with twenty-one homers.

On the mound, Luis Tiant led the pitching staff, posting a 20–13 mark, Bill "Spaceman" Lee went 17–11, John Curtis broke even at 13–13, and rookie left-hander Roger Moret went an astounding 13–2. Veteran hurlers Bob Bolin posted fifteen saves, and Bob Veale notched eleven. It still wasn't enough. The Sox finished second in the AL East at 89–73, eight games behind Baltimore.

Despite four consecutive winning seasons, Kasko was given his walking papers at the end of 1973, replaced by Darrell Johnson, a former part-time catcher.

|||||||

In the off-season, Boston finally granted Reggie Smith his wish, sending the perpetually disgruntled outfielder and pitcher Ken Tatum to the St. Louis Cardinals for pitcher Rick Wise and outfielder Bernie Carbo. Two months later, the Sox sent three pitchers—Curtis, Lynn McGlothen, and Mike Garman—to the Cards for pitchers Reggie Cleveland and Diego Segui and utility man Terry Hughes.

Expecting a good return from his youngsters, new manager Johnson convinced the Sox to release veterans Aparicio and Cepeda before the 1974 season. Boston was in the process of assimilating a large crop of young players, including outfielders Dwight Evans, Rick Miller, and Juan Beniquez, first baseman Cecil Cooper, and shortstop Rick Burleson.

But the Red Sox had shortchanged themselves by trading away Curtis and McGlothen. Among the starters only Tiant improved, going 22–13 with an ERA of 2.92. Lee again won seventeen games, but lost fifteen. Yaz led the team with a batting average of .301.

Poor play and injuries caused the Red Sox to drop to an 84–78 record in 1974, good for third place in the AL East. But better times were coming. Aside from the promising crop of young ballplayers already on the club, the Sox would add "The Gold Dust Twins," outfielders Freddie Lynn and Jim Rice in 1975.

Virtually everything went right for Boston in 1975, up until the very end. The Red Sox handily won the division, posting a record of 95–65. Center fielder Lynn won Rookie of the Year honors and was selected as the American League Most Valuable Player, the first time in baseball history that a rookie simultaneously won both honors.

Lynn hit .331, with twenty-one home runs and 105 RBIs. Left fielder Rice, did almost as well, batting .309, hitting twenty-two home runs and knocking in 102 runs. However, he was lost late in the season when he suffered a broken wrist after being hit by a pitch. Carlton Fisk, too, was injured, missing most of the year, but hit .339 in limited service. Young Cecil Cooper spent most of the season as the Red Sox designated hitter, appearing in 106 games and batting .311.

Likewise, the pitching held up well, with Rick Wise going 19–11, Tiant 18–14, Bill Lee 17–9, Moret 14–3, and Reggie Cleveland 13–9. Although the relief corps was shaky at times, the Sox bolstered their bullpen in July when right-hander Jim Willoughby, who saved eight games in twenty-four appearances, was called up from the minors, doing yeoman's duty.

The Sox swept the powerful Oakland A's in the ALCS, behind stellar performances on the part of Tiant, Wise and Yastrzemski. "We weren't given a chance to beat the three-time defending world champions," Wise said. "It was a wonderful feeling."

In the 1975 World Series Boston would face Cincinnati's Big Red Machine, possibly the most dominant team of the decade. It would prove to be a World Series for the ages, rated by many baseball aficionados as the best Series ever.

The ageless Tiant was absolutely masterful in Game One, throwing a complete game, five-hit shutout, with the Sox cruising to a 5–0 win.

"Spaceman" Bill Lee started Game Two. With the Sox leading 2–1 in the top of the ninth inning, rain caused a lengthy delay. When play resumed, Lee had lost his edge. Boston gave up two runs, and the Reds won, 3–2. The key play was a missed call at second base when the umpire called Reds shortstop Dave Conception safe. Television replays clearly showed he was out.

Moving on to Game Three in Cincinnati, the Reds jumped out to a 5–1 lead, but the Sox battled back, courtesy of a Fred Lynn sacrifice fly and home runs by Bernie Carbo and Dwight Evans. Carbo's pinch-hit homer sent the game into extra innings.

In the bottom of the tenth, with Reds' Cesar Geronimo on first base, pinch-hitter Ed Armbrister attempted to sacrifice the runner to second. He laid down a bunt, with the ball bouncing several feet in front of home plate. Armbrister stood stock still, forcing Boston catcher Carlton Fisk to push him aside. Fisk then threw the ball wildly into center field, allowing Geronimo to reach third as Armbrister advanced to second base.

There was no question that it was a clear-cut case of interference, and the Red Sox argued that Armbrister should be called out.[19] But umpire Larry Barnett, who later termed the play "a simple collision," allowed the play to stand.

Cincinnati's Joe Morgan then lofted a drive to deep center field to win the game, 6–5.

The Sox remained incensed, with Yaz issuing a profanity-laden blast at the umpiring crew. Fisk was stunned, remarking, "I'm an infielder on a play like that. Well, why isn't the man out?" And in the *Boston Globe*, Ray Fitzgerald wrote, "I have been in many sullen and snarling locker rooms in the last decade, but none as bitter as the one last night. The Grinch had stolen Christmas from the Red Sox."

Luis Tiant, who took the mound in Game Four, pitched his way in and out of trouble all night long, giving up four runs on nine hits, walking four, and striking out only four batters. But the right-hander threw a complete-game victory, throwing a whopping 163 pitches and winning the contest, 5–4.

19 The rulebook states that, if a batter or runner fails to avoid a fielder who is attempting to field a batted ball, the batter or runner will be called out.

"Luis Tiant belongs in the Hall of Fame," declared Sox VP Bresciani. "When he had the opportunity to pitch in the postseason or in big games, he always came up big. He was a money guy. Just look at what he did in '75 in the playoffs with Oakland, then the Reds in the World Series.

"You'll never see another complete, nine-inning, 163-pitch game again—in the World Series, no less! They just don't play that way anymore. You'll never see the bases loaded in the bottom of the ninth with the starting pitcher in there. He was a tremendous competitor, and he still is a great guy."

The Reds again took the lead by drubbing Boston 6–2 in Game Five behind the pitching of Don Gullett and Rawly Eastwick.

Back in Boston for the final two games, the storm clouds again rolled in. Rain delayed Game Six three times. By the time the weather cleared, manager Johnson reversed the order of his pitching rotation, naming Tiant to start Game Six, and holding Bill Lee for Game Seven, if necessary.

Facing Reds hurler Gary Nolan, the Sox erupted for three runs on a Fred Lynn blast, but then Tiant finally ran out of gas. He gave up six runs by the eighth inning, and the Reds were six outs away from a world championship.

Then Lynn singled, third baseman Rico Petrocelli walked and, after two outs, Carbo hit *another* pinch-hit homer to tie the game. Both teams threatened in the ninth, but couldn't score. The game went into extra innings. Dwight Evans made a remarkable catch at the short wall in right field and then turned it into a double play to end the eleventh. Wise pitched out trouble the next inning. And then . . .

In the bottom of the twelfth inning Fisk led off against rookie Pat Darcy, who had been untouchable for two innings. Fisk took ball one, then sent a high fly ball down the left-field line. The

usually unflappable Fisk sidestepped down the first base line, frantically waving his arms and screaming, as if willing the ball to land
fair. It glanced off the foul pole.

"Home run!" shouted Red Sox announcer Ned Martin. "The Red
Sox win, and the Series is tied!"

Fisk jumped up and down, clapping his hands, then began rounding the bases. The 35,205 fans at Fenway Park went berserk. Organ-
ist John Kiley struck up the "Hallelujah Chorus," accentuated by the
cheers of the fans and the whooping of Fisk's teammates.

Years later Fisk recounted what he said just prior to his dramatic
at bat. "I did have one specific thought as I stood in the on-deck
circle with Fred Lynn. I said, 'Fred, I think I'm going to hit one off
the wall, so drive me in.' But as it turned out, I hit one off the [foul]
pole and it ended the game, and the rest is history. But Fred and I
were just ready to go home. We were tired!"

Thirteen years later, *TV Guide* reported, "Fisk's home run remains the ultimate moment in TV sports, not for its drama but because of its sheer beauty—an American dream come true."

In the rubber game of the Series, Bill Lee pitched perfect baseball for five innings, taking a 3–0 lead into the top of the sixth. Then,
with a man on base, he violated the scouting reports regarding the
always-dangerous Tony Perez, the Reds' first baseman. Lee had
been warned not to throw Perez any off-speed pitches, in particular
his parabolic curve. But Lee threw his "eephus" pitch anyway, and
Perez hit it out of the park.

Wrote Stout and Johnson in *Red Sox Century*, "Lee was usually
playing more than one game at a time. The one on the field always
had to compete with the one in his head that was scored according to
a discreet set of rules that only Lee himself could account."

Lee left the next inning, after Cincinnati tied the game. In came

Jim Willoughby, who shut down the Reds to close out the seventh inning, and pitched a flawless eighth.

Then, with two outs in the bottom of the eighth inning, Johnson incomprehensibly pulled Willoughby for a pinch-hitter, Cecil Cooper. There were two outs and no one on base, and the Red Sox bullpen was spent. But after Cooper struck out, Johnson brought in rookie righty Jim Burton.

The minds of the Fenway faithful were boggled, stunned, as if they knew what was to come.

Burton, who had appeared in twenty-nine games for Boston during the regular season, walked Ken Griffey Sr. to start the inning. Geronimo sacrificed Griffey to second base and pinch-hitter Dan Driessen advanced him to third with a grounder to second base. After a walk to Pete Rose, Joe Morgan provided the *coup de grâce*: a looping single to right field to bring in the winning run with Rose famously belly flopping into third base.

In anticlimactic fashion Boston went quietly in the bottom of the ninth inning, with Carl Yastrzemski making the final out.

The heartbreak was indescribable—again.

14

THE ENIGMA OF
TOM YAWKEY

In the wake of Boston's heartbreaking seven-game World Series loss to the Reds, fans throughout New England were confident that the Sox would continue to return to postseason play. But throughout the Yawkey years, appearances were *always* deceiving.

In November of 1975, the Sox bolstered their starting pitching by trading for right-hander Ferguson Jenkins, a pitcher of some renown. However, like so many others during the Yawkey regime, the trade proved to be a bust. During his two years with the club, Jenkins went 22–21, a far cry from the future Hall of Famer's production with the Cubs and the Rangers.

The year 1976 got off to a shaky start. Free agency had come into being, and the owners locked out the players. Tom Yawkey, who was deathly ill with leukemia, found himself in the middle of a firestorm with free agency on the horizon and players—notably Fisk—threatening to play out their options. Yawkey became bitter and felt betrayed, even though he had spoiled and overpaid his ballplayers for years. He refused to be bullied into paying bloated salaries unless it was on *his* terms.

The Sox began the season playing mediocre baseball, but righted themselves in May, although they still trailed the Yankees by six games. Bill Lee, off to a horrendous start, took the mound at the newly remodeled Yankee Stadium on May 20.

With the Yankees leading 1–0 in the sixth inning, New York outfielder Lou Piniella tried to score from second base on a single to right field. Dwight Evans threw a perfect peg to Carlton Fisk, who was bowled over by Piniella. Fisk came up swinging, and Lee joined in the ensuing melee. Lee was punched by Yankee outfielder Mickey Rivers, and then New York's massive third baseman, Graig Nettles, picked up Lee and dropped him on his left shoulder. The left-hander was done for the year.

Team spirit plummeted, and when the Sox traded World Series hero Bernie Carbo to Milwaukee for pitcher Tom Murphy and outfielder Bobby Darwin, morale sunk even lower.

General manager O'Connell almost pulled off the deal of the decade in June when he paid $1 million each for Oakland A's outfielder Joe Rudi and future Hall of Fame closer Rollie Fingers. He also made a play for the A's lefty ace Vida Blue, but baseball commissioner Bowie Kuhn stepped in and negated the deals "for the good of the game."

On July 9, 1976, Tom Yawkey succumbed to leukemia at the age of seventy-three. Even in death, Yawkey would continue to throw a long shadow over the team he had alternately coddled, ignored and—either deliberately or inadvertently—undermined.

To this day, Yawkey, an intensely private man who battled myriad demons, remains an enigma to many of the reporters who covered the franchise. One of the *Herald-American* reporters who wrote Yawkey's obituary didn't even know Yawkey had an adopted daughter, instead identifying the woman as Yawkey's "adopted sister" living in Connecticut. In the obituary, Yawkey was described as "an autocratic but benevolent despot who spoiled his ballplayers . . . [and] who regarded his ball club as a hobby and who ran the show by whims and fancies."

The Red Sox owner rarely received press scrutiny, said Brian Willett, a long-time sports reporter at the *Norwich* (Connecticut) *Bulletin*.

"Yawkey was never criticized by the media," Willett declared. "They didn't question any of his moves, anything. He owned the Red Sox."

Yawkey often lashed out at his critics who maligned him for overpaying his ballplayers. "If trying to treat the players as human beings is spoiling them, then I spoil them. But I was brought up to treat a human being as a human being, until he proves unworthy of it."

Everybody bought Yawkey's soft-shoe routine, said season ticket holder Dennis Burke.

"They just accepted his behavior. The media [scrutiny] simply wasn't there. The cronyism certainly was. He hired people who drank with him. It was, 'The Red Sox can do no wrong, win or lose.' And that was it. It was a family-run business like a local five-and-dime store operation."

Indeed, the team was run like Yawkey's private playground, and many journalists and baseball historians have confirmed that the bigotry that beset the franchise emanated from the very top.

"The funny thing about the Yawkey regime is that they didn't like anybody," asserted Clark Booth. "They didn't like blacks. They didn't like Catholics. They didn't like Jews. The Anti-Defamation League brought a suit against the Red Sox in 1959 for discriminating against Jews."

Yet Yawkey once declared, "I don't care if the man is a Chinese, Indian, Negro, or white man. I want to see him play baseball. Race, color, and creed don't matter to me: it's the individual. To me a guy is a guy."

But George Kimball, former sports editor for the Boston *Phoenix*, and later a reporter for the *Boston Herald*, disagreed. "It's sort of like saying that a benevolent slave-owner in the 1850s wasn't a racist because he was kind to his field hands. [Yawkey] presided over the organization that was the last to integrate—and even having made a token breakthrough dragged its feet in the matter of black players for almost another quarter-century—and consistently hired men who implemented those discriminatory practices. Since they operated at his pleasure, you'd have to assume that Yawkey approved of this institutionalized racism, whether it was at his behest or not."

Red Sox vice president Dick Bresciani, who has been with the club since 1972, insisted Yawkey didn't have a prejudiced bone in his body. "I don't believe Tom Yawkey was a racist in any way, and I think it showed in the way he treated the [black] people who worked for him down South where he lived and had his estate, and how he treated people around [the Red Sox organization]. You couldn't be a racist and treat people that way, and be that nice to everybody."

"I don't think it stemmed from Tom Yawkey, but I do think it continued because of [him]," declared author Glenn Stout. "Racism had been the norm before Tom Yawkey, but after the war there was an impetus to integrate due to the deaths of so many African-Americans during World War II. He had ample opportunity to integrate the Red Sox, and many had called for him to do just that. In fact, every time he had the opportunity to be in the vanguard of social change he avoided it. I personally find it reprehensible that he was the first pure owner elected to the Hall of Fame."

Retired *Norwich Bulletin* sportswriter Brian Willett said the media has to be held accountable for glossing over the race story.

"I don't believe I was aware of the racial implications," he ruefully admitted. "I should have been."

Clark Booth is blunt about Yawkey's shortcomings. "I don't think Yawkey was a very good owner. He was behind the times and retarded the growth of the team in many ways. The racial issue was the most dramatic and obvious one. And I think it was deliberate. I don't believe he was simply a product of the times who just followed along. I think he was a racist and it affected his judgment and his recruitment of players for half a century."

In *What's the Matter with the Red Sox?* the late Al Hirshberg defended Yawkey against charges of racism. "My own conviction is that [the racism] was deliberate, but not in the way people think. The problem was not at the top, as many Red Sox fans and observers thought. Yawkey wanted a black ballplayer almost from the beginning, although he never made a big deal about it because he trusted his farm system to sign promising ballplayers regardless of their color."

Hirshberg added the problem wasn't with Cronin either; it was the scouts who refused to honestly evaluate black ballplayers.

George Kimball agreed that there may be some credence in Hirshberg's theory. "Regarding the scouts, I think there's some truth to that, but it wasn't necessarily confined to the Red Sox. In particular, back then the scouting profession in general seemed to be dominated by rednecks, but God knows the Sox had plenty of those. You'd watch them when they got together at spring training and they looked like they could have been sitting on the front porch of some Mississippi general store chewing Red Man."

Part of the problem may have stemmed from the pervasive effect of alcoholism.

Author Richard Johnson says a good example of the impact of alcohol on club operations occurred when Yawkey forced Billy

Evans to leave. "Tom Yawkey had been out drinking one night with Joe Cronin, who resented others encroaching upon his territory. He persuaded Yawkey to fire Billy Evans, the farm director. A drunken Yawkey called Evans at his home in Cleveland and fired him. A day later, Yawkey called Evans again and offered him his job back but Evans refused. To this day, Evans is the only person associated with the Red Sox who is in the Hall of Fame [as an umpire] but not listed as such in any Red Sox publication."

Perhaps the most mystifying chapter in Tom Yawkey's life involved his silent ownership of an infamous South Carolina brothel known as the Sunset Lodge. A year after Yawkey purchased the Red Sox, he moved the whorehouse from Florence, South Carolina, to Georgetown, South Carolina.

Michael Carter, the former sheriff of Georgetown County, said Yawkey initially bankrolled the operation. "I don't know how long he actually owned the operation but . . . he did to begin with. He opened it [in 1934] and he would bring groups from Boston down here often because he owned an [estate]. They'd take a train down here and stop [at the bordello] in Florence. Yawkey hired the lady who used to run the place in Florence."

After Yawkey bought the property in Georgetown, he turned it over to madam Hazel Weiss who ran the operation until 1969, Carter said.

Georgetown author Elizabeth Huntsinger Wolfe confirmed Carter's story, declaring, "[Yawkey] instigated it. He saw the need for a house of leisure in Georgetown . . . and he'd come down by train to Florence and catch a connection to Georgetown. He met the madam, Hazel Weiss, and convinced her to move the operation to Georgetown."

After Yawkey bought the property in Georgetown, he turned it over to the woman who ran the operation until 1969, Carter said. "It was common knowledge back in the early days that he owned it, and gave [Weiss] the property."

Georgetown Times reporter Clayton Stairs said, "The Sunset Lodge was known throughout the region and Georgetown was known for it. Old-timers have told me that if they mentioned they were from Georgetown to strangers, the strangers would immediately say, 'Sunset Lodge.'"

The bordello was actually internationally known, according to the *Boston Globe*.

"I heard Tom Yawkey drove [his second wife] Jean there once and she was furious," one man told the *Globe* in 1989.

Michael Carter, who served as sheriff from 1979 to 1993, said his father, Woodrow, shut down the whorehouse in 1969 after *he* was elected sheriff, while Michael was serving as a state trooper.

"He closed down the Sunset Lodge during his first elected term. He promised folks when he ran that he'd close it down. So that's what he did. As far as I know [my father] told the lady who was running it to shut it down and she did so. From my understanding he gave her so many days to shut down the operation. And that's what she did."

Red Sox vice president Bresciani said that Yawkey was always ready to help struggling club employees. "I had the good fortune to know Tom and work with Tom from '72 until he died in '76, and I got to believe, along with all the other employees around here, what a wonderful human being he was. First of all, he treated everyone equally no matter who they were in the organization, and he was always around speaking to them all, asking about families.

"He was helpful to many people behind the scenes, whether they were in financial difficulty or they had some problem. He did countless things that were never known publicly because he was that type of individual."

Stout agreed, but maintains it simply may have been a psychological quirk.

"He liked being the father figure, and to a degree purchased good will," he said.

To this day, Yawkey's reputation as a "gentleman/sportsman" persists, and his philanthropy is likewise well recognized.

Yawkey was a fervent supporter of charities, predominantly the Jimmy Fund—the Children's Cancer Research Foundation. What many fail to realize is that he *inherited* that charity from former Boston Braves owner Lou Pereni when the Braves left Boston for Milwaukee.

Hazel Weiss, the woman who ran the Sunset Lodge, was always ready to open up her purse for local charities, according to former sheriff Michael Carter. "The lady who ran the place did a lot in the community, making donations to the local hospital, and spent a lot of money locally."

Tom Yawkey and his wife, Jean, were also heavily involved in charitable work, including supporting the Tara Hall Home for Boys, a local orphanage, although Wolfe—who once worked for Tara Hall—said she suspects Jean was the moving force behind much of the benevolence. "They did a lot for Georgetown County, especially for Tara Hall, and for both races," Wolfe said. "Tara Hall, at least, ran a color blind operation. It was founded in 1970 by a [Roman] Catholic priest, Father Owen O'Sullivan."

The long-time owner of the flagship franchise had other peccadilloes, however—and, in the wake of his death the media simply lionized him, whitewashing many of his faults and negative tendencies.

|||||

BASEBALL'S NO. 1 FAN IS DEAD, extolled the front page of the *Boston Globe*, going on to call Tom Yawkey "the last of a baseball breed that could be identified by the obsolete term of Sportsman with a capital S."

"[Yawkey] gave so much to this city over the years, so much pleasure, so much excitement and always so much class," declared Boston mayor Kevin H. White.

Certainly, Tom Yawkey was a complex man, who put critics on notice early on when he declared, "What's mine is mine." The reclusive and taciturn owner proved unyielding when it came to conforming to social mores and that, perhaps, proved to be the reason for the failure of his beloved team to win a championship during the decades he owned the club.

Mayor White may have uttered Yawkey's most lasting epitaph when he said, "the spirit of Tom Yawkey's contribution to Boston in the last four decades will live on long after the rest of us are gone."

For indeed the specter of racism would continue long after Yawkey's death.

|||||

By the time Yawkey died it became apparent that the team wasn't going to shake off its malaise. O'Connell fired manager Darrell Johnson in mid-July, replacing him with third base coach Don Zimmer.

The team limped to an 83–79 record, finishing in third place, fifteen games behind the Yankees. The Yankees won the American League pennant three years running (1976–78), and were world champions in both 1977 and 1978.

15

HAYWOOD AND BUDDY ARE KILLING THE SOX

Twenty years before Yawkey's death, a trust had been established to oversee the franchise, although in reality the Sox owner still called the shots. With Yawkey's passing, the four trustees—Yawkey's widow Jean, Red Sox secretary Joseph LaCour, Dick O'Connell, and Yawkey associate James A. Curran—would operate the team until either the trust was broken up or the team was sold.

A free agent draft was conducted November 4, 1976. Boston selected Twins reliever Bill Campbell who, in 1976, had picked up seventeen wins and twenty saves, signing him to a five-year, $1 million contract. O'Connell's other proposed moves were thwarted by Haywood Sullivan, a Red Sox executive who previously had served as a bullpen catcher. At Sullivan's behest, Jean Yawkey ordered O'Connell to stop spending "her money." Outraged at the sums that owners were forced to pay in the new world of free agency, Sullivan had the ear of Jean Yawkey; in reality, he was more of a surrogate son than he was an employee. The writing was on the wall for O'Connell.

Instead of attempting to acquire free agent infielder Bobby Grich and pitcher Don Gullett (and trading for the A's Mike Torrez) as planned, Boston reacquired former Red Sox George Scott and Bernie Carbo from the Brewers for Cecil Cooper.

Cooper was a budding star, and would spend eleven years with Milwaukee, hitting over .300 in each of his first seven seasons. He was named to the American League All-Star team five times.

In spite of the 213 home runs that Sox batters hit in 1977, Don Zimmer proved unpopular, completely alienating the pitching staff, by juggling everyone except Luis Tiant and Fergie Jenkins between the bullpen and the starting rotation. But perhaps the most critical event that occurred during the season was the formation of the "Buffalo Head Gang," a group made up of pitchers Lee, Jenkins, Wise, and Willoughby, and outfielder Carbo. The group was so named because, declared Jenkins, Zimmer looked like a buffalo, and "buffaloes are the ugliest [and dumbest] animals alive." Lee went one step further, telling the media that Zimmer was like a gerbil because "he has fat, pudgy cheeks, and kids like him."

Ultimately, one by one the "Buffalo Heads" were discarded by the club, which won ninety-seven games in 1977, but still finished third to the powerful Yankees.

The Sox obtained a gritty, hard-hitting second baseman in December 1977 who quickly became a fan favorite. Jerry Remy, a native of Somerset, Massachusetts, was obtained from the Angels for pitcher Don Aase. Oft injured due to his never-say-die style of play, Remy made the 1978 All-Star team, and hit over .300 twice for Boston during his seven years with the club.

After retiring he attained even more popularity when he became a Red Sox television baseball announcer. Affectionately known as "Rem Dawg," he was recently elected as the unofficial president of Red Sox Nation in a widespread poll.

Before the 1978 season rolled around, former team vice president

Sullivan and Edward "Buddy" LeRoux, were awarded the franchise in return for $16 million, of which $15 million was borrowed money. When opposing factions complained that *they* had offered more money, league officials concurred, and Jean Yawkey was forced to join Sullivan, LeRoux, and other "minority" partners, and put up even more up-front money.

The oddest member of the trio was LeRoux, who had served as trainer for the Boston Celtics from 1958 to 1966, and trainer of the Red Sox from 1966 to 1974. He had been unceremoniously fired by Tom Yawkey in 1974 after, against Yawkey's wishes, LeRoux continued to solicit ballplayers to invest in various schemes.

"I think Buddy was brought into the ownership troika for a couple of reasons," former reporter Kimball suggested. "One was that he was perceived to have money, or at least access to money, which Haywood didn't. Two, he was considered at the time to be some sort of financial wizard with a Midas touch. He had not only invested wisely (though not as wisely as advertised, it turned out) with his own money but also steered several players toward lucrative investments. As with a lot of self-made millionaires at the time, Buddy's fortune turned out to be largely predicated on a house of cards. He didn't turn out to be Donald Trump, but he did pretty well for a guy who started out wrapping ankles and handing out jocks."

There may have been another reason, said Kimball, as Sullivan wasn't the sharpest knife in the drawer. "While I'm reluctant to psychoanalyze people I didn't know very well, Mrs. Yawkey may also have felt that while she loved Haywood like a son, he was in way over his head intellectually and might need Buddy to navigate the waters when she was gone."

Meanwhile, O'Connell, the most successful general manager in Red Sox history up until Theo Epstein, found himself unemployed.

(Soon cars sported bumper stickers that read, "Haywood and Buddy Are Killing the Sox.")

"There was a lot of jealousy involved when Dick O'Connell was fired," asserted Glenn Stout. "I think everybody else wanted to take credit for everything. O'Connell, in a lot of people's minds, had been given too much credit." [20]

In the meantime, charter "Buffalo Heads" Wise and Jenkins were traded, and replaced by Dennis Eckersley, then a starter, and ex-Yankee hurler Mike Torrez. And Bernie Carbo left for the second time.

Jenkins, who was intensely disliked by manager Don Zimmer, went on to win sixty-nine more games before retiring. All told, he won 284 games, had a 3.34 ERA, and struck out 3,192 over a nineteen-year career.

One of the three Boston players originally sent to Texas for Jenkins was outfielder Juan Beniquez. Beniquez, a Puerto Rican, played four years in Boston, hitting better than .290 twice in limited service. Once he was freed from "The Plantation," like many other minority players, he blossomed. He played for another thirteen years, hitting .300 or better four times.

|||||

The Sox put together a terrific run in 1978, amassing a fourteen-and-a-half-game lead over the Yankees before succumbing to the so-called "Boston Massacre," when New York decisively swept Boston in two late season series. Bill Lee found out just how much of an anathema he had become to the stubborn Zimmer when the manager

---

20 O'Connell died in August 2002, while LeRoux passed away on January 7, 2008 before he could be interviewed for this book.

demoted him to the bullpen and replaced him with forgettable rookie Bobby Sprowl.

The club ended up trailing New York in September before rallying and ultimately tying the Yankees on the final day of the season to force a one-game playoff. That was the notorious game in which light-hitting Yankees shortstop Bucky Dent hit a three-run homer over the Green Monster to help propel New York into the American League Championship Series and ultimately the World Series.

An anonymous fan summed up the season when he murmured, "They killed our fathers and now the sons of [guns] are coming after us."

The new owners then began even more cost cutting, in the process losing the greatest Sox hurler of the era, Luis Tiant, allegedly thirty-eight years old. Team executives Sullivan and LeRoux refused to offer Luis more than a one-year contract. "Before you think about becoming a free agent," LeRoux warned, "think about your age. I hope you have a lot of money in the bank."

The strong-arm tactics offended the proud Tiant. "After what I'd done all those years, bringing in more people than ever into the ball-park every time I pitched, here and away, they said they only wanted to give me a year. And I said, 'No. I want two years.' They said, 'No, but you come to spring training [on a one-year contract] and [if] you make it, we'll give you another year.'"

Instead Tiant went to Boston's archrival Yankees—on a two-year contract.

"The Yankees called me, and they were the only team [to offer a free agent contract], and they offered me two years. And, you know, it was sad because after all those years [the Sox] treated me like that. It was a tough situation but I didn't have any other choice."

Carl Yastrzemski summed up everybody's feelings by declaring,

"When they let Luis Tiant go to New York, they tore out our heart and soul."

More mismanagement was soon to follow, when Zimmer prevailed over common sense, convincing the Sox to jettison Bill Lee following the heartbreaking 1978 season. Lee was sent packing to Montreal for Stan Papi, an infielder of no distinguished playing ability. The Spaceman went on to win twenty-five games for the Expos over four years. On the other hand Papi hit a whopping .188 for Boston during a single season before hiking his average to .224 with Detroit in 1980. The deal triggered graffiti in Boston subway stations that posed the rhetorical question, "Who's Stan Papi?"

Lee tried to explain why he and Zimmer, a light-hitting former infielder whose severe injury from a pitch ball ruined a promising career with the Dodgers, didn't get along. "Most managers are lifetime .220 hitters," Lee postulated. "For years, pitchers have been getting those managers out [during their playing careers] seventy-five percent of the time, and that's why they don't like us." Of course, terming your manager a "buffalo" and a "gerbil" didn't help, either.

The 1979 Sox chalked up a record of 91–69, good for third place in the AL East. They registered an 83–77 record the next season, falling to fourth place, triggering Don Zimmer's leave-taking. Former Yankees and Tigers manager Ralph Houk replaced him. Houk was universally considered a "dinosaur" who could no longer relate to the players he managed.

The year 1980 was marked by another Red Sox milestone when in December management failed to offer contracts to Hall of Fame catcher Carlton Fisk and outfielder Fred Lynn on time. The club sent Lynn and shortstop Rick Burleson, who had demanded a big contract, to the Angels in separate deals.

Fisk, however, was another story. The matter hinged on the post-mark on the contract offer, but George Kimball believed that the Red Sox deliberately allowed Fisk to leave. "I did think that not even Haywood was that stupid," he said. "If nothing else, they could simply have altered the date on the office postage meter and it probably would have held up in court.

"I think the organizational feeling was that Fisk's best days—at least as a catcher—were behind him. He might not have been worth what [the Sox would] have had to pay him, but they didn't want to alienate the fans by unceremoniously unloading a loyal New England son. My assumption is that missing the contract deadline was an intentional ploy, not a 'blunder,' and when he did go elsewhere, the hope was that fans would blame greed, Fisk's agent, or the climate of free agency rather than the Sox's penury."

Glenn Stout didn't think that was the case. "I'm not sure if they were smart enough to do that on purpose—to do something procedurally to get rid of someone like that. But you had a bullpen catcher [Sullivan] who'd worked his way up his way to general manager. What's that tell you?"

Fisk's career was in such a sad state he went on to play another thirteen seasons for the Chicago White Sox, set numerous catching records, and would end up enshrined in Cooperstown, although his Hall of Fame plaque depicts him wearing a Red Sox cap.

Boston limped through the next several seasons, fielding credible teams but never able to grasp the brass ring. The years were, however, marked by several additional significant management gaffes. Meanwhile, the Yankees won another division title in 1980 and were the AL champs in 1981, putting them in the postseason five times in the six years since the Red Sox went to the 1975 World Series. Baltimore won the one season (1979) that New York missed.

Then Buddy LeRoux attempted to wrest control of the franchise from partners Jean Yawkey and Haywood Sullivan. What would become known as "Coup LeRoux" occurred on June 6, 1982, just prior to a game that was intended to honor the gravely ill Tony Conigliaro, who had suffered a massive heart attack and later a stroke. (The tragic Tony C. would die in 1990 at the age of forty-five.)

That June afternoon, at 4:42 PM, LeRoux, flanked by former GM O'Connell, strode into the press room at Fenway Park to announce that he and the minority partners were taking over the club. He termed the takeover "a reorganization of internal management."

Immediately after LeRoux's announcement, Sullivan staged his own press conference, to assure the media that he and Jean Yawkey were still in control.

Kimball, formerly of the *Herald*, says he found the entire "Keystone Cops" routine laughable. "To me it unfolded with considerable amusement. It was sort of like [Secretary of State Alexander] Haig revising the Constitution to declare himself 'in charge' after Reagan was shot. I remember a few years later when there was a brief and unsuccessful coup in Russia, [Peter] Gammons's first reaction was 'Did Buddy LeRoux have anything to do with this?'"

Blared the headline in the *Globe*, "Sox owners go to war for control of club."

Dick Bresciani—then responsible for public relations—said it was the biggest nightmare he has ever endured during nearly forty years of employment at Fenway Park. "The timing was tremendously terrible. It was probably the worst day I've ever spent with the Red Sox organization. We were in first place, or tied for first place. We'd just come off a road trip. It was the beginning of June. We were going to be on national television that Monday night—ABC, Howard

Cosell. We had brought in all of Tony Conigliaro's teammates . . . with the Jimmy Fund involved, to help raise money for Tony.

"It was a huge night, a huge event. So to have all of that happen, with special press conferences and all kinds of things that clouded the situation, and injunctions, and who's in charge. It was a terrible situation."

Bresciani said that the management trio significantly disagreed over club operations.

"Buddy was a guy who had certain beliefs in how the club should be run, and certain things he wanted to do," Bresciani said. "And, after his initial good years with Haywood and Mrs. Yawkey, [he] started to differ with them. He wanted to do some things that I guess they didn't believe should be done at that time for whatever reason . . . and they just split so far apart that he decided he should take control of the team and he felt he . . . could gain control of the team. So he decided to make this big announcement."

The squabble ended up in court for nearly a year, with Jean Yawkey and Sullivan ending up the victors. But the public brouhaha remained indicative of just how comedic the Red Sox organization was.

The next significant imbroglio traces its genesis to 1972 when Tommy Harper first joined the team. Harper became upset that an Elks Club in Winter Haven, Florida offered temporary memberships to Red Sox players during spring training each year. The problem was that only *white* players were afforded the complimentary memberships. Larry Whiteside of the *Boston Globe*, the first, full-time black baseball beat reporter in Boston, learned about the matter in 1973, but Harper begged him not to write about it.

Harper rejoined the team in the eighties as a coach, only to find the situation hadn't changed. He then chose to break his silence.

"The Elks Club thing didn't originate with Tommy Harper," Kimball declared. "He was just the first to make a fuss about it. It's probably more significant that it had been going on for so long before it *did* become an issue."

To this day author Glenn Stout remains agog at the way the matter was handled, as Harper was fired by the club following the 1985 season, and the Sox brain trust played dumb. Ultimately Harper won a case before the Massachusetts Commission Against Discrimination. But before he obtained a new coaching job years later with another team he ended up working as an auto mechanic within earshot of Fenway Park.

"Again, it demonstrates just how deeply the institutionalized racism was—that, as late as the 1980s you could be doing something like that, and then be surprised that people might make it an issue," Stout said. "Now it seems so anachronistic that things were ever like that."

Long before that happened, Peter Gammons—then a *Boston Globe* baseball writer—spoke with Red Sox executives about the matter in 1979, and was assured the practice had been stopped. Gammons didn't write the story. According to author Howard Bryant, "[Gammons] believes that taking the Red Sox at their word was one of the most questionable journalistic decisions he would ever make."

The Elks Club fiasco was only the tip of the iceberg, Kimball pointed out. "The Elks was just part of an ongoing situation in Winter Haven. Years prior to that several of us were going to dinner at a local restaurant—I believe Dennis Eckersley was in our party—and I phoned ahead to make a reservation. They told me they didn't take reservations for parties of less than eight, but would seat us first-come, first-served and we could wait at the bar, so we did.

"While our group was waiting at the bar, I saw [Jim] Rice walk in with his wife and kid. The manager met him at the front door, and next thing I knew [Rice] was headed back to the parking lot. When I ran out to ask what had happened, Rice told me they had told him he couldn't get a table that night because he didn't have a reservation.

"Jim left with his family. I went back inside and confronted the manager. Caught in an obvious lie, she tried to claim the real reason they turned Rice away was because he had his kid with him, although there were other children in the place with their parents. We walked out and never went back there again.

"When I spoke with Jim about it the next day he asked me not to write about it. I'm sure he might have felt differently had it happened years later, but at that point he didn't want to be the one who rocked the boat. It took Tommy Harper to do that."

Kimball recalled that the situation in Winter Haven was threatening for a journalist who was decidedly left wing. "For years I often ridiculed the Klan and poked fun at the rednecks in Winter Haven, but since they never saw the *Phoenix* [an underground weekly] down there, the locals didn't take much notice. But then in 1980, my first year with the *Herald*, I nearly got run out of town when they reprinted one such column in the local paper. I was getting death threats and all kinds of [things].

"Nobody was happier than I when the Sox decided to move to Fort Myers, which I reasoned might not be much better but at least it wasn't Winter Haven. Just before the move [Red Sox outfielder] Mike Greenwell, who grew up in North Fort Myers, pulled me aside and warned me, only half-jokingly, that while the ones in Winter Haven might have made threats to do so, 'those rednecks down there [in Fort Myers] *will* shoot you.'"

And so it went.

16

1986 AND
SHAUGHNESSY'S CURSE

Sports Illustrated summed up Boston's heartrending collapse in the 1986 World Series by quoting the first paragraph from Charles Dickens's *A Tale of Two Cities*, "It was the best of times, it was the worst of times . . . it was the epoch of belief, it was the epoch of incredulity . . . it was the spring of hope, it was the winter of despair, we had everything before us, we had nothing before us, we were all going direct to Heaven, we were all going direct the other way."

How appropriate, since the team had the world championship in its grasp or, as many have put it, were "one strike away."

Sox general manager Haywood Sullivan's ineptitude had finally caught up with him, and he had been shuffled aside in 1983, replaced by the well-respected Lou Gorman, formerly an executive with the New York Mets.

Picked by most prognosticators to finish no better than fifth in 1986, Boston, under manager John McNamara, boasted solid pitching with Roger Clemens, Bruce Hurst, Dennis "Oil Can" Boyd, Al Nipper, and Tom Seaver (acquired during the summer but unable to pitch in the Fall Classic due to an injury), and hitting from Jim Rice, Wade Boggs, Bill Buckner, and Dwight Evans. Along with Don Baylor, Dave Henderson, and Tony Armas, this was an arsenal no other American League club could match.

The Sox staged a tremendous come-from-behind victory in the ALCS when, after being on the brink of elimination, they stunned the California Angels. Dave Henderson's two-out home run sparked a comeback after the Red Sox were "one strike away" themselves from being eliminated in five games. They rallied to beat the Angels in seven games and then took the first two games of the 1986 World Series from the New York Mets—on the road.

Boston returned to Fenway only to be trounced mightily, 7–1, and 6–2. The Red Sox held on to defeat the Mets in Game Five, 4–2, sending the Series back to New York, where the unthinkable happened.

Starter Roger Clemens, who had steamrolled the American League all season, had to leave the game when he developed a blister on one finger and then tore a fingernail on another. To this day, it remains disputed whether Clemens asked to be removed or whether McNamara yanked him.

McNamara's questionable managing—failing to have his batters move runners along, failing to send in pinch hitters, failing to substitute defensively—led to the bitter loss that handed the game, and eventually the world championship, to the Mets.

Behind 5–3, with two out in the bottom of the tenth inning, the Mets rallied, as Gary Carter and Kevin Mitchell hit singles. Ray Knight singled in Carter. McNamara pulled pitcher Calvin Schiraldi, who had come in for Clemens in the eighth inning, replacing him with Bob Stanley. Stanley, the only pitcher remaining from Boston's 1978 meltdown, promptly threw a wild pitch that allowed Mitchell to cross the plate and tie the score.

Mookie Wilson then hit a ground ball to first baseman Bill Buckner. The ball skipped under his glove, allowing Knight to score from second to win the game. Buckner, who had played hurt all season, was inexplicably still in the lineup, despite McNamara's routinely replacing him in late innings with the more defensively capable Dave Stapleton.

Buckner was later forced to move his family from Massachusetts after being harassed so much about his miscue.

At the end of the game, Sox owner Jean Yawkey leaned over to Gorman and hissed, "Do you understand what I'm telling you? Your manager cost us the world championship."

Game Seven was another anticlimax. Left-hander Bruce Hurst started for Boston, but was ineffective, as were Boston's relief pitchers. Temperamental southpaw hurler Dennis "Oil Can" Boyd was slated to pitch but McNamara opted to start Hurst after a day's rain. Boyd was heartbroken. "I wanted the call, but I didn't get [it]," he sobbed after the Sox fell, 8–5. The mercurial Boyd never fully recovered from the snub. (He repeatedly ran afoul of the Boston brass, which had forced him into counseling during the season.)

"You knew the ending," declared the *Baltimore Sun*. "You just didn't know how. They are the Red Sox . . . Just as Hamlet dies every night, the Red Sox die every time they take the stage."

The 1986 World Series proved to be Boston's last hurrah in the Fall Classic under the Yawkey regime that spanned nearly sixty-nine years. In four World Series—1946, 1967, 1975, and 1986—the Sox fell in seven games.

|||||

True to form, the Red Sox followed their World Series appearance with a lackluster season, and failed to contend in 1987. Boyd, who was 16–10 in 1986, won exactly one game. During spring training an arrest warrant for Boyd was issued after he failed to return several pornographic videos he had rented, prompting the press to dub the affair "Can's Film Festival."

Catcher Rich Gedman, who filed for free agency, found himself frozen out of a job due to collusion between club owners, who would pay a stiff price for their actions. (Owners would later be forced to pay for working together to keep free agents from changing teams during the mid-eighties.) The Worcester, Massachusetts native and former All-Star would remain in Boston but never be an effective major league hitter again.

Roger Clemens, the AL's 1986 Cy Young Award winner and Most Valuable Player, held out following his 24–4 season, and opened 1987 with a 4–6 record, though he did rebound to finish 20–9 and win his second straight Cy Young. Stanley posted an overall 4–15 record.

Meanwhile, Jean Yawkey began leaning on long-time aide John Harrington, freezing out Sullivan, and complicating Gorman's job.

McNamara was let go in mid-1988 after the team was embarrassed by revelations involving All-Star third baseman Wade Boggs. Boggs, married with children, had for years traveled with a girlfriend, Margo Adams. Adams sued Boggs for palimony. The perception was that McNamara had lost control of the club. And being tied for fourth place, nine games out in mid-July, cut down on the complaints about his termination.

Another grizzled baseball veteran, Joe Morgan of suburban Walpole, was named manager. Morgan was initially viewed as an interim skipper, but the team reeled off nineteen wins in twenty games, combined with the press hailing "Morgan Magic," prompted the club to drop the "interim."

Almost immediately Morgan alienated slugger Jim Rice, who was on the down side of his career. He dropped Rice to seventh in the batting order. Then, during the club's seventh consecutive win, the manager sent light-hitting substitute shortstop Spike Owen to the plate in place of Rice. Enraged, Rice pulled Morgan into the runway leading to the clubhouse. Returning to the dugout, the furious manager declared, "I'm the manager of this nine!" Rice was suspended for three games.

"Morgan magic" quickly dissipated in the postseason, with the team falling apart and being swept by Oakland. The malaise continued throughout 1989 in spite of the highest payroll—$19 million—in the American League. Players got hurt, under performed, or simply imploded. Many were buried on the bench or in the bullpen. It was typical Red Sox.

Despite a half-hearted effort during 1990, Boston emerged as the division champions, but Boston was eliminated in the playoffs when the team again dropped four straight games to Oakland. Roger Clemens threw a tantrum in the second inning of the clinching game; he was ejected, along with Morgan and second baseman Marty Barrett.

|||||

Dan Shaughnessy's fairy tale *The Curse of the Bambino* was published in 1990. Shaughnessy appropriated the concept from a *New York Times* column entitled "Babe Ruth Curse Strikes Again" written during the 1986 World Series. Shaughnessy termed trading Babe Ruth "baseball's original sin," and blamed every miscue, mistake and misfortune the franchise ever incurred on his tall tale.

It was easy to buy into such a fantasy, said former Sox hurler Bill Lee. "There's nothing in the world like the fatalism of the Red Sox fans, which has been bred into them for generations by that little green ballpark, and *the wall*, and by a team that keeps trying to win by hitting everything out of sight and just out-bombarding everyone else in the league. All this makes Boston fans a little crazy, and I'm sorry for them."

The idea of a curse took root amongst the casual fan, so much so that many of the fallacies propagated in the book were regurgitated in the script of the movie *Fever Pitch*, which centered on a romance involving a rabid Sox fan. The fictional fan was the character that spewed those myths. (The screenwriters, the Farrelly brothers, are Rhode Island natives.)

"In its essence, of course," asserted *Boston Globe* sportswriter Tony Massarotti in his book, *Dynasty*, "the curse was nothing more than a clever gimmick concocted by Dan Shaughnessy."

Added pitcher Curt Schilling, who perhaps has been pilloried in Shaughnessy's *Boston Globe* columns as much as Ted Williams was in Dave Egan's, "The Curse has served as nothing more than one man's cash cow, period."

Long after the book's publication, Shaughnessy would try to shrug off the theory, stating, "The Curse of the Bambino is a handy expression for all the woes endured by the Sox and their fans over the last three-quarters of a century. The Curse helps us explain the unexplainable. It's superstition over science, a tidy excuse . . . The Curse is part of Boston folklore and serves to soothe citizens of the Red Sox Nation when bad things happen to good teams."

Shaughnessy ignored repeated requests for interviews for this book.

The Curse of the Bambino is now in its twenty-first printing, and despite several revised editions, it remains rife with glaring errors.

Shaughnessy contends that Harry Frazee left an estate of $50,000 when he died; that Tom Yawkey was once prepared to hire Babe Ruth to manage the Red Sox (instead of acquiring player-manager Joe Cronin); and that Yawkey didn't own "Pee Wee" Reese outright while the young infielder was toiling in Louisville. He identifies Ed Barrow as the business manager of the Yankees, not the club's president and general manager; he misrepresents many matters concerning the Boston franchise; and he glosses over the bigotry that permeated the Red Sox during the Yawkey ownership. Moreover, Shaughnessy cites no sources whatsoever.

Even worse in the eyes of many diehard Red Sox fans, Shaughnessy seemed to revel in Red Sox Nation's misery. In the wake of Boston's 2004 world championship, he was quoted as declaring, "The Curse isn't over until I say it is! I wrote the book!"

Shaughnessy told the Boston *Phoenix* that his book prompted many Red Sox fans to despise him.

"I think it's hard to know why one is singled out, or why one attracts a particular amount of venom," Shaughnessy said. "But I think *The Curse of the Bambino* had a lot to do with it. People think that meant I'd either invented the dark history of the Red Sox or was hoping they would lose to keep it going."

According to the writers of *Mind Game*, "The truth is that for nearly a century the Red Sox never found the courage, or the competence, to change things that could have been changed. Boston has been victimized by some of the worst owners and administrators in sports history. There is no Curse of the Bambino, unless the curse is construed to visit on its victims astonishing incompetence, complacency and bigotry."

Red Sox designated hitter David Ortiz scoffed at the idea. "There never was no . . . curse. The only curse there was is 'The Curse of the Big Papi.' And that was on the Yankees."

Boston third baseman Mike Lowell, the 2007 World Series Most Valuable Player, declared, "It's about time somebody set the record straight."

Even ESPN's Peter Gammons ridiculed the idea, writing that the Curse was, "a silly, mindless gimmick that is as stupid as the wave."

At this writing, *The Curse of the Bambino* can be purchased for as little as one cent on Amazon.com.

17

MANAGERIAL MISCUES

Again, under the auspices of the Yawkeys—in this case, Jean Yawkey—the Sox switched gears and went back to spending big bucks on talent, as opposed to looking to the club's farm system to produce young, quality players.

General manager Lou Gorman made what were among his worst player deals during his tenure with the Sox in the wake of the 1990 season, signing free agents Danny Darwin, Jack Clark, and Matt Young to lucrative contracts.

Darwin, who won a grand total of thirty-four games over four seasons for Boston, became, at the time, the highest paid player in Red Sox history. Clark spent two years in Boston before retiring, hitting thirty-three home runs but striking out 220 times. Young was even worse, amassing a record of 3–11 and appearing in only twenty-four games over two years. While with the Red Sox he lost a no-hitter—on walks.

Previously, Gorman had sent future All-Stars Brady Anderson and Curt Schilling to the Baltimore Orioles for pitcher Mike Boddicker. Boddicker, although winning thirty-nine games for the Red Sox over three years, bolted as soon as he could. Schilling won 163 games and was named the co-MVP of the 2001 World Series before rejoining the Boston organization. Anderson would become a three-time All-Star, hit fifty home runs in 1996, and steal 315 bases during his lengthy career.

Gorman also sent top minor league prospect Jeff Bagwell to the Houston Astros for journeyman reliever Larry Andersen on August 30, 1990 while Boston was enmeshed in a race for the AL East title. Andersen finished the season with the Sox, pitching in only fifteen games, then left for free agency, a move he clearly had telegraphed when acquired by Boston. Bagwell went on to be named National League Rookie of the Year in 1991 and National League MVP in 1994, and made four All-Star teams before retiring in 2005. His 2,314 hits, 449 home runs, and career batting average of .297 give him a decent chance to be elected to the Hall of Fame when he becomes eligible.

Gorman still defends the trade. "None of our talent evaluators [properly factored in] Bagwell's power . . . the report was that he couldn't play third base . . .   It also said that he had hit for average only—not for power."

Gorman voiced a strange philosophy when he declared, "Everything goes against the Red Sox. They're star-crossed lovers in a sense. The wrong thing always happens to the Red Sox."

Joe Morgan, who took the blame for the club's 1991 mediocre performance, was fired and replaced by minor league manager and former Red Sox third baseman Butch Hobson. Still sporting the highest payroll in the American League, the Sox limped to an 84–78 finish.

Jean Yawkey suffered a stroke in February 1992. She died six days later, leaving the club in the hands of John Harrington. Harrington controlled two of the three votes to govern the team against

Sullivan's single vote. Sullivan ended up selling his shares back to the Yawkey Trust.

The Sox continued to limp along. The front office slashed the team payroll, and allowed All-Star third baseman Wade Boggs, who had led the American League in batting five times, to go to the hated Yankees via free agency.

In 1993, Harrington replaced general manager Gorman with thirty-five-year-old Dan Duquette. Previously Duquette served as the general manager of the Montreal Expos, where he had excelled in picking up low cost cast-offs to maintain the club's roster while building a strong farm system.

Many wondered if Harrington hired Duquette because the organization intended to operate as a small market team, without the resources to keep its stars. "Duquette," wrote author Peter Golenbock, "had run a bargain-basement operation in Montreal, selling off high-paid players and signing subs from the slap-heap of rejects, over-the-hillers, suspects, and never-weres."

Certainly a look at the Red Sox payroll during the initial five years of the Duquette era indicates that Boston's front office indeed *was* looking upon the franchise as a small market operation.

"I think he did okay in recognizing the talent, but Harrington was trying to spread this fiction that the Red Sox were a small market team," Glenn Stout declared. "They weren't, but [management] tried to cry poor mouth all the time and part of that stance was to let big money guys go, and trash them on the way out."

Sox management was entirely unimaginative: eighty-one home games a year. Period. No fan fests, no special occasions, no concerts, no nothing! No wonder the front office was altogether prone to handwringing and crying poor mouth.

Like other Red Sox GMs before him, Duquette quickly became

the face of the franchise, but his tight-lipped and secretive ways in freezing out the press brought few accolades.

"In general, I think it was unfortunate that he was put in position to be the public face of the franchise, a position he was not equipped for," said Stout. "Of course, he helped hire some people who could have filled that role, but his managers weren't equipped to do so either."

Despite the fact that Duquette made some significant deals—most notably obtaining Pedro Martinez, Jason Varitek, Derek Lowe, and Manny Ramirez—and obtained several blue-chip ballplayers such as Nomar Garciaparra via the amateur draft, he also forced superstars Roger Clemens and Mo Vaughn to leave, famously declaring that Clemens was "in the twilight" of his career.[21]

Many pundits have theorized that Duquette simply felt no affinity toward Clemens and Vaughn because he hadn't had anything to do with acquiring them. "I think that's natural, to a degree," baseball historian Stout agreed. "You want to win with *your* guys—and [Duquette] had to denigrate [Clemens and Vaughn] to make letting them go seem inevitable."

At first, Harrington maintained strong ties to the media, according to former *Herald* beat writer George Kimball.

"Duquette was secretive to the point of being paranoid, but then John Harrington became that way the more imperious [Duquette's] regime became," asserted Kimball. "When I first knew [Harrington] he was almost friendly and gregarious, but he and Dan both became so inaccessible that when you got a one-on-one with them it was almost like being granted a papal audience, and they were so guarded that when they let something slip, you know it hadn't been an accident."

---

21 Clemens went on to win another 162 games (and four Cy Young Awards) for the Toronto Blue Jays, the Houston Astros—and the New York Yankees. His name, however, has come up in regards to performance-enhancing drugs.

Another Duquette blind spot was public relations, and the team was routinely criticized for refusing to answer even the most basic—and banal—questions posed by reporters.

"Duquette was as paranoid as they come," Boston-based sports commentator John Molori said. "He had total control over media coverage and his interviews were as monotone and meaningless as any in history. [However,] Duquette did a lot of good things for the Red Sox. He opened up the Latino and Asian markets, and signed Manny Ramirez, but his [administration] had no concept of public relations and using the media to improve the organization."

As the team crawled through the nineties with very few high notes Duquette was guilty of a half-dozen miscues for every successful move he made. Ironically, Duquette was much like the very successful current Red Sox general manager, Theo Epstein, but with several blind spots, ultimately dooming the Duke's efforts on the part of the club. In *Mind Game*, Baseball Prospectus aptly summed up Duquette's regime by terming Duquette a "failed Epstein prototype."

Duquette's initial season proved to be a disaster. A player strike that ran from August 1994 until April 1995 created considerable fan disenchantment. By the time the strike ended the 1994 season, the Sox had a horrendous 54–61 record. During the strike, Butch Hobson was fired, and former Texas manager Kevin Kennedy came aboard. Sox payroll was $36.3 million—seventh in the American League, outspent by Kansas City, among others!

During the 1994 season Duquette shuffled forty-six players—including twenty-three pitchers—on and off the roster. "As he picked through baseball's pile of discards," wrote Stout and Johnson in *Red Sox Century*, "he ran players in and out of Boston almost every week. To his supporters, he was a genius. To others it appeared he was throwing so much up against the wall that some of it inevitably had to stick."

Attempts to obtain reliever John Wetteland, starting pitcher Kevin Appier and outfielder Sammy Sosa were nullified when the Players Association won a court ruling that negated the deals.

With Kennedy at the helm Boston roared back in 1995, winning the divisional title behind the hitting of first baseman Mo Vaughn and shortstop John Valentin. And after a slow start, outfielder Jose Canseco became an offensive threat.

Pitchers Tim Wakefield and Erik Hansen combined for twenty-nine wins. Roger Clemens, who was injured during the abbreviated spring training, notched only ten victories, with a 4.18 ERA. Then Duquette obtained closer Rick Aguilera from the Twins. Aguilera pulled a hamstring during Boston's first playoff game against Cleveland (which the Sox lost), and obtained free agency after the season concluded with Boston being swept in the division series (a new round of play that resulted with the Red Sox losing their thirteenth straight postseason game). Aguilera ended up re-signing with Minnesota, a move he previously announced before going to the Sox. Boston's payroll of $38.1 million was the second lowest in the AL East, although fifth league-wide.

After Mo Vaughn, who was the AL MVP in a tight vote, signed a three-year, $18.6 million contract in 1996, both Roger Clemens and Jose Canseco publicly ripped Duquette for his hardball contract negotiation methods. Vaughn, who had lost front office support after an altercation at a Boston nightclub during 1995, blasted Duquette for "dissing" Clemens. Kennedy took the players' sides, too.

In the wake of a desultory 85–77 club record in 1996, Clemens left the Sox as a free agent and Canseco was traded to Oakland. Duquette also fired Kennedy, replacing him with former Toronto manager Jimy Williams after being rebuffed by two other field bosses with more credible résumés. The *Boston Herald* topped its story on the change by asking, "Sox Fans Say Jimy Who?"

The niggardly Boston management had only jacked up the 1996 payroll by a paltry $400,000, with player costs ranking at seventh league-wide, but trailing even Seattle, Cleveland, and Texas, among others.

Not only did the American League entry in New York grab the pennant, but the Yankees were world champions that year; won the AL wild card in 1997 (they'd also won it in 1995); then took both the pennant *and* the World Series from 1998–2000, in addition to the AL title in 2001. The Yankees' dynasty was again in full flower.

To replace the departed Clemens and Canseco, Duquette signed sore-armed lefty Steve Avery and problematic infielder Wilfredo Cordero. While Clemens rolled to his fourth Cy Young Award in Toronto, Avery posted a mediocre record of 6–6 with a 6.57 ERA. Cordero, long coveted by Duquette, was arrested in midseason after allegedly clubbing his wife with a telephone. Vaughn also ran into more trouble, this time at a Cleveland strip club. Cordero was suspended for the remainder of the season, while Vaughn never recovered the widespread respect he once enjoyed.

The Sox stumbled to a fourth place finish in 1997, with a record of 78–84. The single bright spot was rookie shortstop Nomar Garciaparra, who hit .306 and was named the American League Rookie of the Year. Although the Sox increased player payroll by $2.1 million, the franchise was ninth in the league, outspent by, among others, Seattle, Anaheim, Baltimore, and Cleveland.

Meanwhile, Vaughn remained involved in a protracted contract dispute with the intractable Duquette. Since the general manager spent in the vicinity of $150 million on contracts during 1997, Vaughn was insulted at the treatment he received. Things would only grow worse. "Either the club wants to pay a fair-market deal or they don't," declared the big first baseman.

While the rancorous negations with Vaughn played out publicly, Duquette shipped two minor leaguers to Montreal for the National League Cy Young Award winner, Pedro Martinez. It was a stroke of genius. Flying into Logan Airport following the trade, Martinez was greeted by hundreds of fans. "That night," Martinez declared, "I said to someone, 'I think I love Boston already.'" Indeed, the city's long-suffering fans would quickly take the slight right-hander to heart.

And with reason. From 1998 through 2004, Martinez posted a sterling 117–37 record, and only once had an earned run average over 3.00.

Duquette's downfall was his constant tinkering with the Red Sox roster and his inept handling of both the fans and the media. Among his worst acquisitions were outfielders Dante Bichette, Carl Everett, and Shane Mack, pitchers Avery, Dustin Hermanson, and Bryce Florie, and infielders Tony Clark, Rico Brogna, and Mike Lansing. Everett played a pivotal role in Jimy Williams' termination, as Duquette refused to back the manager when Everett repeatedly failed to show up for workouts, physical therapy, and games. (Everett was also suspended for ten days after head-butting an umpire.)

In addition, Duquette lost two blue-chip draft picks, Pat Burrell and Mark Teixeira, when he tried to strong-arm them into signing contracts. Both have had All-Star careers. Only two of his picks have played a critical role with Boston: Kevin Youkilis and Nomar Garciaparra. A third draft pick, who might have developed into an impact player, infielder Shea Hillenbrand, proved troublesome and was traded away by Duquette's successor, Theo Epstein. Duquette's trade options proved limited after he alienated many general managers; more than half of his seventy trades were made with only eight clubs.

Boston registered a pathetic 78–84 record in 1997, after Clemens and outfielder Mike Greenwell left the team.

IIIIII

Pedro pitched masterfully in 1998, winning nineteen games after signing a six-year, $75 million contract, an amount that refuted Harrington's long-time claim that the Sox were a "small market" club. John Valentin also signed another lucrative contract, as did manager Jimy Williams—and Duquette himself.

Those signings sent Vaughn over the edge, but on opening day he hit a walk-off grand slam, prompting the crowd to chant, "Sign Mo now!"

The Sox's second place finish with a record of 92–70, qualified them for the AL wild card. After winning the first game against Cleveland—ending the consecutive game postseason losing streak that traced its genesis to the 1986 World Series—the Sox dropped the next three contests. Martinez begged to start Game Four, but was denied.

"It won't matter [what the Red Sox do]," remarked an angry Vaughn prior to the playoffs. "I'm going to test the waters. I owe it to myself." He left in November, signing with the Angels for $85 million, prompting Duquette to sign Jose Offerman, who turned out to be another notable flop.

A patchwork club, led by Martinez performed above all expectations in 1999. Ignoring the availability of several quality starting pitchers, Duquette instead signed the fading Kent Mercker and Rod Beck, along with designated hitter Butch Huskey, who hit .266 with seven home runs.

Pedro Martinez posted his best regular season ever with a 23–4 mark, striking out 313 and crafting a miniscule ERA of 2.07, but at mid-year the club dumped pitcher Mark Portugal, second on the team in innings pitched.

The Sox won the Division Series over Cleveland; they then fell to the Yankees in the ALCS.

In the off season, Duquette sought a left-handed pitcher, signing Jeff Fassero, who posted an 8–8 record and a 4.78 ERA in 2000.

The club had announced plans for a new Fenway Park during the 1999 season, but the plan was rife with problems, one of which was that the land acquisition would require an investment of $500 million, money that the franchise didn't have. (Curiously enough, the Web site and brochure for the new stadium featured an artist's rendering that sported five infielders.)

The fact is that under the Yawkey Trust (as with Tom and Jean) there were no well-perceived incentives to improve—or even clean up—Fenway Park. Even routine maintenance was consistently ignored. The amenities were horrible—and the Trust wasn't about to sink a single dime into improving the stadium. Instead, they wanted the public to underwrite New Fenway Park.

After a fast start in 2000, Boston bottomed out by dropping a late-season series to the Yankees. And although the Yankees faltered in September, the Sox still couldn't catch them.

Duquette tried to force first baseman Rico Brogna to go on the disabled list even though he wasn't injured, yet another maneuver that soured everyone on Duquette. He also released the popular Mike Stanley in midseason, angering the players. "I think it's horrible for our ballclub," said Garciaparra. "[Stanley] has been such a great leader." Left unsaid was the fact that Stanley had previously been on the disabled list for three weeks, even though *he* wasn't hurt.

After Duquette was publicly criticized by second baseman Jeff Frye, Frye was shipped to Colorado, prompting *Globe* columnist

Shaughnessy to deliver one of his best lines. "Duquette must have majored in Machiavelli at Amherst College."

On October 6, John Harrington finally threw in the towel and announced the team would be put on the open market to the highest bidder.

There *was* a light at the end of the tunnel after all.

18

NEW MILLENNIUM, NEW DAWN

Although John Harrington swore a new ownership would be in place by the start of the 2001 season, that proved to be as much of a pipe dream as "New Fenway Park" was. He vowed to sell the franchise to "a diehard Red Sox fan from New England."

Perhaps Stout and Johnson put it best in *Red Sox Century* by declaring, "over the next year and a half . . . the sale process would not just be protracted, but nearly proctological." No more apt words have ever been uttered.

To his credit, Dan Duquette didn't sit still. He signed free agent outfielder Manny Ramirez to an eight-year, $160 million contract. Aside from the deal for Pedro Martinez, it would be Duquette's most shining moment as general manager.

Having Ramirez—a pure hitter of the first order—bat behind Nomar Garciaparra, who hit .372 in 2000, the Sox would feature two very potent batters. And the club brain trust was hoping that Carl Everett would straighten out, but that simply wasn't going to happen. After Everett was suspended for skipping a bus trip during spring training, Garciaparra suffered a split tendon in his wrist. Ramirez also immediately became problematic, balking at shifting from right field to left field, and demanding to serve as the designated hitter. Then he developed shoulder problems and was sidelined.

Even after Duquette left the franchise in February 2002 (after the change in ownership took effect), he continued to defend his handling of the Everett fiasco. "The best interest of the team is more important than that of the individual," he told author David Laurila. "In the case of Carl Everett, we had a multi-year financial commitment to a player that was guaranteed. Jimy wanted him off the team, and Carl didn't want to play here anymore. One of the tenets of the Yawkey owner-ship was that the team was not going to release players with multi-year financial commitments; either we were going to keep a player on our roster and play him, or we were going to trade him."

After Martinez was injured in June 2001, the club fell behind the Yankees, who were heading toward their fourth consecutive World Series. Garciaparra rejoined the team in late July, with Martinez soon to follow. Duquette sent pitcher Tomo Ohka to the Expos for closer Ugueth Urbina, but inexplicably Jimy Williams refused to use Urbina in that role, relying instead on Derek Lowe and Rod Beck.

On August 16 Duquette fired Williams, hiring pitching coach Joe Kerrigan to fill the managing post. "Joe knows our players, he knows our team and he knows our market," declared Duquette. "Over the last ten days, I just really didn't like the look of the team. It looked to me like everyone was standing around waiting for the club to make a change."

Duquette later expounded on his relationship with Williams. "Jimy did a good job for us, especially in 1999. We had some issues where I thought the interests of the organization were more impor-tant than his perspectives as manager, but those things are going to happen. But it was never a situation where I dictated what he did. As manager, he was in charge of the team, the clubhouse and the lineup. Jimy had as much autonomy as any manager in the business during his tenure in Boston." Many who heard that just shook their heads in disbelief, especially considering the ongoing soap opera with the supremely difficult Carl Everett.

When Duquette then demoted pitching coach John Cumberland to bullpen coach, Garciaparra reacted angrily, saying, "That's why nobody wants to [expletive] come play here." Duquette then infuriated Martinez when, after two months on the disabled list, Pedro learned that he had a torn rotator cuff, yet the club had sent him back into action. Duquette upset the team when he claimed the pitcher wasn't really hurt. Ultimately, though, Martinez was shut down for the remainder of the deteriorating season.

The 2001 season turned out just the way most others had under the Yawkey regime, although Duquette remained in charge, paying $30 million for first baseman Tony Clark and center fielder Johnny Damon. Only the Damon deal would bear fruit; Clark hit an anemic .207 and just three home runs in his lone year with the club. But the Sox finally jettisoned Everett by sending him to Texas. The Sox met the Yankees in a late season series and were swept in the three-game set. With that, Boston had lost eight straight games; then the club lost three more in a row to the hard-charging New Yorkers during the second week of September.

IIIII

The story of the sale of the franchise is both torturous and convoluted. After obtaining numerous bids for the club, Harrington announced in November that the list had been whittled down to six, and the team's price tag was estimated at more than $600 million.

The finalists were real estate developer Frank McCourt, who later bought the Los Angeles Dodgers; cable TV mogul Charles Dolan; concessionaire Joe O'Donnell; financier Miles Prentice; Boston Bruins owner Jeremy Jacobs; and a hybrid group headed by Florida Marlins owner John Henry that included television producer Tom Werner, ski magnate Les Otten, the New York Times Company, and former U.S. Senator George Mitchell.

John Henry was a billionaire commodities trader, a self-made man, who had devised several mathematical models to successfully predict the futures of such commodities as soybeans and pork bellies. An avid baseball fan, Henry had owned the Marlins for several years, but it was a losing proposition. He had been searching around for another club to buy; when former Baltimore and San Diego executive Larry Lucchino approached him about joining forces with the Werner-Otten group to buy the Red Sox, Henry jumped at the chance.

Shortly thereafter, Major League Baseball approved the sale of the Florida Marlins to Montreal owner Jeffrey Loria. To assuage the Boston locals, particularly an extremely hostile media that openly backed the Joe O'Donnell/Steve Karp partnership (Karp is a mall developer), John Henry offered O'Donnell and Karp a piece of the pie for roughly $250 million. But the two men backed out, leaving Henry's group intact. Ultimately, the Henry consortium paid in the vicinity of $720 million, including the establishment of a so-called "super charity."

John Molori, who has covered Boston sports since 1991, said taking sides was understandable, but insisted the sale to the Henry group wasn't a foregone conclusion. "I would not call the sale a 'bag job.' Clearly, Major League Baseball is going to choose and support any ownership that will improve and increase revenue for a big market team. And it has worked out great for the team, city and league."

Baseball historian Stout demurred, taking the position that the deal was in fact a "bag job," arranged by MLB commissioner Bud Selig and John Harrington. "I think they knew way ahead of time that [the sale to the Henry-led group] was going to take place. It was a setup."

Ownership of Major League Baseball clubs is a closed society, Stout said. "Baseball doesn't and didn't want individuals to buy baseball teams outright. They wanted bigger money and wanted to tap into Wall Street. It's syndicate baseball, which goes back to Ban Johnson. They let [Henry] do it, but like so much of the stuff it's circumstantial. How can you own part of two teams simultaneously? The [Steve] Karps and Joe O'Donnells weren't those kind of people." (Henry also owned a small percentage of Yankees stock at the time of the Red Sox sale.)

Even in 2008, writer Tony Massarotti asserted the sale may have been suspect. "Looking back, I'm not sure our suspicions about the sale *process* were unfounded. Let's not confuse the issues. Regardless of whether Henry and Co. got control of the Red Sox through some sort of 'favorable' treatment, the fact is that they have proven quite capable at running the franchise and turning the Red Sox into a power for years to come."

And O'Donnell had some harsh words after the sale, declaring, "It was such a screw job. Everybody in town knew it was a screw job. But Selig wanted these small market guys to get the team."

After the Karp/O'Donnell and Henry consortium merger fell through, Karp and O'Donnell withdrew their independent offer for the franchise. Not exactly the makings of a "bag job."

The other top bidders had problems with their bids. Charles Dolan violated the rules of the bidding process; before backing out

Karp and O'Donnell were balking at ponying up their entire bid up front; and Miles Prentice didn't have all his financing in place.

The Yawkey regime, ineptly running the club since 1933, was—finally and mercifully—history.

The Henry group took over franchise operations in February 2002. They fired Duquette later that month and Kerrigan a week later. Assistant general manager Mike Port was named interim GM and career minor league manager Grady Little, most recently a bench coach with Cleveland, replaced Kerrigan. The appointment of Little as field manager was met with overwhelming approval by the players, who broke into applause when he first entered the clubhouse. "Buckle up," Little said. "We're getting ready to have a good ride."

Red Sox Nation's expectations couldn't have been any higher. The Henry regime decidedly proved "fan friendly," with Ramirez, Martinez, and Garciaparra, among others, greeting fans as they arrived at Fenway for opening day. "I cleared a path for Manny to get to the gate," said Trot Nixon. "I was like a fullback."

The Henry consortium publicly announced that they wanted to save Fenway Park, putting an architect on staff to determine how the park's capacity could be increased from its inadequate 33,000 seats.

The 2002 season's starting rotation was solid, and Derek Lowe threw a no-hitter on April 27. But after a fast start, the Sox lost Manny Ramirez for a month after he broke a finger on May 11. Despite the loss of Ramirez, the Sox posted a 25–6 record on the road in the first two-plus months of the season. The squad slumped when it returned to Fenway for several interleague series, first losing a three-game set to the world champion Arizona Diamondbacks. Curt Schilling beat the Red Sox 3–2, in the second game of the series, after which a fan shouted to Schilling, "Wish you were with the Red

Sox!" The big right-hander retorted, "I was." "Please come back!" urged the fan. Two years later he would.

Although the Sox took two of three games from the Rockies, they lost two of three to Atlanta, beat San Diego two of three, and then dropped a three-game set against the Dodgers.

After going 5–10 in interleague play, they fell out of first place, dropping a half game behind the Yankees. They then dropped another three games to Atlanta, finishing the month of June with a grim 10–16 record.[22]

The Sox finished the first half of 2002 with a record of 52–33, but after the All-Star break, the team played .500 ball. The players were also troubled by a potential strike, but, worried about its effects, the Players Association hammered out a new agreement with the owners.

As the team faltered, Dan Shaughnessy lobbied for manager Grady Little's termination, indicative of the writer's "sky is falling" approach. *Globe* reporter Michael Holley wrote that the blame shouldn't be directed at Little, calling on Sox president Larry Lucchino to hire a general manager, "who can remix and resuscitate the Sox." For his part, Little expressed disappointment. "When you have a ballclub like we have, and you say you want to be in contention to win the American League East, and if not, you want to be in contention to be a wild card team, you just can't go out there and let pop-ups that hang in the air for twenty seconds fall. You can't miss

22 On July 5, 2002, Red Sox Nation went into mourning when the incomparable Ted Williams passed away from heart failure at the age of eighty-three. In a macabre twist Williams's son, John Henry Williams, shipped his father's remains to a cryonics lab in Arizona. At least one of John Henry Williams's sisters would accuse the young man – who made a living off of selling his father's memorabilia—of having Ted sign a blank sheet of paper on which John Henry Williams wrote the request to freeze the older Williams' body. The oil-stained piece of paper had been in the younger Williams's car trunk. The situation proved so disquieting that Red Sox principal owner John Henry insisted that he be identified as "John W. Henry" during the memorial service for the fallen slugger.

the opportunity to turn double plays that are routine. You can't forget to cover first. You can't have a guy hit a double with no outs and not make something happen. It's a lot of little things. When we win, it's a ballclub effort. When you lose, it's a ballclub effort too."

By the close of the season the Sox had posted a record of 93–69, certainly not a dismal mark, although they failed to make the playoffs for the third straight year.

As chief executive officer, Lucchino wasn't one to stand pat, first hiring statistics expert Bill James as an adviser. He then set his sights on Toronto general manager J. P. Ricciardi, whom the Blue Jays quickly signed to a contract extension. He then pursued Oakland GM Billy Beane, who backed out of a deal at the last minute.

Lucchino turned to someone in-house, a young man recommended by Ricciardi, Beane and San Diego general manager, Kevin Towers—twenty-eight-year-old Red Sox assistant general manager, Theo Epstein. It was a stroke of genius. "It will be clear to you over time that this is a gifted person with a real opportunity to have a profound impact on this franchise," said Lucchino.

"We've selected him for his intellect; we've selected him for his character. We've selected him for his passion for baseball, his knowledge and history and passion for the Red Sox, for the breadth of his work experience, and for the ability to bring people together and work together in new and innovative ways. We think Theo Epstein has a chance to be an outstanding long-term general manager of the Red Sox."

The Yale-educated Epstein, grandson of the co-author of the screenplay for the movie *Casablanca*, is the son of the head of Boston University's creative writing program. Subsequently an embarrassed Epstein had to tell his proud parents not to distribute any more baby pictures to the press.

Epstein had interned with the Baltimore Orioles, and then went to San Diego with Lucchino, where he served as director of baseball operations. When Lucchino took over as Sox president, he hired Epstein as assistant GM. "The Red Sox are very much in my blood," said Epstein, who grew up in Brookline, Massachusetts. "I grew up second-guessing Red Sox general managers."

He promised to bring a world championship to the thirsty city. "It's going to happen. We're going to become a championship organization and win a World Series." Indeed from the very beginning, Epstein's playbook was composed of three parts, according to Seth Mnookin, an author who had unprecedented access to the Red Sox organization for more than a year.

"When he was named general manager in 2002," wrote Mnookin, "he set three immediate goals for himself: winning a World Series, rebuilding the team's minor league system, and managing the transition away from the team dominated by the 2004 free agent class."

It only took him two years.

19

A FAILURE TO COMMUNICATE

From *Boston Post* beat writer Paul Shannon to *Globe* columnist Dan Shaughnessy, the press has exerted a disproportional impact upon Red Sox operations, vacillating between serving as the conscience of the franchise and blithely ignoring the warts that the club exhibited.

The press has always played an active—and often detrimental—role in franchise operations. As far back as 1907, when Nick Flatley of the *Boston Journal*, in an article announcing Boston's new nickname (the Boston Pilgrims) failed to include details concerning the jettisoning of the five players highlighted in the sub headline, the press has often ignored seminal matters concerning the club. Conversely, the media has often overblown issues that really didn't warrant such coverage.

Eleven years after his 1907 piece, Flatley penned an article for the *Boston American* during the 1918 World Series that detailed the abortive players' strike. Although Flatley widely quoted Ban Johnson, he failed to mention that Johnson was stone drunk when Johnson convinced the players to take the field.

The Boston press bought into Johnson's smear campaign against Harry Frazee, who alienated reporters when he cut off the free food and liquor they'd become accustomed to. He also banned reporters who wrote articles critical of the club.

"The press had been intensely courted by Johnson, and in retrospect it's understandable that the newspapers in town simply picked up Johnson's war cry against Frazee," declared author Richard Johnson. "I think [Frazee] knew it was inevitable that he'd lose the battle to retain control of the team."

After Frazee's sale of Ruth to the Yankees his alienation of the media came back to haunt him—with a vengeance.

"Frazee's mistake—and the cause of the fossilization of his legacy as the man responsible for the media-constructed Curse of the Bambino—had everything to do with his failure to ally himself more strongly with the local press," postulated author Seth Mnookin. "Many of Boston's sportswriters were already friendly with Ban Johnson, and Frazee . . . [and that] gave the city's scribes further reason to line up against him. There was also the lingering suspicion that Frazee was Jewish (he wasn't), a definite black mark in the early-twentieth-century, heavily Irish-Catholic Boston. This wouldn't be the first time the members of Boston's sporting press would take it upon themselves to decide the proper way to run the Red Sox."

Boston's newspapers then took another significant step to pay Frazee back for all his slights—real and imagined—by cutting back their Red Sox coverage. Some barely covered the club during Frazee's last years of ownership. When Frazee sold the club in 1923, the media afforded Bob Quinn kid-glove coverage, a practice that continued after the team was sold to Tom Yawkey.

Stout and Johnson noted Frazee was even slandered after he was in his coffin. "Paul Shannon's obituary of Frazee in the [*Boston*] *Post* is most notorious for its inaccuracies, and he again raised questions over Frazee's religion . . . The [*New York*] *Times* made a particularly egregious error, reporting that Frazee died nearly broke."

Ted Williams probably wouldn't have been forced into volunteering for the military during World War II if it hadn't been for the incessant howling of the press, as Williams had a legitimate deferment. It's quite conceivable that, with the additional five years Williams missed serving in the Navy and Marines, he'd have broken every batting mark ever established.

Perhaps the most enigmatic journalist ever to cover the Red Sox was Dave "The Colonel" Egan, who wrote for the *Boston Daily Record* and the *Boston Advertiser*. Egan repeatedly took unfair swipes at the mercurial Williams. Williams was repeatedly victimized by scurrilous stories that were widely disseminated in the press when the media clearly knew the stories were false.

"Williams was a particular target of the *Boston Record* columnist Dave Egan, who ripped Williams with a style and frequency that would make Dan Shaughnessy blush," wrote Bruce Allen, founder of Boston Sports Media Watch. Allen pointed out that Egan tore into Williams for failing to wear a necktie the day Williams reported for duty during the Korean War. "On the day that Williams was leaving to serve his country and [putting] his life on the line, Egan rips him because he prefers not to wear neckties. [Egan's] worried that America's youth will be tarnished because Ted Williams will not wear a tie."

Yet Egan was also the reporter who wrote the piece that forced general manager Eddie Collins to give tryouts to Jackie Robinson, Sam Jethroe, and Marvin Williams, although the press paid but cursory attention to the affair.

"I don't think there were any stories before the day of the tryout, and they weren't really stories, just brief paragraphs," author Stout remarked. No narratives of the tryouts were ever published.

Into the fifties and sixties the press continued its laid-back coverage, although long-time Boston broadcaster Clark Booth countered that the media did its job well. Yet the press completely failed to hold the franchise accountable for its often-overt racism. As detailed in Howard Bryant's masterpiece on race and Red Sox baseball, the media malpractice stretched into the early nineties, long after Yawkey was dead.

"I think the media was reasonably candid and tough in the old days," said Booth. "The contemporary media are a bunch of pussycats compared to the old crowd. I think the attitudes then were much tougher."

Alcohol consumption, skirt chasing, and carousing were tacitly acknowledged, but accepted. "It was a different era," he explained. "People had a different attitude about baseball. They didn't hold athletes to a higher standard. [Ballplayers] were expected to be rowdy [and] . . . certain members of the team were alcoholics. Everybody drank. It permeated the front office. I was amazed when I got onto the scene to see how much they drank. Everybody. From two hours before the game to three hours after the game. So you didn't overreact to the situation. It was to be expected."

Stout insisted the press never mentioned the incident at the Cloud Nine bar when Earl Wilson was traded because reporters feared retribution. "To write about race while covering the Sox at the time was to risk being cut off."

In an article published in *Esquire* magazine in 1980, former *Boston Herald-American* reporter Marie Brenner wrote of a disturbing incident involving newspaperman and radio sports talk host Clif Keane.

Keane, who had been so incensed about the "nigger" comment during the Robinson tryout, hollered at Boston's black George Scott before a game at Fenway: "Hey Boomer, you old bush nigger!" Keane shouted. "You gonna get out there and hit some taters?"

Keane, manager Don Zimmer, and general manager Haywood Sullivan all laughed at the slur, according to Brenner. She reported that Zimmer later claimed Keane simply called Scott "an old bush."

Keane also drew widespread criticism when he and radio partner Larry Claflin hosted Scott on their "Clif and Claf" program and joked with the big first baseman about eating fried chicken and watermelon.

Disturbingly, many white writers frequented the notorious Winter Haven Elks Club, according to former Boston *Phoenix* sports editor George Kimball.

"I was never in the Elks Club but some players, white coaches, and managers frequented it, and most of the beat writers and columnists when I first started—Keane, [Bill] Liston, Claflin, [Fred] Ciampa, Dave O'Hara for sure, along with [Sox broadcasters] Ken Coleman and Ned Martin—routinely went there without questioning the racial policy, and this went on right through the 1970s," asserted Kimball.

Overt and implied racism continued to rear its ugly head into the nineties, as black 600 Club manager Thomas Sneed had a photo of his white girlfriend defaced in 1998. Again, the case ended up before the Massachusetts Commission on Discrimination. Essentially the press ignored the story.

Media relations under Duquette were an utter nightmare, said Tony Massarotti, who's covered the Sox since 1993. "Most media people . . . resented Duquette and the Red Sox for how they conducted their operation . . . Getting the Sox to address even routine matters was sometimes a chore. Coupled with the team's inability to win a world championship, this left the Sox open to a great deal of criticism."

The Boston media also seemed to have resented professions of faith. When Curt Schilling took the mound in the 2004 ALCS with his right ankle tendon stitched in place, he later credited God for his ability to pitch, drawing snickers from the media. Schilling, a Christian since 1997, subsequently leaned heavily upon his faith to get through his wife Shonda's bout with melanoma.

"It's amazing to me the sheer bitterness that was in that pressroom when the words 'Jesus Christ' came out of my mouth," said Schilling. "I never said I prayed to him to let me win, or to help us win. I prayed for one thing: the ability to compete that night and after all that had happened, all I had gone through, he gave me that."

When John Henry first took the reins of the club, he scheduled fifteen-minute long meetings with Boston's key media players, a stroke of genius, according to the *Globe*'s Massarotti. "Clearly, the Red Sox were interested in improving relations between the media and the club, which they have done," he said. "At the same time, we can never be allies. Regardless as to whether the Sox truly believe we are important, they went out of their way to make us *feel* important . . . I give the Red Sox all the credit in the world for at least taking the time to acknowledge the media's role and responsibilities."

Sports commentator John Molori agreed. "The team was absolutely trying to make 'nice-nice' with the media," he asserted. "After the Dan Duquette reign, they *had* to do that. Did they bend over backwards? Yes. Did they fawn over the media? Yes. There is no question that 'job one' was to create an era of good feeling, at least initially, with the press. Quite simply, previous regimes did not care one bit about what the media thought."

From the sidelines, George Kimball said the press-cognizant new management tickled him: "The new regime [has been] enormously cooperative even on stories they knew might not cast the team—or the owners—in the best light and established a bond of trust almost right away but trust me, after what we'd had for thirty-five years or so . . . it was a breath of fresh air."

The city's sports media has become such an institutional powerhouse that Boston Sports Media Watch, a Web site focusing on the market's sports media, has become wildly popular.

Press coverage of the Red Sox was turned upon its head after the Sox won the 2004 world championship, according to Bruce Allen.

"The biggest shift in the impact of press coverage came after the first World Series win, not the sale to the Henry group," Allen said. "The local media had always been fatalistic about the Red Sox and played that angle up big. Once the so-called 'curse' disappeared, many of these people had to completely change the way they covered the team. That's a huge shift. It's hard to be cynical and snide about a team that has been as successful as they have been since 2004."

20

THE IMPOSSIBLE DREAM
MADE POSSIBLE

The Red Sox again came agonizingly close to realizing their dream in 2003 after cruising to a wild card spot in the American League playoffs.

Even before the season started, Theo Epstein slashed $33 million in payroll to have some room to work. He jettisoned mediocre players: Tony Clark, Dustin Hermanson, Jose Offerman, Darren Oliver, and Ugueth Urbina, whom the media termed "one of the nastiest men ever to set foot in a major league clubhouse." Urbina, who fortunately declined a contract extension, was out of baseball within two years, and imprisoned in his native Colombia after being convicted of attempted murder.

Epstein, who acquired second baseman Todd Walker from Cincinnati, made a losing bid for Cuban defector Jose Contreras. Instead the Cuban expatriate signed with the detested Yankees. "It's very difficult to bid against a team that has an unlimited budget," declared John Henry. "With an unlimited budget, you can buy anything you think you need." However, Larry Lucchino wasn't so calm about losing Contreras, calling New York "the Evil Empire."

Lucchino's outburst prompted a terse response from Yankees owner George Steinbrenner. "I made it a New Year's resolution not to respond to George's petty personal attacks and gross mischaracterizations of my record," retorted Lucchino. "But I may underline those dates when the 'Empire' visits Fenway Park."

Epstein attempted to engineer a trade with Montreal, a team forced to sell off one of its blue-chip pitchers, either Bartolo Colon or Javier Vasquez. Montreal GM Omar Minaya wanted Casey Fossum, while Epstein was offering third baseman Shea Hillenbrand and infielder Freddy Sanchez, (who would later become a star with Pittsburgh). The Yankees managed to stymie the Sox when they engineered a three-team deal with Montreal and the Chicago White Sox. Colon went to Chicago; Vasquez stayed with the Expos. When New York general manager Brian Cashman inexplicably denied orchestrating the trade, *Globe* journalist Bob Hohler ridiculed the notion. "Sure," wrote Hohler, "and the Cross Bronx Expressway is paved with gumdrops." (Vazquez would be traded from Montreal to the Yankees after the season.)

Epstein wasn't through, however. He signed first basemen Kevin Millar and David Ortiz, and third baseman Bill Mueller. He also picked up pitchers Chad Fox and Mike Timlin. All but Fox played key roles in the Red Sox 2004 world championship.

"From one to nine, we have some tough outs, on-base skills, and power as well," Epstein declared. "I think we're going to score a lot of runs."

If the Sox had a weakness it was that they lacked a closer. Adviser Bill James had long advocated a "closer-by-committee" approach, and Boston was the first to try the idea. The plan failed, and Pedro Martinez openly criticized the club for letting Urbina go.

Epstein then sent the temperamental and problematic Shea

Hillenbrand to Arizona for former Diamondbacks closer Byung-Hyun Kim. With Fossum failing as a starter Epstein planned on utilizing Kim in a starting role.

The Sox rolled on offensively but their pitching was thin, and both Pedro Martinez and Fossum spent time on the disabled list. The bullpen proved suspect, blowing games to the Pirates and Brewers. Pitcher Brandon Lyon imploded against St. Louis even though the Sox scored seven runs. When Martinez returned, he stopped the bleeding, but while he was out, the Sox amassed a record of 9–13. And the bullpen blew four games in relief of Pedro. "There are some guys [in the bullpen] whose wives shouldn't be buying green bananas," Little cracked.

Despite the mediocre play, Boston clung to first place in the AL East.

Right fielder Trot Nixon pulled a Little League level gaffe in mid-June when, after catching a fly ball, he hurled it into the stands. Unfortunately there was only one out. An Angels runner scored, Boston lost the game—and Nixon's errant souvenir toss ended up on ESPN's *SportsCenter* for a week.

The media and fans rallied to the Sox because of stellar public relations. Newcomer Kevin Millar, a Texan, coined the phrase, "Cowboy Up," a rodeo term that caught on.

However, underlying problems remained. Manager Grady Little greatly upset the front office by disregarding statistically oriented information, in favor of relying solely on his instincts. It would ultimately cost him his job, but in the meantime, Epstein and Lucchino talked Henry out of firing the manager more than once.

The club still couldn't put the Yankees away, although Ramirez made a game-saving catch in left field against New York after the All-Star break. Then Manny—who was just "Manny being Manny"—

flopped onto his back in left, giggling uncontrollably while the fans went berserk.

Martinez, Lowe, and Wakefield won just enough games to secure the wild card spot, and the Sox captured ninety-five contests, two more wins than they had in 2002.

Boston faced Oakland in the divisional services. After falling behind two games to none, the Sox roared back to take three in a row. The Yankees were next.

As the clubs squared off, so did Martinez—against Yankee coach and former Sox manager Don Zimmer. In Game Three at Fenway, Zimmer charged the mound after Pedro threw a pitch in the vicinity of a batter's head. Pedro turned and dumped the aged and overweight coach to the turf. Later in the game, two Yankees took umbrage at a Boston groundskeeper's taunting, and beat him up.

With each club having won three games, Little left Martinez in the eighth inning of the seventh game, although Pedro was faltering. That season he became a different pitcher when the slight right-hander threw more than 100 pitches in a game, and Little had been ordered to pull him at 100 pitches or seven innings, whichever came first (in 2003 batters hit .370 against Pedro once he reached 105 pitches).

In fact, Martinez later said after his highly successful seventh inning he had told Little to "get the lefty [reliever] ready, and Tim Wakefield," who had already won two games against New York. But Grady left Martinez in the game which cost the Red Sox a World Series appearance—and cost Little his job.

Within days John Henry ordered Little's firing. Henry was also tired of Ramirez's shenanigans (Manny had become a problem child, was perceived to be a cry baby and sometime malingerer, and constantly demanded to be dealt to another club). The outfielder was placed on irrevocable waivers. Predictably, there were no takers.

Lucchino, Epstein, and assistant Jed Hoyer flew to Arizona over Thanksgiving to meet with pitcher Curt Schilling. They convinced him to waive his "no trade" clause and approve a deal that would bring him back to Boston.

"Being able to engage a large number of Sox fans on Sons of Sam Horn [an exclusive Web site about the Red Sox] over the few days of the negotiations drove home some pretty startling points," Schilling declared.

He said the fervent Boston fans persuaded him to approve the trade. "In addition to being incredibly impressed with Theo and Jed . . . it dawned on [my wife] Shonda and me that during the Thanksgiving holiday, there were actually people in this world *praying* that we would choose to come to Boston. It was mind-boggling and I knew it was also an incredible motivator. If I came here, and we did anything short of win it all, it would be a failure."

The Schilling deal will go down in history as one of Epstein's greatest coups.

"I want to be part of bringing the first World Series [championship] in modern history to Boston," Schilling publicly declared at the time. "I guess I hate the Yankees now."

Simultaneously the Sox hired a new manager, Terry Francona, who had been a coach with Oakland, Schilling's former manager with the Phillies, and a former major league player whose career had been marred by injuries.

Epstein signed free agent closer Keith Foulke, a "lights out" reliever who periodically had given the Sox fits when he played for Oakland.

The Sox also tried for weeks to trade Garciaparra and Ramirez in order to obtain Texas Rangers shortstop Alex Rodriguez and White Sox outfielder Magglio Ordonez. The deal soured after the

Major League Baseball Players Association refused to allow the Sox to alter A-Rod's astronomical contract. Almost immediately, the Yankees sent second baseman Alfonso Soriano to Texas in return for Rodriguez, who agreed to move to third base since Derek Jeter manned the shortstop position in New York. The deal ignited Boston, but the Sox had alienated their talented, oft-injured shortstop Nomar Garciaparra, who caught wind of the discussions while on his honeymoon. The moody infielder soured completely on the Olde Towne Team.

John Henry was incredulous at New York's audacity, declaring, "The Yankees are going insanely beyond the resources of all the other teams." To which New York's Steinbrenner responded, "Unlike the Yankees, [Henry] chose not to go the extra distance for his fans."

The battle lines had once again been drawn. Under the Henry regime, the Red Sox's 2004 motto was reaffirmed as "Beat the Yankees, no matter what!"

For his part, Garciaparra said he was physically hurt and emotionally distraught, although he maintained that he still wanted to stay in Boston. On March 31, he claimed he had strained the Achilles tendon in his right foot when he was struck by a batted ball earlier in the month. Nobody with the club could recall the March 5 incident, but Garciaparra was placed on the DL, and the club didn't expect him back until May. No matter, he would never again be the same player who—at that point—had hit for a lifetime average of .323.

After getting off to a fast start in spite of the loss of Garciaparra, Nixon, and Kim, the Sox leveled off and played .500 ball against teams with worse records. Nomar returned in late June but underperformed, and grew even more disillusioned when there was public speculation that he was beyond his prime.

The Yankees met Boston at the Stadium at the end of June and—with the biggest game of the season looming on July 1, which was Boston's chance to close the gap in the AL East—Nomar sat it out, allegedly nursing a sore Achilles. A-Rod played well, and New York shortstop Derek Jeter dove into the stands to catch a foul ball in extra innings, bruising his shoulder and cutting his chin—but holding onto the ball. The play prompted one anonymous Red Sox official to declare, "The difference between the two teams was obvious that night," a slam at Garciaparra.

New York swept the three-game set, but the difference in desire prompted the Sox front office to begin thinking that perhaps it *was* time to say goodbye to Nomar. Before that happened though, Boston hosted New York at friendly Fenway in late July, desperately needing a sweep.

But Schilling, the ace of the staff, who had performed magnificently all year, couldn't stave off New York in the first game, and the Yankees defeated the Sox, 8–7. Then lightning struck in Game Two in front of a national audience.

In the midst of a Yankee rally, Sox hurler Bronson Arroyo hit Rodriguez with a pitch and, when the angry third baseman charged the mound, Sox catcher Jason Varitek intercepted him, and attempted to make Rodriguez eat his catcher's mitt. Varitek later said he had used some "choice words" in telling Rodriguez to go to first base. Obviously Rodriguez didn't listen, triggering a brawl that ended with both players, Boston outfielder Gabe Kapler and Yankees outfielder Kenny Lofton, ejected. Boston manager Terry Francona was also tossed for arguing a call at second base in the fifth inning. Several days later the league suspended and levied fines against Varitek, Rodriguez, Kapler, Nixon, and Yankees reliever Tanyon Sturtze, and fined Schilling, Ortiz, and Lofton. Schilling later said the importance of Varitek's interception of Rodriguez was incalculable. "My fondest memories [include Varitek's] face plant on A-Rod for no other reason than that was an igniter for us and a catalyst for so many other things," he declared.

With the Sox trailing by two runs in the bottom of the ninth, Garciaparra doubled, Kevin Millar singled him in, and third baseman Bill Mueller hit a two-run, walk-off homer off Yankees closer Mariano Rivera. Francona ran on to the field barefoot from the clubhouse to congratulate Mueller. It was the beginning of a Red Sox resurgence. "It's the most draining [win]," said Francona. "It was the most physical. It's a huge win for us, and it will be bigger if we make it bigger. If we have this catapult us and we do something with it, that's what will really make it big." The Red Sox again beat the Bronx Bombers the following day.

Boston prepared to put Nomar Garciaparra back on the disabled list because his foot was troubling him again, even though he had hit nearly .400 in July. Within a week, Garciaparra, once the Red Sox poster boy, would be Boston history.

The Sox turnaround was nearly complete at the trade deadline, July 31, when Theo Epstein pulled the trigger on Garciaparra. In a stunning four-way deal, he was sent to the Chicago Cubs, while the Sox acquired shortstop Orlando Cabrera from Montreal and first baseman Doug Mienkiewicz from Minnesota. In a separate transaction, speedy Dodgers outfielder Dave Roberts also joined Boston.

The deals provided the Red Sox with much-needed defense and speed, as well as eliminating an often-hurt defensive liability and clubhouse malcontent in Garciaparra. Epstein felt badly about trading away a Boston icon. "You never want to trade a player of Nomar's caliber," Theo said. "He's been a great Red Sox [player], one of the greatest of all-time. I wish him and his family nothing but the best in the future."

Nomar's teammates also had mixed feelings. "We just traded away Mr. Boston, a guy who meant so much to the city and just like that he's gone," said Johnny Damon.

"You're surprised, obviously. But I don't think it was unexpected," remarked Curt Schilling. "Obviously, the three guys they brought in here, all three are very good to well above average defensive players. So [the front office is] addressing a concern."

At the time Boston's record stood at a mediocre 43–43.

A week after the trade, the team was rocked in Detroit when the usually sunny Kevin Millar threw a fit when he was told he would not start at first base for the seventh consecutive game.

"I'm not going to be lied to," he told reporters. "I didn't know they traded for [Mienkiewicz] to be the everyday first baseman." Millar had been hitting .469 with six home runs and 16 RBIs over his last fourteen games. He ended up playing left field, got on base three times, and drove in a run after Ramirez sat out the contest, complaining of a sore throat.

The Red Sox then caught fire, taking three out of four from Tampa Bay. After dropping two of three to the White Sox, they swept the Blue Jays at Fenway, followed by a three-game sweep in Chicago, then took two of three in Toronto.

After a slow start, Orlando Cabrera won games with both his glove and his bat. Moving back to Fenway, the Sox swept Detroit in a four-game series. Suddenly they were only three and a half games behind the Yankees.

When the club cruised to the wild card berth, the ever-critical press chided the Sox for drinking champagne in the clubhouse after securing the playoff spot. Manager Francona slammed the reporters. "It's their right to do what they want," he growled. "If they're excited to be in the playoffs, they have a right to be excited." The first round of the playoffs saw Boston sweep the Anaheim Angels. Schilling blew away the Angels in Game One. Then Pedro shut them down in Game Two. But young Bronson Arroyo gave way to Mike Timlin in the seventh inning of Game Three; Timlin allowed a game-tying grand slam to Vladimir Guerrero. Forgotten man Derek Lowe, who had been dropped from the starting rotation took the mound as the game went into extra innings. A David Ortiz blast over the Green Monster uncorked yet more champagne. Days later, Boston was headed to New York to face the Bronx Bombers in the ALCS—again!

That series would prove to be the biggest comeback in the history of professional baseball: the first time a team had ever lost the first three games of a postseason series and still win in seven games.

"Someone gave me a hat that said 'YH' on it and it took me a while to figure out what it [meant]," former Red Sox catcher Carlton Fisk recalled. "It turns out that it means Yankee Hater, and for us former Red Sox players, it's extra special, considering it came against the Yanks in the ALCS."

Boston's next opponent was St. Louis in the World Series, their seven-game tormentors in 1946 and 1967. This time the Sox swept.

Game One of the 2004 World Series was an error-marred slugfest, with the Sox playing like the Keystone Kops in the field, surrendering numerous leads. But after blowing leads of 4–0, 5–2 and 9–7, Boston defeated the Cardinals, 11–9, on second baseman Mark Bellhorn's two-run homer in the bottom of the eighth inning.

Curt Schilling, still suffering from a torn tendon sheath in his right ankle, superbly shut down the Cardinals in Game Two at Fenway, pitching in forty-eight degree weather to secure a 6–2 victory.

In St. Louis, Pedro Martinez pitched his heart out in what would be his last game as a member of the Red Sox, leading Boston to a decisive 4–1 win. He held the Cards to no runs and was removed by Francona after seven innings just shy of 100 pitches.

Derek Lowe, whose comeback in the playoffs was described by owner John Henry as "just an incredible thing," threw seven shutout innings en route to a 3–0 win in the fourth game. Finally the Boston Red Sox secured their first world championship in eighty-six very long years.

It took the Henry regime only three short years to accomplish it. "Bag job" or not, the Henry consortium proved to be the right choice to operate the previously perpetually inept franchise.

For the Red Sox Nation, the joy was indescribable!

Much like 1967, many of the club's ballplayers reveled in their newly minted fame. With his flowing locks and heavy beard making him look more Christ-like than ever, Johnny Damon traded repartee with David Letterman on late-night television.

Regarding the history-making comeback against the Bronx Bombers, Damon couldn't resist declaring, "As everyone's been reading and hearing, you know, we're a bunch of idiots. We didn't really know what we were up against."

He also marveled at Curt Schilling's guts—and performance. "That was an awesome feat," Damon cracked. "The thing is, after the game, we're carrying him to the bus, because he can't walk. And, you know, he's a pretty big dude. Our backs were hurting for a few days."

The city of Boston's massive duck boat–borne parade was another topic of conversation.

"It was amazing. Of course, we all know how great those Boston fans are," Damon continued. "There they are, diving into cold water and freezing to death and police have to go rescue them and save their lives." And in California, David Ortiz, Derek Lowe, Mike Timlin, Dave Roberts, and Alan Embree walked on stage in the midst of Jay Leno's *Tonight Show* monologue to raucous cheers, showered with red, white, and blue confetti.

21

AFTERMATH

The euphoria was unbelievable. For months, the Red Sox Nation savored the 2004 World Championship. But the sweet dream then took a U-turn when the front office contributed missteps that doomed the team's efforts for the next two seasons.

Two days after Boston's Series victory, twelve players filed for free agency: Lowe, Varitek, Kapler, catcher Doug Mirabelli, first baseman David McCarty, infielder Pokey Reese, and pitchers Pedro Astacio, Terry Adams, Scott Williamson, Ramiro Mendoza, Curtis Leskanic, and Mike Myers. Pedro Martinez would soon follow.

General manager Theo Epstein had grown disenchanted with chief executive officer Larry Lucchino as Epstein began the third and final year of his contract. The rift, which began after Boston lost the A-Rod sweepstakes, widened when Epstein traded Garciaparra. It would soon worsen.

Schilling had to postpone the surgery on his right ankle because of the suturing done by team physician Dr. Bill Morgan during the playoffs (in spite of his novel solution to Schilling's dilemma, the club soon fired Morgan).

Schilling successfully went under the knife on November 9. The pitcher, who posted a 21-6 record and an ERA of 3.26 in 2004, was expected to be out until the early part of the 2005 season.

Both the Red Sox and Pedro Martinez were closemouthed about their on-going negotiations, although Epstein was determined not to overpay the pitcher. Martinez, who had declared his free agency before the November 11 deadline, met with the Sox and both New York-based clubs. The discussions between Boston and Pedro turned acrimonious, and Martinez ended up signing with the Mets. "I never had the feeling that he wanted to re-sign," John Henry told author Seth Mnookin.

At his introductory press conference in New York, Martinez took some shots at Boston's brain trust. "I have all love and respect for the fans of Boston. I'm deeply touched, and sorry for the fans. I will always love them. I hope to once be able to pay them my respects. It's too bad we couldn't work it out. Now, it's a new beginning for me. I'm sure the fans will understand that I have a life and have to go forward. But I gave [the Red Sox] every opportunity to keep me."

Francona nevertheless remained optimistic about the support he'd get from the front office.

"I have a lot of confidence in Theo and ownership that when we head down to Fort Myers [for spring training], we'll have a good team," he said.

During the first week of December, Epstein announced the signing of righty Matt Mantei, a reliever who served as Arizona's closer in 2003, but was sidelined with tendonitis for much of 2004. Another previously injured pitcher, Wade Miller, also penned a contract with the Sox, as did left-hander John Halama. Theo then signed free agent southpaw David Wells, age forty-one, and thirty-year-old righty starter Matt Clement. All were bargain basement players compared to the departed Martinez and Lowe.

The Sox re-signed team leader Jason Varitek to a four-year contract, and formally named him captain. Pitcher Tim Wakefield was ecstatic. "Everyone knew he was the captain before it was actually acknowledged, but I think it's a great honor that the Red Sox were able to put the 'C' on his jersey and officially call him the captain of the team. It means a tremendous amount not only to me personally, but to the team, and most important, to the city of Boston and Red Sox Nation."

The club also agreed on a multi-year deal with former Cardinals shortstop Edgar Renteria, a four-time All-Star and two-time Gold Glove winner, who had, ironically, made the last out of the 2004 World Series. According to Theo, signing Renteria might not have been possible if the club had kept Martinez.

Outfielder Dave Roberts was sent to San Diego for outfielder Jay Payton and utility infielder Ramon Vazquez. Second baseman Bellhorn and pitcher Arroyo were then tendered contracts, but first baseman Mientkiewicz was shipped to the Mets for cash and a prospect. Thus the roster was set for Fort Myers and spring training.

Unfortunately for both the franchise and Red Sox Nation, Epstein's maneuverings failed to pay off in 2005. Renteria buckled under media scrutiny, failing to hit *and* field. Clement had a good first half, but then bottomed out. Wells posted an overall record of 17–10 with an ERA of nearly five runs per game over parts of two seasons. Schilling ended up on the disabled list in April from recurrent ankle injuries.

In contrast with the enthusiastic Dave Roberts, Jay Peyton quickly became a clubhouse distraction. Miller, Mantei, and Halama were among those who didn't live up to their potential. Bellhorn hit a desultory .216 with seven home runs and 109 strikeouts before he was released.

Two months into the 2005 season, the Sox were 32–29. They then reeled off twelve wins in their next thirteen games. But a faltering Foulke went on the disabled list, replaced as closer by Schilling, who still wasn't healthy. Johnny Damon blasted the club, asserting that setup man Mike Timlin deserved the job. Millar threw a tantrum when the Sox signed veteran John Olerud to a minor league contract May 1 (Millar had quickly become ineffective, clubbing only nine home runs and fielding poorly). "They became the biggest bunch of prima donnas ever assembled," one anonymous Sox executive admitted. "It's a problem with a veteran team, especially one that's had some success."

A *Sports Illustrated* article reported that Ramirez wanted out of Boston—again. The phrase "Manny being Manny" grew tiring due to his constant antics throughout much of the season. Much like the on-the-field activities of the late Ted Williams, lackadaisical performances would be followed by acts of sheer brilliance.

Clement, who was hit in the head by a line drive, posted a 13–6 record, albeit with a horrible 4.57 ERA. Schilling was moved back to the starting rotation but never regained his form. He went 8–8, saved nine games, but posted a 5.69 ERA.

After leading the AL East for much of the year, the Sox had slipped into second place when the Yankees visited Fenway Park for a final three-game set on September 30. After Boston took two out of three, the teams tied with identical 95–67 records. However, the Yankees took ten of nineteen games between the two clubs overall, earning New York first place in the division.

In the final analysis it really didn't matter because the Red Sox were completely overmatched as the wild card entry in the first round of the playoffs, getting swept by Chicago. The Yankees were bounced by the Angels.

It proved to serve as an ignominious end to a half-baked season. But the situation in Boston only grew worse after the club was eliminated from the playoffs.

Theo Epstein and player development director Ben Cherington were preparing to conduct a massive overhaul of the club roster, but Epstein's contract was due to expire on October 31. He had grown disenchanted with both Lucchino and public affairs chief Charles Steinberg, feeling they had hung him out to dry on more than one occasion. "If I'm going to commit to staying," he declared, "I need to know we're all in this together."

Principal owner John Henry had recognized that Epstein was ruffled and weary. Henry wanted to retain Theo, and assigned the contract negotiations to Lucchino. He forced them to sit down on October 11. "It didn't work," Henry said. "It blew things up. It drove them further apart as opposed to bringing them together."

The media then weighed in, with many beat reporters upset that it seemed that Epstein's contract negotiations were not being conducted on the up-and-up. "How in the name of John Harrington does that happen, particularly to an organization that has otherwise taken so many strides?" asked Massarotti. "Not so long ago, the Red Sox front office was perceived as being badly out of touch . . . [This] reminds all of the old days."

After it appeared as though there finally had been a meeting of the minds and Epstein would agree to terms with the club, the acerbic Shaughnessy wrote a column on October 30 entitled, "Let's iron out some of this dirty laundry." Epstein was convinced either Lucchino or Steinberg had planted the column. (Apparently many of Shaughnessy's comments had been heard previously from the mouths of others in the Sox front office.)

Epstein resigned the following day, e-mailing Henry, asserting,

"I have a huge pit in my stomach. But it's nowhere near as big a pit as I'd have if I'd already signed a contract." He left Fenway's executive offices on Halloween dressed in a gorilla suit to avoid the voracious media, an altogether appropriate end to a tragicomedy of epic proportions.

But it wasn't over. The *Globe* ran an October 31 article claiming that Epstein would sign a new contract valued at $1.5 million a year. Ultimately Lucchino and Epstein offered convoluted explanations for the younger man's leave-taking.

Two days later Henry and Epstein held a joint press conference with Henry lamenting, "This is a great, great loss. I feel responsible." After Henry questioned his fitness as principal owner of the club, he fingered the press. "I can tell you that one of the problems in this process was the media did not have access to what was going on so they had to rely upon unnamed sources . . . there were things that were said that were inaccurate."

Both Henry and Epstein made it clear that the problems didn't stem from *their* relationship. Jed Hoyer and Ben Cherington were named as co-general managers.

Meanwhile, Lucchino sent top minor league prospect, Hanley Ramirez, and three minor leaguers to Florida for pitcher Josh Beckett, relief pitcher Guillermo Mota and third baseman Mike Lowell. Beckett had been the most valuable player of the 2003 World Series, while Lowell, a solid infielder with a large contract who was perceived as a throw-in following a sub-par 2005 season, would become the 2007 World Series MVP for the *next* Red Sox world championship squad.

The merry-go-round spun again later in the off season, with the Sox losing fan favorite Johnny Damon, who signed a four-year contract with the Yankees. John Henry blasted Damon's agent, Scott

Boras, for misleading the club during negotiations to retain the popular outfielder.

Mueller signed with the Dodgers, Olerud retired, Mirabelli was sent to the Padres, and Myers left. Millar also departed, signing a multi-year deal with Baltimore, while Boston signed first baseman J. T. Snow and second baseman Mark Loretta. The club also sent Renteria to Atlanta for minor league third baseman Andy Marte. Pitcher Julio Tavarez also joined the club.

And in late January, so did Theo Epstein.

"On behalf of all of the partners as well as the entire management of the Boston Red Sox, I can tell you that we are exceedingly happy to have Theo returning as general manager," Henry said in a prepared statement. "Despite the attempts of some to portray Theo's return as a win for someone and a loss for someone else, this is a win/win situation."

Epstein was the epitome of tact in his statement. "Throughout November, John Henry, Tom Werner, Larry and I held discussions to see what lessons could be learned in the aftermath of my departure," he explained. "Gradually, with the benefit of time and greater perspective, we tackled not only our personal conflicts but also the differences regarding our thoughts for the organization. We emerged, ten weeks and many spirited conversations later, with the comfort of a shared vision for the future of the organization, including the role of the baseball operations department."

Henry and Tom Werner apparently had conducted some serious fence mending. "Tom and I are very happy to see Larry and Theo working together again," Henry said. "People sometimes disagree. I don't think you can have healthy relationships without disagreements and an organization is not going to evolve beyond mediocrity without them. This is not the same organization that Theo left.

There was enough discord then to give Theo legitimate reasons to move on."

Lucchino was likewise gracious.

"Theo returns as general manager to an organization that is different from the one he left on October 31," he said. "The fourteen-year relationship between Theo and me, and the passage of time over the last three months, have helped to put behind us the friction that developed during last year's negotiations."

The Sox engineered a deal with the Indians, acquiring outfielder Coco Crisp, pitcher David Riske, and catcher Josh Bard. In return Boston relinquished Marte, Mota, and catching prospect Kelly Shoppach. Crisp, who hit .300 with sixteen homers, 69 RBIs and fifteen stolen bases in 2005, was a superb fielder. Former Boston reserve outfielder Gabe Kapler became a non-roster invitee to spring training, and the Sox signed free agent shortstop Alex Gonzalez. And just before the start of the season the Red Sox shipped starter Bronson Arroyo to Cincinnati for outfielder Wily Mo Pena.

The club got off to a tremendous start in 2006, then collapsed in August. Between the first and the twenty-second, Boston dropped from first place to six and a half games behind the Yankees. Medical problems abounded. David Ortiz developed an irregular heartbeat, and rookie lefty Jon Lester was diagnosed with non-Hodgkin's lymphoma. Closer Jonathan Papelbon was disabled in September with a dislocated shoulder after saving thirty-five games. Matt Clement went 5-5 with a 6.61 ERA before requiring major reconstructive surgery. After 125 games Manny Ramirez claimed he had hurt his leg, and sat out the remainder of the season. Varitek, Gonzalez, Timlin, Nixon, Crisp, Wakefield, and Wells all spent time on the disabled list.

The Sox finished the year with a record of 86–76, falling to third place in the AL East, and failing to make the playoffs for the first time since 2002, the year John Henry & Co. took over the club.

Things could only get better, but nobody knew just *how* much better they would get.

22

THE JOY OF SOX

True to form, the Red Sox actively worked to improve their roster during the 2006 off-season, signing free agents shortstop Julio Lugo and right fielder J.D. Drew. However, their biggest acquisitions came from overseas.

Boston ponied up more than $103 million to sign Daisuke Matsuzaka, a right-handed pitcher with a stellar track record in Japan's major leagues (Matsuzaka is such an icon that pitchers from the high school he attended still won't throw from the practice mound he threw from). While pitching in Japan, Daisuke (commonly called Dice-K) sported a miniscule earned run average and had a repertoire that included no fewer than five stellar pitches.

Boston bid more than $50 million simply to obtain the rights to negotiate with Matsuzaka. Even at that, Daisuke's agent, the notoriously difficult Scott Boras, was ready to torpedo the contract negotiations until Matsuzaka instructed him to come to terms with the club.

John Henry was effusive in praising Epstein's efforts at finalizing a deal with Boras.

"When Leslie Epstein's twenty-eight-year-old son became general manager of the Red Sox, he gave [Theo] two words of advice:

'Be bold.' The day that we took over this organization, people in this organization to a man, to a woman, on all levels . . . we've been bold and this was I believe a bold move."

Boston bid $51,111,111 for the rights to negotiate with Daisuke, more than $13 million than the Sox's closest competitor, the Mets. Henry came up with the figure, superstitiously basing it upon "Investor 11," the anonymous notation he used during his bid to buy the Red Sox.

The Sox also signed Matsuzaka's countryman, Hideki Okajima, a lefty reliever with a solid track record. Okajima's price tag was considerably less, a little more than $3 million.

With young left-hander Jon Lester sidelined due to cancer, the addition of Matsuzaka proved critical to Boston's success in 2007. The team, however, still lacked a legitimate closer. Jonathon Papelbon, who did a tremendous job in 2006, volunteered to go back to the bullpen during spring training. The Sox leapt at the offer, despite Papelbon's shoulder problems at the end of the 2006 season. Once again, Papelbon threw well, beyond all expectations.

The 2007 season got off to an inauspicious start when the Sox (behind Curt Schilling) were defeated on opening day by the woeful Kansas City Royals. But both Beckett and Matsuzaka followed with wins, as did knuckleballer Tim Wakefield.

On April 18, when Wakefield recorded his second victory of the young season, the Red Sox vaulted into first place in the American League East, and never relinquished it. Two days later, at Fenway, Boston engineered a five-run rally in the bottom of the eighth inning, to snatch a 7–6 win from the struggling Yankees. The losing pitcher in the contest was Mariano Rivera, New York's long-time top closer. Two days later the Red Sox hit four consecutive home runs off Yankee rookie Chase Wright, only the fifth team in major league history to accomplish the feat. Even at that, the Sox needed a three-run four-bagger from Mike Lowell to win the game, 7–6. That home run barrage took Matsuzaka off the hook after he gave up six runs to the Yankees in his first-ever appearance at Fenway Park. "I wanted very badly to record my first win at Fenway Park," Matsuzaka said through an interpreter. "The opponent being the Yankees and the fact that my teammates had already defeated them twice made me want to win even more."

Boston again humiliated New York five days later at Yankee Stadium when they raked Rivera for four runs in one-third of an inning. The final score was 11–4. New York's woes were only beginning, as in spite of a career year for Alex Rodriguez, the team fell as many as fourteen games off the pace set by the division-leading Bosox.

Beckett was proving virtually unhittable, while Wakefield ran off a double-digit number of victories. Both Schilling and Matsuzaka were throwing well, Papelbon was untouchable as the club's closer, and Okajima proved a pleasant surprise as a setup man for him. When a right-handed setup man was required, Boston native Manny Delcarmen stepped in, proving himself invaluable throughout the season.

The Sox were getting timely hitting from a number of unexpected sources: first baseman Kevin Youkilis, third baseman Lowell, and rookie second baseman Dustin Pedroia.

However, designated hitter David Ortiz was struggling; late in the year the Sox learned that the slugger was suffering from a bad knee that would require off-season surgery. And the team's two big free agent acquisitions as position players—shortstop Julio Lugo and right fielder J. D. Drew—both struggled at the plate, while Manny Ramirez wasn't hitting up to par either. Center fielder Coco Crisp was even worse.

Boston received some potentially disturbing news in early May when Roger Clemens announced he was returning to Major League Baseball once more, but again, as a New York Yankee. The Sox had made a strong offer for the pitcher, but the New Yorkers outbid Boston roughly by a prorated $10 million to again secure the services of the player who for years had been the face of the Red Sox franchise. [23]

Boston's players took the news stoically. "It would have been nice to have him, but we didn't need him. We don't need him," declared Curt Schilling. "It's May. We have a long way to go. But I like this team. I feel like we are legitimate World Series contenders without him."

The Sox engineered another miracle on Mother's Day, when, trailing the Baltimore Orioles 5–0 in the bottom of the ninth inning, they rallied for a 6–5 win. Four days later they swept a day/night doubleheader against the reeling Detroit Tigers.

But in spite of the burgeoning optimism on the part of Red Sox Nation, manager Terry Francona urged caution. "We preach so much to stay in the moment. What we did last week is gone. What we're going to do, or have to try to do next week, if you look at it, you kind of get overwhelmed."

Yankees hurler Scott Proctor opened the month of June 1 in New York City by bouncing a pitch off Kevin Youkilis's batting helmet. Considering the bad blood between the two teams, Sox fans held their collective breath, hoping that every remaining contest between the clubs wouldn't automatically trigger World War III. The strangest aspect of the beaning was the fact that New York was leading

---

23 In light of the Mitchell Report on the use of performance-enhancing drugs, released in December 2007, it may have proved to be a blessing that the Sox didn't procure Clemens's services after all. There's little doubt that Clemens availed himself to PEDs off-and-on from the 1999 season through the early years of the new millennium.

by six runs at the time, although Youkilis was nearing the end of a twenty-three-game hitting streak.

Schilling made a strong bid for immortality when he nearly threw a no-hitter against the Oakland Athletics June 7, surrendering a clean hit to Shannon Stewart with two outs in the bottom of the ninth inning. He had shaken off catcher Jason Varitek's call for a slider, to Schilling's everlasting chagrin. "With two outs, I was sure I had it," the forty-year-old Schilling said. "I shook off [Varitek] and now I'll have to deal with a 'what-if' the rest of my life."

Unfortunately for Schilling, the one-hitter proved to be the highlight of his regular season, as shoulder woes put him on the disabled list for two months following his next start. Fortunately for the Sox, Josh Beckett was proving to be nearly unbeatable, raising his season mark to 10–1 with his defeat of Atlanta on June 19.

As the squad prepared to take a couple of well-deserved days off thanks to the All-Star break, six members of the Red Sox packed their overnight bags to travel to San Francisco, the site of the 2007 All-Star classic: Mike Lowell, David Ortiz, Manny Ramirez, Josh Beckett, Jonathan Papelbon, and Hideki Okajima.

The team continued to maintain its stranglehold on first place, sporting a ten-game lead, having occupied first place for eighty-four consecutive days. And that in spite of the lack of production from Ortiz and Ramirez. However, Francona argued that the two sluggers shouldn't be counted out: "They can produce. They are two phenomenal hitters. They have the ability to sometimes produce when they're getting pitched around. The production is not quite there yet. I firmly believe they'll be some numbers up there where everybody goes, 'Boy, they sure got hot.'"

Echoed J. D. Drew, in the throes of what was close to a season-long slump, "It's a 'feel' thing. You go through things as the season goes along. You can never explain them. It's not always a fun thing but that's just the way the baseball season plays out. You play so many games and eventually something is going to happen and you go through a span where you can't really find your stroke. You're a little fatigued and sometimes you even feel too strong or you're trying to do too much. It's just one of those situations where it will all fall back into place for sure."

In fairness to Drew, he had to be distracted by the plight of his infant son, Jack, who underwent surgery for developmental displacement of his hips. Drew missed a three-game series in Boston, but found himself on a flight to Seattle in early August.

On the bright side, after battling anaplastic large cell lymphoma for nearly eleven months, young Jon Lester returned to the club on July 23, facing a fearsome Cleveland lineup. Lester proceeded to handcuff the Indians, throwing six strong innings for a 6–2 victory. His gutsy performance earned him a feature spot on the ABC Evening News. "We thought Jon was a pretty special young man before all this transpired," Francona smiled. "To handle it with the grace he did, he's a tough guy not to pull for."

Lester had posted a stellar 7–2 in fifteen starts for the Sox in 2006 before the cancer felled him. His efforts proved to be one of the top feel-good sports stories of 2007.

However, by the time Lester returned Matsuzaka had started to falter due to stress on his arm. The hurler had been used to pitching once a week in Japan; American major league clubs generally use a five-man rotation.

At the trade deadline, Boston made a significant roster move, acquiring former standout closer Eric Gagne from the Texas Rangers. In a comeback effort with Texas, Gagne had performed admirably in 2007. The former National League Cy Young Award winner had missed the better part of two seasons and undergone surgeries for arm woes, including one major reconstruction. The Sox were intent upon using Gagne as a setup man, augmenting the efforts of Mike Timlin, Delcarmen, and the ailing Okajima, also suffering from fatigue.

Gagne was enthused, even though he'd be giving up the closer's role. "I wanted to be with the Red Sox and help them win the World Series. That's all I care about. There [are] guys that play fifteen, twenty years and can't even taste a World Series. That's what I'm here for."

Unfortunately, Gagne proved to be a disappointment. Although he was effective in his initial outings, he quickly blew three consecutive games. Baltimore roughed him up on August 10, then again on August 12. Five days later the Angels rallied against him to beat the Sox, 7–5, after Gagne had entered the game with a 5–4 lead.

Meanwhile, the Yankees were slowly but surely creeping back into the picture, on a 23–8 tear since the All-Star break.

"[The Yankees are] playing a whole lot better than we are right now, it's that simple," said Curt Schilling. "They're winning, and we're not. But the answers are here in this [clubhouse], and we're going to find them."

Starters Josh Beckett and Tim Wakefield were carrying the club. Beckett became the first fifteen-game winner in the major leagues on August 11, while Wakefield notched twenty-six consecutive decisions as a starting pitcher, one shy of tying the all-time record.

Lester returned to the squad in mid-month after a stint in the minors, throwing a no-decision game against the Devil Rays, although the Sox rallied for a dramatic 2–1 win.

Rookie righty Clay Buchholz joined the club in mid-August, and was immediately thrown into the fray, overcoming a bout of wildness early in his major league debut versus the Angels. Varitek was impressed with Buchholz's poise.

"He had an outstanding outing," declared Varitek. "He kept his poise with the lead, and he threw strikes—didn't really walk people. He had a good changeup—you've seen his curveball—and I found out later he had a pretty good sinker, too."

Francona had announced that Buchholz would throw a limited number of pitches. "I don't care if [Buchholz] is throwing a no-hitter," Francona declared. Little did Francona know that Buchholz would accomplish that very feat in his *second* MLB start.

At the end of August Boston and New York were gearing up to play what seemed to be another of their annual, crucial end-of-the-season matches. The Yankees had steadily gained ground on the division-leading Sox, and Boston wanted to avenge their 2006 mid-August meltdown.

New York proceeded to replicate that feat in the closing days of August 2007. The Yanks dominated Boston in the first game, 5–0, highlighted by two fastballs hurled behind the head of Kevin Youkilis by New York fireballer Joba Chamberlain. The missiles sent the right-hander to an early shower. "If that young man is trying to get our attention, he did a very good job," said Francona.

By the time the smoke cleared, the Red Sox had again been swept in the three-game series. In the wake of scoring an amazing forty-six runs in a four-game set versus Chicago just prior to the New York series, Boston's bats had gone cold, and both Manny Ramirez and Ortiz were ailing. Later Youkilis would join them in the ranks of the walking wounded.

Then Clay Buchholz promptly made Francona a prophetic genius by hurling a 10–0 no-hitter against the Baltimore Orioles in his second major league start. Buchholz had been recalled from Pawtucket to make a spot start in place of Wakefield, who was suffering from back problems.

Late in the contest Red Sox management even debated whether Buchholz should continue pitching despite his looming no-hitter. "There was a lot of discussion going back and forth about what we do if he goes out in the ninth at 105 pitches," Epstein admitted.

Boston needed that shot in the arm, as the relief corps was growing thin. Okajima's sixty-five and a third innings pitched represented his highest seasonal total since 2000. After giving up a game-winning home run to Toronto's Vernon Wells, Okajima acknowledged that he was both physically and mentally fatigued.

Previously, the Sox had shelved Gagne in the hopes of restoring the right-hander's psyche. Francona sent Buchholz to the bullpen, and the youngster beat Baltimore in relief on September 6, five days after his no-hitter.

Matsuzaka continued to falter, hammered by Baltimore for six hits and eight runs over two and two-thirds innings. The loss left his record at 14–12, with an earned run average of 4.44. Pitching coach John Farrell said he felt Matsuzaka was over-throwing and relying too much on his fastball. "I think he's sacrificing location. He's somewhat gone away from his off-speed pitches, and hitters have had a chance to go in and look hard and not really have to guard too much against anything soft in a pitch mix."

Matsuzaka's losing effort meant the Sox were five and a half games ahead of the Yankees in the AL East.

Then Jon Lester took center stage again, beating the Orioles, 4–0, on September 7. Lester had finally gotten his groove back. "[I] just felt like I had a clue on where the ball was going. I knew how to correct the mistakes and the misfires and go from there."

Three days later Ortiz was forced out of the lineup because of a torn right meniscus. He had been hobbled by the injury since June of 2006 and hoped to make it through the remainder of the 2007 season before having surgery. Left fielder Ramirez, who at that point had missed thirteen consecutive games with a strained left oblique, also was hurt.

Headed into Fenway Park for another showdown with the Yankees, the Sox needed to play well to secure the division. Boston's top two relievers—Okajima and Papelbon—were hammered in the series opener, blowing a 7–2 lead, and surrendering six runs in the eighth inning to lose, 8–7. The lead was suddenly down to four games.

They managed to win the second game after Youkilis was struck on his right wrist by a pitch. Rookie outfielder Jacoby Ellsbury pinch-ran for the first baseman, sparking the Sox to a solid victory via his legs and his bat. The win snapped a five-game losing streak to the New Yorkers that went back to June. Beckett was the winning pitcher, picking up his nineteenth victory.

X-rays on Youkilis were negative, but he was listed as day-to-day. Losing him hurt, and the Sox bats went silent again. The team managed to score only five runs in a three-game series at Toronto. They lost all three, and their AL East lead dropped to a mere one and a half games over the surging Yankees.

Gagne again threw poorly in the final loss to the Blue Jays, and Okajima was shut down in the wake of the Yankees' debacle. He didn't seem too concerned about needing to sit for a few games. "Similar things happened to me in Japan, too," he said. "Nothing overly shocking. I want to be game ready when I go out and pitch instead of in so-so condition. I believe that I'll be pitching sometime between now and before the playoffs start." Manny Ramirez was still out, joined by Coco Crisp, who was suffering from a bad back.

In spite of the injuries and uneven play, Boston clinched the AL East title on September 29, and the team readied itself for the Los Angeles Angels.

Beckett, the man on the mound when they opened at Fenway Park in the divisional series, continued his postseason mastery: He threw a four-hit, complete game 4–0 shutout, striking out eight Angels and walking none.

Beckett said it was all in a night's work. "You go out there and you find out what kind of pitcher you are that day and you just go from there, and get into pitch by pitch execution," he explained. "Just exploiting hitters' weaknesses."

Manny Ramirez finally unlimbered his bat in Game Two, crushing a walk-off home run off of Angels closer Francisco Rodriguez in the tenth inning for a 6–3 win. It was only the fifth walk-off postseason home run in club history.

When the series moved to the West Coast, Curt Schilling got the start for the Sox. He didn't disappoint, throwing seven shutout innings, allowing only six hits and a walk in Boston's 9–1 series-clinching victory.

"I thought Schilling was outstanding," commented Francona. "I thought from the beginning, he commanded, especially the command of his fastball to both sides of the plate—in and out, up and down. He really pitched."

Schilling's transition from a pure power pitcher to one relying upon stealth was nearly complete.

As the Sox rolled on to victory over the Angels, the Yankees—the AL wild card entry—were falling to Cleveland. At least temporarily New York's stranglehold on the American League was in limbo.

A relaxed and rejuvenated David Ortiz said he liked the Sox's chances. "You have to be excited about what's going on with this team," declared Ortiz, who went five-for-seven with two homers in the series. "We're playing good [and] hopefully the four or five days off [won't] affect us."

After a four-day hiatus, the Cleveland Indians prepared to meet the Sox at Fenway in the American League Championship Series. Cleveland had upended the Yankees in four games. Again, Beckett—Major League Baseball's only twenty-game winner of 2007—Matsuzaka, and Schilling would take to the mound for Boston in the best-of-seven series, with Schilling scheduled to start the second game.

Beckett shut down the potent Indians' bats, assisted by an awesome display of hitting by Ramirez and Ortiz, who combined to reach base ten times in the lopsided 10-3 win. At that point Ortiz had reached base in sixteen of his eighteen postseason plate appearances, while Ramirez had reached base in thirteen of eighteen at bats.

The hopes of Red Sox Nation soared—until the Indians trounced Boston in Game Two, 13–6, in eleven innings. Schilling faltered, getting a no-decision after leaving the game trailing by the score of 4–3. Things went from bad to worse when the series continued in Cleveland. Matsuzaka threw poorly in Game Three and Cleveland hurler Jake Westbrook quieted Boston's bats, 4–2.

Reflecting back upon the club's 2004 ALCS heroics, Ortiz remained guardedly hopeful. "We've been in worse situations than this and have bounced back and gotten it done."

It was then Wakefield's turn to try and keep the Red Sox out of a 3–1 hole. It didn't happen. After retiring the first thirteen hitters, Wakefield's knuckleball failed. The bullpen couldn't silence Cleveland's bats either, and the Sox fell 7–3.

The lone bright spot was a mammoth home run clubbed by Ramirez, who remained optimistic following the loss. He insisted the club's bats would come around.

"We've got a lot of confidence in our teammates. . . . We have to keep grinding it out and see what's going to happen."

The ball was again placed in the capable hands of Josh Beckett for Game Five at Cleveland's Jacobs Field. He didn't disappoint, securing his third postseason victory of 2007. By defeating Cleveland for the second time, Beckett forced the Indians to face Curt Schilling, one of the greatest playoff performers in baseball history. In Game Six, back in Boston, Schilling drew the Sox even with a stellar performance as Boston cruised to a 12–2 win. "He really, really pitched like the guy we need," lauded Francona. "I don't know if he had his best fastball tonight, but he located it very well and used his off speed [pitches] really effectively."

Only ten of sixty-five MLB teams had ever come back from a 3–1 game deficit to win a best-of-seven series, with the 2004 Red Sox the last to do so. And Game Seven would be the first at Fenway since the Sox overcame a 3–1 deficit to defeat the Angels in the 1986 ALCS.

The game was anti-climatic, as Boston pummeled the Indians, 11–2. Starter Matsuzaka pitched well and closer Jonathan Papelbon registered the last six outs. He punctuated the victory by dancing an Irish jig (clad only in a tee shirt and spandex shorts) in the infield after recording the last out, a performance that quickly became an ESPN classic.

The Colorado Rockies faced the Sox in the 2007 World Series in what was billed as "The Rox versus the Sox." Colorado was on a tremendous roll, having won twenty-one of twenty-two games prior to the World Series.

Going into Game One in Boston, the Rockies faced the formidable Josh Beckett. Boston steamrolled Colorado, 13–1, featuring a seven-run fifth inning as Beckett simply overpowered them.

In Game Two, Boston edged out the Rockies, 2–1, behind Schilling, Okajima and Papelbon. Schilling jokingly called the relief effort "the Oki-Paps Show." The Rockies fared no better in Denver, as Okajima's countryman, Matsuzaka, backed by five Sox relievers, earned his first-ever World Series victory.

Jon Lester notched Boston's win in Game Four, with home run help from Mike Lowell and Bobby Kielty, with the latter's coming on his lone at bat of the Series.

By sweeping Colorado the Sox drove a stake even deeper into the heart of the Curse of the Bambino. And in the wake of rebounding from that three-games-to-one deficit in the 2007 ALCS, the curse was completely and totally dead and gone, once and forever.

23

FULL CIRCLE

Boston's second world championship in four years not only quashed any vestiges of a demonic cloud—darker than the darkest Stephen King novel—that hung over the franchise for eighty-six years, it also elevated the Red Sox to a dynastic level similar to the one that spanned the first eighteen years of the club's existence.

John Henry, Tom Werner, Larry Lucchino, and Theo Epstein, backed by their highly professional front office, have established a new benchmark for major league franchises. Astute draft picks, accurate analyses of potential acquisitions, and scientific field managing combined with more than a modicum of gut-level coaching have become the hallmarks of Red Sox operations. It has also engendered a sense of loyalty among the players who pour their hearts and souls into a grueling, 162-game schedule—plus playoff contests.

In comparison with other Major League Baseball franchises, Curt Schilling insisted the fans make all the difference.

"That in a nutshell is what makes the experience of wearing this uniform so uniquely different than anything I've ever experienced," said Schilling. "It's like a 162-game [Green Bay] Packers season, or 143 playoff games and nineteen World Series games before the post season begins. The energy and expectations are stratospheric and an incredible rush to play in."

Red Sox Vice President Dick Bresciani—who has served under Tom Yawkey, Jean Yawkey, Haywood Sullivan, Buddy LeRoux, John Harrington, and the present ownership—declared that the current front office is unique.

"I think this ownership believes in utilizing everything possible to try to help win," he said. "We have to face the Yankees every year, and no other club has that real stone dragging them down. It's always the Yankees. And our fans want us to compete with the Yankees above all. So, year-in and year-out we're faced with that. For many years we've been second to them. They've got a great organization, tremendous players, and now we've started to do better.[24]

"Theo Epstein has done a marvelous job, and he has the good fortune to have ownership behind him and supportive of him. They're on the same page, and they give him the funds and the resources. And he's done the job.

"They look for anything [to get an edge on the competition]. This ownership is willing to give Theo all the assets and all the resources to help him and his staff put together a championship team."

Pitcher Manny Delcarmen, a local product who grew up less than a dozen miles from Fenway Park, said the Sox operate their minor league system properly. "They really take the development of young players in the minors seriously. They do it the right way. I got drafted in 2000 so I've been around a little while, and they don't rush you through the system. There's a lot of [player] development down there in preparing you for the big leagues. I think that's a key thing that separates us from a lot of other teams."

24 Repeated requests for interviews with John Henry, Larry Lucchino, Terry Francona, and Theo Epstein through media relations director John Blake were ignored.

Schilling, who played in the Red Sox minor league system in the late eighties, agreed. "There is absolutely no comparison in organizations when it comes to the player development pipeline now in place," he said. "I had some incredibly influential and instrumental men as part of my early career . . . [but] from a player development standpoint this organization was horribly lacking in so many areas my first trip through. I can honestly say that in my first three years of pro ball I had a 'coach' watching me throw my bullpen [sessions] less than twenty-five percent of the time. We had no [full-time] pitching coaches; everyone was a 'rover.'"

The franchise has successfully retained Fenway Park, both expanding it and making it much more "fan friendly." Even before the 2004 world championship, the club had added 1,331 new seats. Ex-catcher Carlton Fisk was pleased because the stadium means so much to the region. "I think Fenway Park is an historical landmark," he said. "There are a couple of concerns: Is it safe and is it big enough to support the team? The team needs revenues, and is it large enough to do that? So far it seems to work real well. It would be a shame to lose Fenway Park."

"While baseball is the Red Sox's highest priority, the club's leadership has put great emphasis on improving Fenway Park and enhancing the experience at a ballgame," added club vice president John Blake. "As a result of the success of the improvements, John Henry, Tom Werner, and Larry Lucchino announced on March 23, 2005, that the club was formally committing to remain long-term at Fenway Park with 'no strings attached.'"

Mike Lowell said he re-signed with the Sox in late 2007 because it's a first-class organization—and because of the clubhouse chemistry. "I think this clubhouse is made up of guys who are on the same page. It's a mix of veterans and young guys and I genuinely believe that we enjoy spending time with each other—and that's a big thing. Because if you don't like whom you're coming to the park with, that can be a divisive factor."

Curt Schilling re-signed with the team because he wanted to finish his career in Boston.

> There really was no decision to be made in my mind. I felt compelled to try and "make up" for the lost few years after 2004 when I was unable to perform to the level of personal and organization expectations. I knew after the final out of the 2007 season that if Boston did not want me to return I would retire. Having multiple offers on the table, or [offers] presented to me as "potential offers," made it easy for me to realize that I could still do this, and teams recognized that, and that Boston would make me an offer.
>
> I think they also knew that this is where I wanted to finish my career and that would mean their offer would come in well under the others. The easy thing about all this was that the money was a non-factor; something above minimum in an offer from the Sox would be enough for me.

Tim Wakefield said the difference is palpable. "It's a matter of character and tradition," said Wakefield, a member of the team since 1995. "The new ownership has done such a great job of building a team around good character and maintaining the tradition of the Red Sox, and that's what made us successful over the last four years."

The incomparable Luis Tiant, one of many former Sox players who had been alienated by the previous management, says the aura around the franchise has changed. "They're completely different. It's a 180-degree turn, you know? They're good to us. They respect us. They respect the game. And . . . they've brought about twenty of us players back to hire us and that's great. They respect us. And that means everything.

"They're not just hiring you and putting you on the sidelines. They'll hire you and look for [feedback], and talk to you. I can go and talk to Lucchino like we're talking now. And Mr. Henry, he treats you like a man, and that's the way I like to be treated. That's the way I like people to behave because that's the way I like to be treated."

Tiant made it a point to say that the new ownership had distributed 2004 *and* 2007 World Series rings to virtually the entire staff, himself included.

Carlton Fisk, who left the club with a bitter taste in his mouth, vowing to wear a White Sox cap if inducted into the Hall of Fame (he didn't, donning instead a Boston cap), and swearing he would never make up with the team that burned him so badly, has come home again. Like many of his Red Sox contemporaries, Fisk has reestablished ties with the franchise.

"As alumni of the Red Sox, we realized how rare and special [the 2004 championship] was. Lonborg, Yaz, Petrocelli, and others from the 1967 team were tied to this team. And those of us from the 1975 team were connected in a way. Everyone who has played for the Red Sox has wished that they could have had the fortunes this team had."

And what about the "Curse of the Bambino?" Schilling asserted the "curse" was due to nothing more than a lack of chemistry. "The only curse in Boston for eighty-six years was a curse of talent. None of the teams in the previous eighty-six years possessed the same talent, passion, drive, and commitment that we did, as a team. Winning a world championship is *never* [solely] about having the most talent, in my opinion. But it is *always* about having the best *team*, and in 2004, and in 2007, that team was the Boston Red Sox."

Sports Museum curator Richard Johnson pointed out one unique connection between the Red Sox world champions from the years 1916 and 1918 and the world champions from 2004 and 2007. "The team experienced nearly an entire turnover between world championships during both eras."

Indeed, there were only four Red Sox players who appeared in both the 1916 World Series and the 1918 World Series—and only six who played on both squads in the World Series of 2004 and the 2007 World Series.

Johnson brought up another interesting point, as well.

"How many World Series did Babe Ruth win in New York?" he asked. "I get all kinds of outrageous answers—six, seven, ten. He was in New York from 1920 through 1933. And the Yankees won four World Series. Ruth was with the Red Sox for five years and the Sox won three World Series."

Red Sox Nation, the franchise really has come full circle. It's a Red Sox Renaissance.

NEAR MISS

Despite its many high points, all in all the 2008 season ended up a disappointing one for the Olde Towne Team, as injuries and clubhouse angst ultimately doomed the efforts of the Red Sox.

By the time spring training was over the team had already lost ace pitcher Josh Beckett and reliever Mike Timlin. Right fielder J. D. Drew was soon to follow. This in addition to the loss of hurler Curt Schilling, who had suffered a serious tear of the muscle in his right shoulder, and who hoped to rehab and return around the All-Star break. Instead he ultimately underwent season-ending surgery in July.

Boston opened its season with an erratic schedule. Starting with the regular-season opener in Tokyo, the Sox returned to the States to play three meaningless exhibitions in Los Angeles, flew to Oakland for a series, then traveled cross-country to play the Blue Jays in Toronto before finally playing at Fenway.

The Sox were plagued with injuries throughout the year, and "Manny being Manny" finally became "Manny being the plague." Mike Lowell suffered a thumb injury and was placed on the disabled list April 11. Rookie outfielder Brandon Moss underwent an emergency appendectomy early on, while pitcher Daisuke Matsuzaka went on the DL in late May. Incredibly, things got worse. David Ortiz, "Big Papi" to teammates and fans alike, tore the sheath surrounding the tendon in his left wrist. He'd be lost for roughly two months, but he never regained his effectiveness at the plate.

Although Boston reeled off a lengthy winning streak at Fenway, the Sox were atrocious on the road. And Manny Ramirez wasn't hitting. Drew carried the club through the month of June.

Ramirez finally *did* find his swing . . . at the Red Sox's sixty-four-year-old traveling secretary, Jack McCormick. During an interleague series in Houston June 28, Manny demanded sixteen tickets for the following day's game. When McCormick told Ramirez he might have trouble getting such a large number at the last minute, Ramirez snarled, "Just do your job," and shoved McCormick to the floor.

"The hard part for me," remarked Curt Schilling, "was this derailed into a train wreck so quick, so fast, and so oddly [after having] the Buddha Zen Master guy [Ramirez] in spring training, reading and [saying] 'Life is good; don't worry, be happy.' And it just looked like he was poised to have a monster season. Physically, he worked his butt off."

It was the second physical altercation for Ramirez in a month. He punched Sox first baseman Kevin Youkilis in the Red Sox dugout several weeks earlier. And suddenly the man/child superstar was making noises about not being appreciated, and demanding that the club pick up the two one-year options it held on him, at $20 million per year (he'd already pocketed almost $160 million from the Sox, from 2001–08).

Then Ramirez began to complain of various ailments, claiming he couldn't play. He said his knee was bothering him but, when pressed, couldn't remember *which* knee! The team finally had MRIs done on *both* of his knees. Both were fine. He again stopped running out ground balls, and took three successive called strikes against the Yankees' Mariano Rivera. The last straw was when—around the All-Star break—he publicly called Sox owner John Henry a liar.

With Boston so anxious to rid itself of this clubhouse cancer, the Sox paid Ramirez's salary with his new team, the Dodgers. He was gone at the trade deadline.[25] In a three-way trade, Boston received Pittsburgh outfielder Jason Bay, who did a marvelous job in Boston, both in left field and at the plate.

Shortstop Julio Lugo tore a quad muscle July 11, sidelining him for the year, while Drew's balky back was once again flaring up. Lowell, the 2007 World Series MVP, partially tore the labrum in his right hip, effectively ending any meaningful contribution on his part. He could hardly walk. Most of the pitching staff spent time on the disabled list at one point or another. The entire soap opera proved to be baseball's version of *General Hospital*.

Yet the club hung tough, staying close to the surprising Tampa Bay Rays, the team that ultimately won the AL crown. Youkilis was a monster at the plate, batting .312, hitting 29 homeruns and collecting 115 RBIs, prompting the Fenway faithful to holler, "Yo-o-o-o-k! Yo-o-o-o-k!" every time he'd come to bat. But outpacing him was little Dustin Pedroia, the tiny second baseman. (Although the *Red Sox Media Guide* lists him at 5'9" he isn't any taller than 5'7".)

---

25 Both Peter Gammons and Bill Simmons of ESPN later asserted that Manny's catastrophic meltdown could be laid at the feet of his new agent, the famously difficult Scott Boras. "Management people point out that Boras proudly orchestrated the Manny Ramirez shutdown in Boston and, as Boras has told GMs, got Ramirez where he wanted him in Los Angeles," wrote Gammons on ESPN.com. "Getting a player to opt out in the middle of his contract and essentially refuse to honor what he'd signed isn't easy." Had Ramirez stayed in Boston for the two option years on his contract, Boras wouldn't have received any commission. After the conclusion of the 2008 season, it was revealed that the Red Sox had formally notified Manny that the team was suspending him for repeatedly failing to take the field. The trade to the Dodgers precluded the suspension.

Pedroia, the 2007 AL Rookie of the Year, wound up winning the American League Most Valuable Player Award, hitting .326, with 17 homers and 83 RBIs in 2008—predominantly batting *second*. And lefty Jon Lester (16–6) not only threw a no-hitter against Kansas City on May 19, but picked up the slack for the oft-injured Beckett, who never did get on track. Finally, although constantly walking batters, Dice-K, in his sophomore major league season, logged an 18–3 record, with a 2.90 ERA.

Clearly the Sox were ailing when they faced the Angels in the American League Division Series after winning the AL wild card. After eking out a hard-fought victory over the 100-win Angels, however, Boston ran into a young juggernaut in the championship round—the Rays. Alas, even though the Red Sox again tried to rally from a three-games-to-one postseason deficit and rallied from 7–0 down in the seventh inning of Game Five at Fenway, Tampa Bay held on to beat the Olde Towne Team for the pennant in seven games.

But there's always next year.

ACKNOWLEDGMENTS

I could fill a book by itself with all the people and organizations I need to recognize both before and during my efforts to complete this project.

First, again I must acknowledge the impact upon my life by my wife and my late father. Thanks for believing, even when I faltered.

I want to thank my son, Joshua Gutlon; my daughter, Alicia Gutlon; my mom, Jeanette (Gutlon) Glazebrook; my brother, Jon Gutlon; my niece, Heather Marshall; my daughter-in-law, Katlyn Gutlon, and my nephews, Wilson and Jon David Gutlon. (Thanks for the limited edition "The Curse is Reversed" rendering, Willie!) Likewise, I want to remember my late stepfather, David Glazebrook, and my late sister, Juliette Gutlon Marshall.

My agent, Jon Malysiak, of Jonathan Scott Literary Agency of Chicago, recognized the project's worth, and tirelessly worked to land a publisher. His advice and assistance were invaluable, and I look forward to collaborating on future projects. Jon's partner in crime, Scott Adlington, also played a role in helping me refine the manuscript.

And, in spite of his allegiance to the "Dark Side," i.e., the New York Yankees, associate publisher Bill Wolfsthal of Skyhorse

Publishing jumped at the opportunity to strip away as much moolah as possible from the fans of Red Sox Nation who will buy this book, hopefully in droves. I also wish to thank Kathleen Go, the editor at Skyhorse, for her diligent work on the manuscript, along with free-lance editor Matthew Silverman and photographer Tyler Gardner.

What can I say about the Pike County–based "Jerry Gutlon Fan Club?"

Two years of covering Pike County government straight from the shoulder and without favor earned me the everlasting gratitude of a large number of West Central Georgians, most whom had never dealt with a reporter who tirelessly endeavors to report the truth, no matter the cost.

My precious friend, the late Lloyd "Bud" Gayton, still moni-tored county meetings, four years after I gave up the beat. Likewise, Carol and Jimmy Bass are two of the finest people God has ever graced the earth with. And Joy Walker is a delightful lady who has always been willing to help and encourage the Gutlon clan. Ditto for Randy Schultz. Many, many more Pike County residents—too many to mention by name—became much more than news sources over the years. You know who you are. God bless you all.

The kernel initially planted in my life for journalism resulted from the encouragement I received from my high school English depart-ment head, Ernest Blake, of Sharon (Massachusetts) High School. He recognized that I had a God-given talent to write and urged me to utilize it to its fullest. Without Mr. Blake's encouragement I prob-ably wouldn't have gone to college—and that no doubt would have relegated me to a place in Southeast Asia called Vietnam.

I must acknowledge some of my brothers in Alcoholics Anony-mous, particularly Henry M., Arnie G., Brian D., Paul W., and How-ie M. You guys are the greatest. And I also want to recognize my friends from Anchor Hospital, who were there when I needed them. Can you believe it? I wrote a book!

My former brother-in-arms in the military, Sgt. 1ˢᵗ Class Joseph D. Burke IV, must have nearly passed out when he learned I had contracted to write a book about our beloved Boston Red Sox. But Joe and his Dad, Joseph "Dennis" Burke III, were ready to help me complete the research in Boston, and assist me in weeding through hundreds of photos to select just the right ones to illustrate the project. My heartfelt thanks to both generations of Burkes! And I forgive you for being New York Giants fans. Brian Willett, a former sports reporter at the *Norwich* (Connecticut) *Bulletin*, joined the Burkes in assisting me at the Boston Public Library.

There are a number of journalists who have inspired me over the years, some who are gone, while others remain active in the field or have simply retired. First, three broadcast journalism professors who truly made a difference in my career, Dick Mallary, later a vice president of Gannett Broadcasting; Arnold Zenker, formerly of CBS Television News; and Bob Perkins, who taught my sportscasting class, all at Grahm, three blocks from Fenway Park. Thanks for believing in my abilities even when my personal life was chaotic, gentlemen!

Likewise, I need to thank another former professor of mine, Louise DeSantis, who gave me more latitude in her classes than I probably deserved, allowing me to write lengthy term papers, both analytical and creative.

I would be remiss if I didn't acknowledge Clark Booth, formerly of WCVB-TV and WBZ-TV, who once urged me to change the world through incisive *news* reporting in lieu of covering the "tacky world" of sports. I'm proud to say that I actually did change the course of history more than once—even though it wasn't on as large a stage as I once aspired. Certainly the activists in Pike County, Georgia and Lake County, Florida would agree that I redirected things for the better!

Several journalists I must recognize have left us: Edward R. Murrow, of CBS News fame, my first news hero; David Halberstam, formerly of the *New York Times*; Peter Jennings of ABC News; and ABC's Jim McKay, who passed while I was writing this book.

I want to thank a vast number of former newspaper, radio, and television employers, and editors and broadcast managers who gave me the opportunity to report news and sports over the years. To those few newspaper editors, including John Pastor, formerly managing editor of the *Daily Commercial* of Leesburg, Florida, whose work actually improved mine (a rarity, believe me!), thank you, thank you, thank you!

Specifically, I'd also like to recognize John Sullivan of the *Griffin Daily News* of Griffin, Georgia, who lobbied to hire me as assistant sports editor during the summer of 2001. Although we butted heads during our two years together, when I returned to the sports department as sports editor during the summer of 2004, no one knew that the Red Sox were about to engineer the greatest comeback in the history of baseball.

And, after Boston blew away the St. Louis Cardinals in the 2004 World Series, it was the *Griffin Daily News* that provided me with the platform to initially publish a column on the mythical "Curse of the Bambino," entitled, "Curse? Bah, humbug! What curse?"

Combined with the wonderful prose of Glenn Stout and Richard Johnson in *Red Sox Century* (and Stout's insightful article on "The Curse" for ESPN.com), the column provided the initial impetus for this work.

Johnson, who also serves as the curator of the (Boston) Sports Museum, personally called me in February 2008 after I signed the publishing contract with Skyhorse. And Glenn Stout, George Kimball, Clark Booth, Bruce Allen, and John Molori all tirelessly answered my myriad questions. I will be forever grateful.

Hundreds of other journalists past and present have contributed to this project, the vast majority unwittingly. My sources have included newspapers, magazines, broadcast outlets, and Web sites. They comprise a list too numerous to mention, although sources are cited in the bibliography.

However, I must specifically mention Stout and Johnson for their landmark work in *Red Sox Century*; Howard Bryant for his wonderful *Shut Out: A Story of Race and Baseball in Boston*; long-time *Boston Herald* reporter and author Tony Massarotti, now of the *Boston Globe*; and Peter Golenbock for *Fenway: An Unexpurgated History of the Boston Red Sox*, especially for his interviews.

Reporter Clayton Stairs of the *Georgetown* (South Carolina) *Times* was instrumental in assisting me in tracking down information concerning Red Sox owner Tom Yawkey's long-time association with that community—and his silent partnership in the Sunset Lodge bordello. I'd also like to thank Michael Carter, former sheriff of Georgetown County, and author Elizabeth Huntsinger Wolfe for sharing their memories of that tawdry operation.

In particular, I also want to extend my gratitude to those journalists who write for MLB.com, and the Boston Red Sox official Web site. Without the resources of that Web site I never could have written such a comprehensive narrative of the 2007 world championship season. I also want to thank those statisticians who maintain the Baseball Almanac site, who—more than once—prevented me from making erroneous suppositions and foolish gaffes.

The staff of the Boston Public Library was unfailingly helpful during the three weeks I haunted the place in May 2008. I especially wish to thank Marta Pardee-King and Aaron Schmidt, without whose assistance this project would've been much, much more difficult.

Thanks, as well, to the Boston Red Sox, particularly John Blake, Pam Ganley, Megan LaBella, and Dick Bresciani. To all those member of the Boston Red Sox, past and present, thank you for sharing your thoughts with me. I especially wish to acknowledge the input from two of the greatest clutch pitchers of all time: Curt Schilling and Luis Tiant. I pray that my children may carry themselves with as much faith and dignity you two gentlemen exude.

Joe McDonald, a prolific reporter for the *Providence Journal*, was especially helpful while I was visiting Fenway Park. I'd also like to recognize Katie Leighton, Curt Schilling's publicist, for assisting in repeatedly peppering that insightful gentleman with questions.

Personal friends, colleagues, and acquaintances have also helped in this undertaking in a variety of very special ways. I'd like to acknowledge Don and Winnie Chase; Frank Peddicord; Master Sgt. (ret.) Chris Simonson, U.S. Army; Gary Corsair; Marci Elliott; Mike Graham; the Rev. Tony Kent of Cornerstone Assembly of God Church; Bishop Tommy Powell, the Rev. Mark Davenport and music minister Damien Wright, along with the rest of the ministerial staff at Harvest Temple Church of God; Doug Gorman; Steve Postlethwait; Kenny Kinsler; Angela "the Angel of Death" Allen; Beth Avery; James Ray; John Mrosek; Leigh Bailey; Demetrius Smith; and attorneys Bill Johnston and Brennan MacDowell, among others. Your encouragement, enthusiasm and input were invaluable in helping me stay the course. Thank you, all—and God bless you.

I also must remember my posse from college, although we've mostly been out-of-touch for decades, a situation largely created through my own youthful stupidity and misbehavior. Going to school around the corner from Fenway Park was a unique experience. Guess I fooled most of you, eh? What a long, strange trip it's been!

I especially want to cite my Grahm classmate and brother-in-Christ, Maurice Tate, who never gave up on this reprobate, or ostracized me even during the worst of my skule daze.

Finally, I want to acknowledge my Lord and Savior, Jesus Christ, without whom this would never have been possible, and who blessed me with the talent to express myself, both verbally and through the written word.

SELECTED BIBLIOGRAPHY

Books

Adomites, Paul, ed. *Cooperstown: Baseball's Hall of Famers*. Lincolnwood, Ill.: Publications International, 1999.
Alexander, Charles C. *Ty Cobb*. New York: Oxford University Press, 1984.
Allen, Maury. *Jackie Robinson: A Life Remembered*. New York: Franklin Watts, 1987.
Angell, Roger. *Game Time: A Baseball Companion*. Orlando, Fla.: Harcourt, Inc., 2003.
_____. *Late Innings*. New York: Simon and Schuster, 1982.
_____. *Season Ticket*, Boston: Houghton Mifflin Company, 1988.
Appel, Marty and Matt Winick, eds. *The Illustrated Digest of Baseball*. New York: Stadia Sports Publishing, 1973.
Asinof, Eliot. *Eight Men Out*. New York: Holt, Rinehart and Winston, 1963.
The Boston Red Sox. *Official Media Guides*, various editions.
_____. *Official Scorebook Magazine*, various editions.
_____. *Official Yearbook*, various editions.
Boswell, Thomas. *How Life Imitates the World Series*. New York: Penguin Books, 1982.
Bryant, Howard. *Shut Out: A Story of Race and Baseball in Boston*. Boston: Beacon Press, 2002.
Clemens, Roger and Peter Gammons. *Rocket Man*. Lexington, Mass.: Stephen Greene Press, 1987.
Coleman, Ken and Dan Vaneti. *The Impossible Dream Remembered*. Lexington, Mass.: Stephen Greene Press, 1987.
Creamer, Robert. *The Legend Comes to Life*. New York: Simon and Schuster, 1974.
Davis, Mac. *Baseball's Unforgettables*. New York: Bantam Books, 1966.
_____. *The Greatest in Baseball*. New York: Scholastic Books, 1962.
Epstein, Beryl and Sam Epstein. *Stories of Champions*. New York: Scholastic Books, 1963.
Frommer, Frederick and Harvey Frommer. *Yankees vs. Red Sox: Baseball's Greatest Rivalry*. New York: Berkeley, 2002.
Gammons, Peter. *Beyond the* Sixth *Game*. Boston: Houghton Mifflin, 1985.
Goldman, Steven, ed. *Mind Game: How the Boston Red Sox Got Smart, Won a World Series, and Created a New Blueprint for Winning*. New York: Prospectus Entertainment Ventures, 2005.
Golenbeck, Peter. *Dynasty: The New York Yankees 1949-1964*. Englewood, N.J.: Prentice-Hall, Inc., 1975.
_____. *Fenway*. New York: G.P. Putnam and Sons, 1992.
_____. *Red Sox Nation*. Chicago: Triumph Books, 2005.
Grossman, Leigh. *The Red Sox Fan Handbook*. Cambridge, Mass.: Rounder Books, 2005.
Gutman, Dan. *Baseball Babylon*. New York: Penguin Books, 1992.
Halberstam, David. *Summer of '49*. New York: William Morrow and Company, 1989.
_____. *The Teammates*. New York: Hyperionbooks, 2004.
Harrelson, Ken and Al Hirshberg. *Hawk*. New York: The Viking Press, 1969.
Helyar, John. *Lords of the Realm*. New York: Ballantine Books, 1994.
Higgins, George V. *The Progress of the Seasons*. New York: Prentice Hall Press, 1990.
Hirshberg, Al. *What's the Matter with the Red Sox?* Cornwall, New York: Dodd, Mead and Company, 1973.
Holley, Michael. *Red Sox Rule: Terry Francona and Boston's Rise to Dominance*. New York: HarperCollins Publishers, 2008.
Honig, Donald. *The Boston Red Sox*. New York: Prentice Hall Press, 1990.
Kahn, Roger. *October Men*. New York: Harcourt, Inc., 2003.
Kaiser, Ken and David Fisher. *Planet of the Umps*. New York: St. Martin's Press, 2003.
Keene, Kerry and Raymond Sinibaldi and David Hickey. *The Babe in Red Stockings*. Champaign, Ill.: Sagamore Publishing, 1997.
Kiersh, Edward. *Where Have You Gone, Vince DiMaggio?* New York: Bantam Books, 1983.
King, Stephen and Stewart O'Nan. *Faithful*. New York: Scribner, 2004.
Langguth, A.J. *Patriots: The Men Who Started the American Revolution*. New York: Touchstone. 1988.
Laurila, David. *Interviews from Red Sox Nation*. Hanover, Mass.: Maple Street Press, 2006.
Lee, William F. and Dick Lally. *The Wrong Stuff*. New York: Viking Press, 1984.
Lindberg, Richard. *Who's on Third? The Chicago White Sox Story*. South Bend, Ind.: Icarus Press, 1983.
Linn, Ed. *Hitter: the Life and Turmoils of Ted Williams*. New York: Harcourt Brace & Company, 1993.
_____. *Inside the Yankees: The Championship Year*. New York: Random House, 1978.
Lieb, Frederick. *The Boston Red Sox*. New York: G.P. Putnam and Sons, 1947.

Mantle, Mickey and Mickey Herskowitz. *All My Octobers*. New York: HarperCollins Publishers, 1994.

Massarotti, Tony. *Dynasty: The Inside Story of How the Red Sox Became a Baseball Powerhouse*. New York: St. Martin's Press, 2008.

McLain, Denny and The Sporting News. *Strikeout: The Story of Denny McLain*. St. Louis, Mo.: The Sporting News Publishing Co., 1988.

Montville, Leigh. *The Big Bam: The Life and Times of Babe Ruth*. New York: Doubleday, 2006.

Morgan, Joe and David Falkner. *Joe Morgan: A Life in Baseball*. New York: W.W. Norton and Co., 1993.

Mnookin, Seth. *Feeding the Monster: How Money, Smarts, and Nerve Took a Team to the Top*. New York: Simon & Schuster, 2006.

Murdock, Eugene. *Ban Johnson: Czar of Baseball*. Westport, Conn.: Greenwood Press, 1982.

Nash, Bruce and Allan Zullo. *Nash & Zullo's Believe it or Else!!* New York: Dell Publishing, 1992.

Neft, David S. et al. *The Boston Red Sox Fan Book*. New York: St. Martin's Griffin, 2002.

Nemec, David. *Great Baseball Feats, Facts and Firsts*. New York: New American Library, 2004.

O'Connor, Dick. *Reggie Jackson: Superstar*. New York: Scholastic Books, 1975.

Ortiz, David and Tony Massarotti. *Big Papi: My Story of Big Dreams and Big Hits*. New York: St. Martin's Press, 2007.

Piersall, Jimmy and Al Hirshberg. *Fear Strikes Out*. Boston: Little Brown, 1955.

Rampersad, Arnold and Rachel Robinson, *Jackie Robinson*. New York: Alfred A. Knopf, Inc., 1997.

A.J. Reach and Company. *The Reach Official American League Baseball Guide*. Philadelphia: A.J. Reach Company, 1902.

Reynolds, Bill. *Lost Summer: The '67 Red Sox and the Impossible Dream*. New York: Warner Books, 1997.

Riley, Dan, ed. *The Red Sox Reader*. Thousand Oaks, Calif.: Ventura Arts, 1987.

Ritter, Lawrence. *The Glory of Their Times*. New York: Macmillan, 1984.

Robinson, Ray, ed. *Baseball Stars of 1960*. New York: Pyramid Books, 1960.

_____. *Baseball Stars of 1969*. New York: Pyramid Books, 1969.

_____. *Baseball Stars of 1970*. New York: Pyramid Books, 1970.

Ross, Alan. *Echoes from the Ball Park*. Nashville, Tenn.: Walnut Grove Press, 1999.

_____. *The Red Sox Century: Voices and Memories from Fenway Park*. Nashville, Tenn.: Walnut Grove Press, 2004.

Roth, Allan, ed. *1967 Who's Who in Baseball*. New York: Harris Press, 1967.

Rust Jr., Art. *Get that Nigger off the Field*. Los Angeles: Shadow Lawn Press, 1992.

Seidel, Michael. *Ted Williams: A Baseball Life*. Chicago: Contemporary Books, Inc., 1991.

Shaughnessy, Dan. *The Curse of the Bambino*. New York: Dutton, 1990.

_____. *One Strike Away*. New York: Beaufort Books, 1987.

_____. *The Legend of the Curse of the Bambino*. New York: Simon & Schuster, 2005.

_____. *Reversing the Curse: Inside the 2004 Boston Red Sox*. New York: Houghton Mifflin Company, 2005.

Simmons, Bill, *Now I Can Die in Peace*. New York: ESPN Books, 2005.

Simon, Scott. Jackie Robinson and the Integration of Baseball." John Wiley & Sons, Inc., Hoboken, NJ, 2002.

Smith, Robert. *Babe Ruth's America*. New York: Crowell Publishing, 1974.

The Sporting News. *The Sporting News Official Baseball Guide*s, various editions.

Stout, Glenn and Richard A. Johnson. *Red Sox Century*. New York: Houghton Mifflin Company, 2004.

Stout, Glenn, ed. *Impossible Dreams: A Red Sox Collection*. New York: Houghton Mifflin Company, 2003.

Stump, Al. *Cobb*. Chapel Hill, N.C.: Algonquin Books, 1994.

Tygiel, Jules. *Baseball's Great Experiment*. New York: Oxford University Press, 1983.

Various. *The Rivals: The Boston Red Sox Vs. The New York Yankees*. New York: St. Martin's Press, 2004.

Vecsey, George. *A Year in the Sun*. New York: Random House, 1989.

_____. *Baseball: A History of America's Favorite Game*. New York: Random House, 2006

Wagenheim, Kal. *Babe Ruth: His Life and Legend*. New York: Praeger Publishers, 1974.

Walton, Ed. *Red Sox Triumphs and Tragedies*. New York: Stein and Day, 1980.

Waterman, Ty and Mel Springer. *The Year the Red Sox Won the Series*. Boston: Northeastern University Press, 1999.

Williams, Dick and Bill Plaschke. *No More Mr. Nice Guy*. New York: Harcourt, Brace and Jovanovich, 1990.

Williams, Ted and John Underwood. *My Turn at Bat*. New York: Simon and Schuster, 1969.

_____. *The Science of Hitting*. New York: Simon and Schuster, 1971.

Wood, Allan James. *1918: Babe Ruth and the World Champion Boston Red Sox*. Lincoln, Nebraska: Writers Club Press, 2000.

Wood, Bob. *Dodger Dogs to Fenway Franks*. New York: McGraw-Hill Book Company, 1988.

Yastrzemski, Carl and Al Hirshberg. *Yaz*. New York: Viking Press, 1968.

Magazines

Baseball Magazine
Boston Baseball
Boston Magazine
Collier's
Esquire
Harper's
Sport
Sports Illustrated
The New Yorker
The Saturday Evening Post
TV Guide
Yankee

Online Resources

baseballalmanac.com
baseballmusings.com
baseball-reference.com
baseballthinkfactory.org
chiff.com
hof.com
mlb.com
mlbtraderumors.com
RedSox.com
red-sox10.tripod.com
searchboston.com
soxsux.com
wikipedia.com
yankeessuck.com

Publications

A 2004 Boston Red Sox World Series Ring, courtesy of Red Sox vice chairman Les Otten
Exhibit A
The Boston Phoenix
The Massachusetts Historical Review
The Sporting News

Newspapers

The Boston American
The Boston Daily Record
The Boston Globe
The Boston Herald
The Boston Herald-American
The Boston Morning Journal
The Boston Post
The Boston Record American
The Boston Times
The Boston Transcript
The Boston Traveller
The Daily Commercial
The Georgetown (S.C.) *Times*
The Griffin Daily News
The New York Daily News
The New York Post
The New York Times
The (North Andover) Eagle-Tribune
The Patriot Ledger
The Portland (Me.) Press Herald
The Providence Journal
The Scrantonian
The (Attleboro) Sun Chronicle
The Worcester Telegram & Evening Gazette

INDEX